A MODEL SPY

Dedicated to "H" and her nieces.
Also Anne Bonny, born c1697 and her spiritual descendants;
VG, Aly, Josie and Phoebe

A MODEL SPY

JOHN RORY MACLEAN

MIRROR BOOKS

MIRROR BOOKS

All of the events in this story are true, but some names and details have been changed to protect the identities of some individuals where appropriate.

1

Published in Great Britain and Ireland in 2026 by Mirror Books, a Reach PLC business.

www.mirrorbooks.co.uk
@TheMirrorBooks

Print ISBN 9781917439657
eBook ISBN 9781917439664

Editing and Production: Christine Costello, Nick Webster
Cover Design: Chris Collins

Photographic Acknowledgements: Alamy, MirrorPix

Every effort has been made to trace copyright, Any oversights will be rectified in future editions.

Printed and bound in Great Britain by
CPI Group (UK) Ltd, Croydon, CR0 4YY

FSC www.fsc.org MIX Paper | Supporting responsible forestry FSC® C013604

CONTENTS

PROLOGUE

"HER ACTIVITIES FOR the last 10 years are certainly consistent with a high degree of espionage, although it has hitherto been impossible to say definitely that she is more than a widely travelled and remarkably well befriended adventuress." Captain J.E.B. Hill. MI5. 7th October 1944.

In the hills behind the Californian coast, not far from the sprawl of Los Angeles, there are several blocks of condos. They're in a gated development set amongst the broad streets and neat houses of suburban America. In the gardens, Bird of Paradise flowers nod their spiky heads in the wind that blows up from the Pacific.

In one of the condos is a box of old documents and photographs. In amongst them, there's the fashion portfolio of a beautiful young woman. She's modelling haute couture by Lucien Lelong, Jean Patou, Maggy Rouff, Bergdorf Goodman and the go to designer in 1940s Germany, Annemarie Heise.

The box also contains a photograph of a young man with dark hair slicked back like the silent film star Rudolph Valentino. On the back of the photograph is written: "I did love you. I do love you. I will always love you."

The woman loved by the young man was Gisela Klein, a model and spy for Germany in the 1930s and throughout the Second World War. The man who wrote of his love was John Profumo, later the British government minister infamous for the 1960s sex and espionage scandal which bears his name. He gave Gisela a green jade ring as proof of his devotion, and she kept it for her whole life.

John – or Jack as he was known to friends and family – Introduced Gisela to the cream of 1930s British society. The Astors; members of the Royal Household and officers of the elite Guards regiments. She modelled in London, New York and Paris and associated with the rich, famous and aristocratic in Cannes. She was the lover of the man who should have been the President of the United States of America; and she socialised with his whole family including his brother John F Kennedy (JFK) who did become President.

Gisela wasn't just a beautiful party girl. British and French intelligence chased her but never found out about her secret link to the two most senior Nazis in Germany, Adolf Hitler and Hermann Göring. She also hid that she modelled for the designer who dressed the women of the Nazi elite, including Hitler's mistress Eva Braun, and she maintained multiple contacts with Germany's intelligence services. Espionage would appear to be a price she paid for the freedom to live the life she wanted outside the stifling confines of Nazi Germany and its restricted vision of the role of women.

It also led her into the greatest danger, imprisoned , pregnant and bargaining for her life.

Hunting the real Gisela Klein through the records has been putting together a jigsaw where some of the pieces are hidden or were lost in the destruction of the Second World War. Much of her life is obscured in the archives and elsewhere by the men around her who were always assigned a more important role despite Gisela clearly being more intelligent than most of them. Even her modelling photographs only partially reveal the woman behind the mask. There was always something held back, a feature of her personality noted by her own children. That mystery only added to her allure. She wasn't a Mata Hari; she didn't have to be unless she chose. She was the "intelligent, witty and companionable" networker who knew everyone, and they were only too happy to tell her everything. She was the look of 1930s haute couture and the real face of the morally complex, part time, sometimes exciting and mostly wearying world of being a spy.

This is a true story. The vital central pieces of the jigsaw lie in these papers and photographs kept by her daughter Lisl and son Horst in California. They were unaware of her secret life until I contacted them. I have changed their names but no others in what follows:

John Rory Maclean, 2025

SUMMARY OF TRACES

Germany

Gisela Klein. The "very beautiful German girl." International model and intelligence asset. Alias: Gisela Kleim; Karin; Madeleine Fontaine; Mrs Edward Adam.

Werner Theodor Schaurte. German industrialist. Member of the right wing nationalist Stahlhelm organisation and later the Nazi Sturmabteilung (SA). A frequent visitor to the UK and the US in the 1930s. A connection of Klein who had personal access to Hermann Göring and Adolf Hitler despite his Jewish ancestry.

Hermann Göring. WW1 fighter pilot. Created the Gestapo in 1933. In charge of the German air force, the Luftwaffe from 1935. In charge of industrial policy. Second only to Hitler. In the 1930s he was running back-channel communications and espionage operations in Britain on behalf of the Nazis.

Wolfgang Krause-Brandstetter. Cambridge educated German Foreign Office spy in the 1930s and during the Second World War. Publisher, propaganda expert and later Abwehr officer for air intelligence. Identified as Klein's control in 1930s Paris. Alias: Wolfgang Ernst, Dr Braun.

Friedrich Carl Hanesse. German Air Military Attache in Paris in the mid 1930s and later General of the Luftwaffe in Paris. Linked to

Klein and Brandstetter. Looted art and treasure for Göring. French intelligence put him in charge of placing sabotage agents in the UK and America in 1944

Margarethe Klimt. Fashion designer and one the leaders of the Nazi fashion front in the 1930s. Labelled a "cultural icon" by Joseph Goebbels. Organised a fashion show for the Anglo-German Fellowship in London.

Annemarie Heise. Berlin couturier to Magda Goebbels, wife of Propaganda Minister Joseph and Eva Braun, Hitler's mistress. Gisela Klein worked in Heise's salon in Berlin as a sales assistant and model.

Rudolf Goldschmidt. Pre-war a suspected "low grade agent for Germany" when he worked for the German subsidiary of the film company Metro Goldwyn Mayer. Gisela Klein introduced him to Nancy Astor's youngest son Jakey in Berlin in 1938.

Heinrich Siegler von Eberswald. Publisher, sportsman, Nazi SA member who worked for Nazi intelligence in Austria in the 1930s and was later an Abwehr intelligence officer in Berlin and Paris. Klein worked with him on an economic espionage plan and secret financial transactions in occupied Paris.

Friedrich Siegler von Eberswald. Brother of Heinrich and a former SA intelligence officer. Involved in the attempted Nazi coup in Austria and fled to Germany. Later Luftwaffe Lieutenant Colonel in Berlin and Paris. Publisher of an economic and political magazine used as a cover for spying, and the Wehrmacht soldiers' pocketbook including special SS edition.

Carl Heinrich von Stulpnagel. German Military Commander of Paris and previously in charge of Military Intelligence for the Foreign Armies Section between 1932 and 1936. Klein claimed he recruited her to espionage work. Executed after 1944 Valkyrie plot to kill Hitler.

Werner Ohletz. Senior Abwehr officer in Berlin and Paris. Linked to Gisela Klein. Like Stulpnagel associated with 1944 plot to kill Hitler but survived.

Britain

John Dennis "Jack" Profumo. Playboy, pilot, jump jockey, soldier and Conservative Minister for War involved in a sex and spy scandal in the 1960s. Klein's lover from the 1930s. Their affair would span the duration of the Second World War only apparently ending in the 1950s.

Jeanne Stourton. Lady Camoys. 1930s Nazi supporter. Lover of Hitler's foreign affairs adviser and German Ambassador to Britain, Joachim von Ribbentrop. She was a spy for him and friend of Jack Profumo.

Nancy Astor. The first woman to take her seat in Parliament. The centre of the alleged "Cliveden set" of influential people who appeased Hitler. She would identify Klein as a spy in 1935 after the German and Jack Profumo spent the weekend together at Cliveden on the Astor estate.

Bill Astor. Conservative MP and Nancy's eldest son. Friend of Jack Profumo whose later lifestyle at Cliveden would be central to the 1960s Profumo scandal.

David Astor. Second World War Intelligence officer and later Editor of *the Observer* newspaper. His mother Nancy asked him to provide Klein's location when she was trying to track her down.

Michael Astor. Son of Nancy. Friend of Jack Profumo and Gisela.

Jakey Astor. Nancy Astor's youngest son. Would meet Gisela Klein in Berlin in 1938.

Diana Russell Clarke. Gisela Klein stayed with her in 1938 and narrowly escaped arrest. Russell Clarke later worked at Bletchley Park on breaking German codes. Called Klein "a very beautiful German girl".

Richard Derek Cardiff. Scots Guards officer who Klein visited in the UK after meeting him in Egypt.

Hanmer "Pat" Cecil Hanbury. Grenadier Guards officer who Klein also met in Egypt and who flew to Paris with her in 1937.

Dorothy "Dodo" Hanbury. First British woman member of the Italian Fascist Party. Pat Hanbury's mother and in love with the pro-German Lord Mount Temple.

Lord Mount Temple. Former Conservative politician Wilfred Ashley. Chairman of the Anglo-German Fellowship, the organisation the Nazis tried to use to influence British policy towards Germany. He vouched for Gisela Klein in 1935 to get her permission to stay longer in the UK.

"Geordy" George Leveson-Gower. 5th Duke of Sutherland. Friend of the Prince of Wales, later Edward VIII. Member of the Royal Household. Former defence minister and probable lover of Gisela Klein in the south of France.

Ronald Sidney Seth. Special Operations Executive. Double, possibly triple agent. Met Wolfgang Brandstetter and Gisela Klein in occupied Paris while training for a German espionage mission to Britain. He didn't realise who she was because she was using another identity.

United States

Joseph Patrick Kennedy Jr. Known as Jack by close friends and family. Groomed to be the first Catholic President of the United States of America by his father. Klein's lover in Paris, Cannes and Copenhagen and probably the United States. Shared his father's antisemitic and isolationist views. An early admirer of the success of the Nazis in apparently tackling Germany's economic problems.

Joseph Patrick Kennedy Sr. Kennedy patriarch. Prohibition bootleg runner, financier, Hollywood executive and isolationist US Ambassador to the Court of St James into the Second World War.

William C Bullitt. US Ambassador to France gave Joe Kennedy Jr. an internship at the Paris embassy and he and his brother Jack Kennedy – later assassinated US President John F Kennedy – stayed with Bullitt's right hand man Carmel Offie in Paris, where Joe was seeing Gisela Klein after she'd escaped arrest in Britain.

1

THE PURGING OF GISELA KLEIN

Paris 1944

IT WAS THE day before her 29th Birthday and she'd come so close to getting away with it all. She'd played the innocent socialite accidentally caught up in events beyond her understanding to square things with the newly arrived American forces in the city and the Paris police, who had their own problems after their obedience to the Germans, had helped her by suggesting she typed out a timeline of her life allowing her to neatly edit some of the inconvenient reality.

None of that mattered now. She'd been arrested and tied to a tree to be publicly humiliated on the most famous street in the French capital. She must have been betrayed by an informant or perhaps her luck had finally just run out.

She would have been absolutely terrified about what was going to happen with very good reasons. The nausea she felt wasn't just because she was in the early stages of pregnancy with her first child. This was Paris in September 1944 after it had been liberated from German occupation. The city was in the grip of what would later become known as the "wild purge" as Parisians tried to cleanse themselves of the guilt and shame of their own behaviour. Hundreds if not thousands in the city would die at the hands of their neighbours.

The Fifi's, as the amateur and out of control Forces of the French Interior were known, had pushed into the restaurant on the Champs Elysees carrying weapons and with the same arrogant power of life and death the German secret police, the Gestapo, had been wielding only a few weeks before.

Her false French ID card had identified her as Gisela Klein, with an occupation of Secretary. They seemed to know how she'd come to possess it and they took her outside. The other diners, most of whom had done business with the Germans would have tried to avoid catching the attention of the Fifi's as they left. The world famous Maxims restaurant on the Rue Royale just over a mile away from where she was now bound and helpless had even offered free food to the influx of American and British officers as protection against too close a scrutiny of its gastronomic service to the German elite including Adolf Hitler's second in command Herman Göring.

Retribution was on the menu from a furious population where many now claimed to have been active in the resistance to the occupying German forces, but in reality had largely collaborated either actively or passively. Those who had genuinely resisted had often been betrayed by French informers and were even hunted down by their own compatriots in the French Fascist paramilitary force, the Milice and in Paris by the black market gang run by German intelligence, who'd diversified into anti resistance and anti semitic activities and were known as the French Gestapo.

None of the truth or detail mattered now. A sewer flood of revenge and self justification flowed through the streets and alleys of the city. The innocent, suspected and actual collaborators were murdered without trial or evidence. Gunshots and cries echoed through the deserted night time streets as the inhabitants hid in their shuttered and dark homes. During the day women were paraded in public to be beaten and abused and have their heads shaved or far worse. Some had taken German lovers or fallen in love with young men in the wrong uniform. The fraternisation of others kept their families fed when the alternative had been starvation. Some were falsely accused out of jealousy or score settling.

As she stood tied and captive on the Champs Elysees, a street where she'd worked for the Nazi run Continental Films and she'd known well since she'd modelled for French *Vogue* in the 1930's, Gisela Klein was the subject of particular hatred. She was to her captors an easy target, a German woman, a living reminder of the four years of humiliation of the self proclaimed City of Light that had done nothing to stop the despised Bosches marching in.

Around her was a chaos of competing factions and power struggles. The Paris police were largely absent from the streets as they worked out which way things were going to go. The official resistance in the form of the Fifi's contained numbers of former collaborators anxious to show which side they were on now by the zeal with which they persecuted people who'd behaved just like them. They operated as freelance squads arresting people and carrying out killings. Communists, Socialists and the followers of the Free French General Charles de Gaulle competed for positions of power and a slice of post war France.

The juidicial and civil administration systems in the city were in tatters. Many of the judges and politicians had been jailed facing charges of collaboration. As a result Gisela was facing a very dangerous and uncertain future. She was completely in the hands of her abductors who could deal with her in any way that they chose and there was absolutely nobody to stop them.

She would, according to the secret file kept on her by British Military Intelligence, end up alongside the French judges and politicians incarcerated in the notorious Fresnes Prison. Conditions inside were said to be worse than when it had been run by the Gestapo who had tortured and murdered with impunity inside its grim walls.

Women were crammed six to a cell designed for one. Many of them were prostitutes, only guilty of working their trade, as if they'd ever had any real choice about their customers. There would be no respite for Gisela. On the same day she was seized from the restaurant she faced a hostile interrogation for the first time. It was undoubtedly the lowest point in her life, imprisoned, alone and pregnant.

She was subjected to many questioning sessions over the weeks and months to come and some of her answers were noted down and preserved in the secret French intelligence files about her. Those transcripts show Gisela Klein still had cards to play. She would take the losing hand she'd just been dealt and bluff for all she was worth.

In reality, the stake was her life and that of her child but her hidden ace was that her beauty helped her to disguise how clever she really was. It meant men made easy assumptions about her which led them away from what she'd actually been doing, and that she knew far more about German espionage both before and during the war in France, Britain, and the United States than her current captors would ever realise.

2

NO PAID EMPLOYMENT

1933

HER NATURAL HONEY blonde hair and green eyes were what the port officials at Harwich on England's east coast noticed first as they checked her papers at Parkeston Quay on that warm dry day in June 1933.

The high wheeling seagulls, the low port buildings and railway station, the oily, seaweed infused smell of the harbour and the sharp sulphur tang of hard British steam coal, distinctly different to the brown coal of her home, were her official welcome to England.

Gisela's visa to land in the UK was granted on the basis the 19 year-old was going to stay with a family in Essex before going on to Oxford University to continue her studies in the English language.

After showing her German passport and clearing customs she went to board the passenger train to London, sitting, waiting, on the other side of the harbour terminal. LNER, the initials of the London and North Eastern Railway, were written in gold on the dusty apple green coach enamel of the steam locomotive pulling varnished teakwood carriages.

A railway porter hurried forward to put her suitcases up and onto the luggage rack in the compartment, accepting the few coins she gave him as a tip.

She must have been excited at embarking on the last part of a journey to somewhere completely new. Constant travel, as if she was running from or to something, was to be a theme in her life. If there were also butterflies in her stomach, from anxiety about the unknown, no one would have guessed from her face, which in public amongst strangers, and always when photographed, gave little away but her ability to attract.

The world around her was in flux. The young woman, along with everyone else, was caught in the tentacles of the great economic depression that had spread out around the world from the 1929 Wall Street Crash in the United States.

The squeeze was now at its worst. Britain's export trade had slumped to half its previous level, creating three and half million unemployed. There were black spots of grinding poverty for working class men, women and children in Scotland, the North and Wales.

The rich and well connected still had plenty, if they hadn't piled into the stock market, and Britain's ruling classes had confidence in themselves and their Empire. The rhythms of life, especially in the countryside, continued much as before.

The young blonde woman was coming from somewhere far worse. Germany's industrial Ruhr, where American capital and investment had fled. This proved disastrous for an economy that had guttered weakly since the First World War. One in three Germans were unemployed. Her once very prosperous and well-connected family were no longer wealthy, and like many other young German women she was looking abroad for her future.

She was one of thousands who would be employed in domestic work as au pairs and governesses in British middle-class households. Many of these were told to listen and report what they heard as part of a German spying operation.

British intelligence would later discover Mrs My Eriksson, a German agent posing as a Domestic worker who kept a list of other domestic staff including one who worked at No 10 Downing Street. Another woman Margaret Newitt who ran a domestic agency for German women was placing staff in households of interest to the German embassy. She was interned during the Second World War.

But listening at keyholes wasn't really Gisela Klein's style. There were other ways of helping her country. A country she cared deeply about. Gisela's patriotism for Germany was born in the turmoil of the Ruhr she'd seen as child.

It was a landscape of right-wing militias of disillusioned and embittered ex-soldiers from the First World War. They were in vicious armed warfare with Communist-led strikers from the huge industrial plants. This chaos and division was compounded by an invasion and occupation of the whole region, including her home city, by French soldiers when she was nine years old in 1923. The troops shot local protestors while seizing goods as part of war reparations imposed by the Treaty of Versailles which ended the First World War.

Like millions of her fellow citizens, Gisela felt Germany had been treated very badly and it was now time for her country to take its place amongst the great nations of Europe. She certainly wasn't going to be pushing at a closed door in Britain, as many agreed with the idea of a resurgent Germany in the 1930s.

As Gisela arrived across the Channel in mid-June 1933, Hitler was cementing his grip on power. He was an admirer of Britain and in particular its Empire. He hoped to maintain friendly relations while pursuing his ambitions for a Third Reich and expansion. It would be wrong to assume however that, because of her views,

Gisela was a Nazi and an ardent supporter of Adolf Hitler. Many German nationalists like her weren't.

Their beliefs were often based on their social class, with the upper, middle and the officer class in the German army having most of the same aims as Hitler; but with massively differing levels of support for the thuggish tactics, antisemitism and policies of the Nazi party.

However, while she publicly told people in Britain she was anti-Nazi, Gisela was being, as she so often was, economical with the truth. She had a personal connection to someone from her home town with direct links to the two most powerful men in Germany: Hermann Göring, who created the feared Gestapo and led the German air force, and the Fuhrer, Adolf Hitler.

The ticket Gisela Klein purchased bringing her to Harwich also came with a hidden surcharge. All travellers outside the German Reich had to pay it. Senior Nazis admired the Soviet Union's devotion to the doctrine of total espionage, and they adopted it. This meant anyone leaving Germany had to gather and report all information possible: social, political, economic and of course military. Gisela would go on to be remarkably successful in this endeavour, developing and maintaining high level contacts in all these spheres in Britain, France and later America.

****

Amongst Gisela Klein's personal papers and photographs in California is a white card with black print. It gives a formal notice of Gisela Hendrina Klein's birth on the 5th of September 1913 and refers to her father Alfred Klein as a lawyer.

She was raised in the hustle and bustle of the river Rhine port city of Dusseldorf on the affluent Goltsteinstrasse. A street that proclaimed the success of its inhabitants. It housed politicians, artists and entrepreneurs and her father Alfred, who was also a book binder, her mother Henriette and her two brothers Werner and Helmut. Germany was one of the most literate countries in Europe and the book and the printing trade was large and highly profitable.

It was a world she would later freeze in the memory of an exile, maintaining a love for her country she never relinquished and although the records show she never actually joined the Nazi Party, that wouldn't stop her working to support Germany. The problem for Gisela was, as with so many of the men she would beguile, her country was not really faithful to her.

Adolf Hitler became the Chancellor of Germany in January 1933 and just two months later, through the innocuously named Enabling Act, he assumed an effective dictatorship and then began ruthlessly suppressing anyone who opposed him. He achieved this in a supposedly democratic system by intimidation, the huge miscalculations and arrogance of other politicians, and the simple expedient of locking up his enemies in the newly created concentration camps. By the end of 1933, 100,000 people would be incarcerated.

Two months before Gisela left Dusseldorf, the Hitler Youth burned what were described as "unwanted" books and paintings in front of the city's Rhine Hall.

That April, the paramilitary Nazi Sturmabteilung known as the SA or Brownshirts surrounded Dusseldorf's monolithic Tietz department store and the Gustav Carsch fashion house as part of the Nazi organised boycott of Jewish businesses. Both would be sold at knock down rates within the year.

The Dusseldorf Gestapo, targeted the artist Paul Klee as a "Galician Jew" forcing him out of his teaching job at the Dusseldorf Academy of Art. He produced an abstract work featuring a black cross called "Struck from the List" marking the event.

On the opposite side of the River Rhine from Dusseldorf in the ancient city of Neuss, a German industrialist marked the Fuhrer's accession to power by using members of his own workforce to create a storm troop of SA Brown shirts. Werner Theodor "Teddy" Schaurte was 36 years old and he and Gisela knew each other well enough for her to keep something he sent her secret for the whole of her life.

He was also born in Dusseldorf. He inherited the top job in what would become the world's largest manufacturer of nuts and bolts, Bauer and Schaurte. His enterprise would be directly funded by Hermann Göring's air ministry. Werner was personally congratulated by Hitler for his application of National Socialist principles to the factory and his creation of the unit of SA storm troopers. The company's products would quite literally hold the German military machine together. But Werner had a problem that meant keeping close to the new powers in Germany wasn't just political, it was absolutely necessary. He had Jewish ancestry.

While Hitler, with his dark hair and little toothbrush moustache, seemed miles away from the image of the Nordic Aryans the Nazis were so keen on, it's also possible the natural blonde Gisela wasn't a full part of their vision of the future either.

Jews were excluded from working for the civil authorities by legislation called the Law for the Restoration of the Professional Civil Service. This was followed by hundreds of vicious and petty orders and laws restricting the lives of the German Jewish population. It led to the first wave of emigration by German Jews.

Young women like Gisela were already being subjected to intense propaganda that marriages between Aryan women and Jewish men, and vice versa, led to Germany's decline, because of a dilution of the pure German blood of the country. While Gisela's looks pointed towards the Aryan future the Nazis envisaged, her ancestry may have pointed in a different direction.

Gisela's mother Henriette, from whom she got her striking appearance, if not her blonde hair, was Dutch. On her mother's side the family were called Kalis and her maternal grandmother's maiden name was Kruisinga, a fairly common name in Holland. The family were from a small town near the border with Germany.

Kalis can be a Polish or Slovak derived name with Jewish heritage. There are also some existing records of a Dutch Jewish Kruisinga family, but there were also certainly branches of the family who were Christians.

However, in Amsterdam, the Institute for War, Holocaust and Genocide Research, found no direct evidence to support the idea that Gisela had Jewish heritage from her mother's side of the family. Gisela, according to her family, would always say she was a Lutheran, and she did at one stage in her life attend Lutheran services, although she was never a great churchgoer.

Her father, Alfred Klein, served in the German army in the First World War – there is a picture of him, which she always kept, standing in a garden with a rustic wooden pergola behind him in a military uniform with high cavalry style boots and holding a riding crop.

According to a family story the Nazis nationalised Alfred's book binding business. It seems possible that what in fact happened was that the business was Aryanised, particularly if Alfred had Jewish ancestry himself or perhaps partners. From 1933 Jews were "encouraged" to sell their businesses to people the Nazis regarded as having pure German blood. One German document does describe Alfred as a Catholic but conversions as part of an integration into broad German society were common enough.

Later British Intelligence would also speculate as to whether Gisela was Jewish. In the British file on her, Major Dick White of MI5's counterintelligence branch, describes her surname, Klein as a Jewish name although pointed out she was of "aryan appearance".

A tacit and common British acceptance of the prevailing Nazi doctrine that someone's appearance could identify them, and there was something that could even be called an Aryan race. He also stated she'd had difficulty renewing her German passport with the consulate in Paris. He doesn't draw any conclusion from this.

Major White was only partly correct about the name Klein. It just means "small" in German, and while many victims of the Holocaust carried the name, there were many non-Jewish Kleins as well. Gisela's difficulty renewing her passport does however coincide with a Nazi move that saw people with Jewish ancestry begin to lose the standard German passports and have them replaced with a marked document with an indelible letter J printed on it. J for Juden.

Her family do not appear in the files of German racial census of 1939 which required people to certify their ancestry back to their grandparents with documentary evidence. The families who provided information on Jewish ancestors had these records sent to a central registry and these largely survived the Second World War. However, they are only 87 percent complete, with those from the Rhine Province, of which Dusseldorf is part, completely missing. The German National Archive notes drily, in a poorly translated reference, that these record cards from the census were "eliminated" in 1945, as, by then, had so many of the people they recorded.

This census was part of the Nazi plan to find and rid Germany of Jews who the Nazis were using as scapegoats for the defeat of the First World War and the turmoil that followed. Many Germans also believed that Communism was some sort of Jewish driven conspiracy.

There was a deadly debate about what made a person Jewish and therefore both non-Aryan, and in the eyes of the Nazis, a non-German. The authorities eventually decided that anyone with three or four religiously practicing grandparents qualified. Later having two Jewish grandparents was enough to threaten your life.

People with a lesser Jewish heritage than that were called "Mischling," a term of abuse that roughly corresponds to mongrel in English. This group included some who were practicing Christians and others who were not only secular but did not identify with the Jewish community at all. Not being able to prove three generations of Aryan blood was enough to label someone and cause them continuing difficulties with the Nazis. The industrialist Werner Schaurte had a Jewish great-grandfather, but even having a suspect name like Klein could trigger problems with petty Nazi bureaucrats.

There is no documentary evidence Gisela's father suffered as a direct result of the activities of the Nazis. Alfred died in 1941, while working as an air raid warden in the block of apartments in which he then lived on Kapellerstrasse. His death was supposed to be from a heart attack; he was said to have put on a lot of weight. Perhaps coincidentally, it was at the same time as the Nazis began their deportations of German Jews to the "East" as the "Final Solution" began.

Gisela's box of papers in California also contained Alfred's death notice which makes no reference to him being a lawyer. The Nazis officially banned most Jews from the profession in 1933 just before Gisela arrived in the UK and you had to be a member of their Lawyers Organisation to practice. Instead, this death notice highlights his service to Germany as a Lieutenant in the Landwehr army and that he was the holder of the Iron Cross second class for an individual act of bravery. He probably served on the eastern front against the Russians in the First World War. Holding the Iron Cross afforded a little protection against the Nazis. Jewish veterans with this award were allowed to continue as lawyers until 1938.

There is another clue to a possible Jewish inheritance from

Gisela's father. Well before Alfred Klein died, Gisela would distance herself from him when questioned by the British authorities. She told them she was being financially supported by her mother who she said was living in Holland. This was conveniently misleading and may well have been to divert their interest into an otherwise unexplained "private income" they'd been told about.

However, it was not a good thing to be regarded as a Jewish refugee from Germany in Britain in the 1930s. There were familiar strident arguments about "economic migrants" taking jobs, some of it an excuse for the antisemitism rife in British institutions and particularly amongst the middle and upper classes.

The British Medical Association opposed German Jewish doctors being allowed entry and there were bans on Jewish shopworkers trying to escape what they could clearly see coming. The British hardline on Jewish migrants, shared by other countries, meant the routes for women out of Germany were limited to domestic work and student studies. Gisela used both.

There's a postscript to the question of Gisela's heritage. When I mentioned the circumstantial evidence to her daughter, Lisl, it transpired that as part of her desire to know more about her mother, she'd taken a commercially available DNA test.

Its results showed a small proportion, just 2.6 percent, of the genetic markers indicative of European Jewish ancestry. It may or may not have come from her mother. Her half-brother, Horst, took the same test and didn't share the result. Siblings don't necessarily inherit the same genes from a parent. However, if Lisl inherited this line from her mother, it would suggest, based on current knowledge, that any Jewish ancestry was further back than Giselas own grandparents. It would not however rule out her father having a Jewish grandparent.

Whatever the case, Gisela certainly could have found plenty of reasons to wish herself away from Germany in 1933. There was an election in March, although it was anything but free and fair. The burning of the Reichstag parliament building the month before had seen the issuing of a decree that suspended freedom of the press and most civil liberties. As Gisela arrived in England the Social Democratic Party was officially banned in Germany. It was the only party to vote against the legislative act that gave Hitler his dictatorial powers. Its leadership fled and would eventually end up in London.

Gisela's family don't know exactly when she started working as a model or mannequin, as they were known then. It's thought it was when she went to Oxford. She was still a fresh faced 19-year-old when she first arrived. One of the pictures in the official file on her in the espionage collection at the British National Archives in Kew, with a bow in her thick hair and a white blouse with a long collar and a grey jacket, makes her look more mature than her years. It's her eyes which look older, as though she has already seen things her more comfortably insulated contemporaries in Britain hadn't.

The photographer Graham Grant, of Wigmore Street in London's Westminster 1, was more analytical about Gisela's "striking" appearance. Noted on a pre-stamped form on the back of a photograph for her modelling portfolio: *Hair: Blonde; Eyes: Grey;* (in fact they were green) *Height: Five feet ten inches; Bust: 34 inches; Waist: 26; Hips: 36; Shoes: size 6; Glove: 6 ¾; Hat: 22.* Usefully, because she wasn't meant to be working while she was in Britain, her name is mis-spelled on the back of the photograph, Kleim not Klein. It was her first recorded use of an alias.

This was an indication of both her practical and pragmatic character, where a mixture of truth and lies to authority were part and parcel of daily life. What would become clear was that she would ignore rules and break laws whenever it suited her. She loved the excitement of risk and men with similar inclinations. She had a vivid imagination sometimes at variance to the truth, whether because she wished it so, or because it served her purpose didn't seem to matter. This was coupled with a self-disciplined drive, a capacity for hard work, a talent for organising and an ambition to achieve a status one way or another both for herself and for her country.

She was the youngest child, a girl after two boys. Her position in the family contributed to her advanced social skills, desire to be noticed and ability to cope independently with life. Having older brothers toughened her and helped her to deal with and keep men as friends and maintain aspiring lovers at a distance. Although that may have been a hard lesson. She would later tell her daughter how embarrassing she had at first found the stares from men her looks seemed to provoke.

****

However, before this young woman could become established as a model and spy, not necessarily in that order, Great Dunmow in Essex was to be her first stop in England.

She changed trains from the Harwich to London Liverpool Street service onto the relatively sleepy Bishops Stortford to Braintree branch line of the London North Eastern Railway. Gisela was coming to live in a classic example of little England of that inter-war period. A small, pleasant and prosperous market town with origins recorded in the Domesday book. The people there were very proud the bacon factory just up the road from the railway station supplied the prestigious London department store Harrods.

The town's war memorial is at the junction of the High Street and New Street. When Gisela first saw it, the names of local men killed in the conflict between Britain and Germany between 1914 and 1918, were still sharp and fresh on the Portland stone pillar and in people's memories.

It was one of the thousands of similar memorials in villages, towns, cities railways stations and businesses fuelling a passionate desire the conflict that had cost nearly 900,000 British combatants and civilians their lives, should never happen again. This was the ultimate driver for the appeasement of Hitlers political demands. It would be the stark dividing line in British political life of the decade. Only in retrospect did it appear to have encouraged the aggression it so desperately wanted to avert.

Great Dunmow was very different to Gisela's home in Dusseldorf. The Klein family townhouse there was originally designed as an artist's residence. It was three storeys high with slightly arched windows and little black iron balconies outside the full-length windows on the first floor. The windows opened onto the street bringing a view of the flowerbeds on the opposite side of the road decorated with ornamental stone urns. These little gardens were backed by a row of Linden trees; the Seufzer Avenue, the Sighing Avenue; and behind them, the canalised river Dussel flowed to its confluence with the powerful River Rhine, making Dusseldorf an important port for the industrial Ruhr.

During the good years, Gisela later told her daughter, she and her brothers were ferried to school in the back of a Rolls Royce motorcar. There were photographs showing her and other teenage girls on trips to the seaside in Belgium and later with young friends, male and female, in other motor cars, a further indication of her privileged upbringing and contacts. Then came the bad times, and she later gave her son a million mark note from the hyper-inflation years and told him how during a family holiday, a river trip on the Rhine, her father carried all the paper banknotes they needed crammed into a suitcase.

In Great Dunmow Gisela stayed in a large old house called Rood End. Like her own home, it looked onto the road, but the pavement here was narrow and the road much busier – it was the main route in the town leading to Bishop's Stortford. Behind the house was a large garden and stabling. Rood End was the residence of Dr Geoffrey Barber, his wife Daphne, and their one-year-old son Nicholas. The Barbers were a prominent family in the town. He was the local doctor running his surgery from home, and Daphne Barber did voluntary work. Gisela was going to be an au pair for Nicholas before officially going on to Oxford to "continue her studies of English".

While Gisela waited for her 20th birthday in September, the Oxford Michaelmas university term of 1933 and helped with the household duties, she would have been a spectator of a traditional event that made the town of Great Dunmow well known in the area.

The Flitch Trials are said to date back to 1104. In these a married couple must convince a jury of "six local bachelors and six local maidens" they have never wished themselves unwed. Those that succeed win a flitch of bacon. Half a pig cut lengthways. The flitches hang on a stand carried on the shoulders of four men and were, (and still are to this day, although no longer annually) paraded along with the prospective couples and the judge and the jury, while the local population enjoy the spectacle. This parade passed Rood End House and so Gisela would only have to have looked out of the windows for a grandstand view.

In August of that year a Mr. and Mrs. Bird from Hammersmith in London; a Mr. and Mrs. Cox from Peckham in London, and a Mr. and Mrs. Mann from Woking in Surrey carried their porcine prizes away. Half a pig in the depressed 1930s was valuable enough to make travelling to Dunmow from outside Essex well worth it.

It must have seemed so very strange and very English to Gisela. Perhaps she found it romantic that a couple could live in wedded bliss and be prepared to declare it for all to see, although she may merely have thought it a quaint custom, no more relevant personally than the tradition of the cartwheeling children of Dusseldorf, an event celebrating the award of City status after a 13th century battle.

That summer, Essex along with most of the rest of the country enjoyed exceptionally fine weather with prolonged spells of sunshine. It was an auspicious start to her time in Britain. She was away from the increasing restrictions of Germany and able to enjoy all the prospects and yearnings that inexperience and vitality offer to the young who are going to live forever. While her line to officialdom was that she was to continue her studies in English, the unofficial version suggests her English was pretty good already. She seems to have had a natural facility with languages, with English and French, some Dutch from her mother and later workable Spanish and Italian on top of her own German.

What would become very clear was that any academic interest she might have had was not really in studying the English language but rather more in learning all she could about young English men of a certain class. Speaking English with a slightly exotic German accent never did the actress Marlene Dietrich any harm, and it was something Gisela, who had a similar but softer style, did her whole life. It opened many doors for her where men, both young and old, were concerned.

One became especially important to her. Particularly with regards to an arms-length relationship with the truth, and a love of risk, they were two peas in a pod. She maintained their romance for two decades, even while they were both on opposing sides of another World War the previous "War to End all Wars" not only failed to prevent but made inevitable.

3

CALL ME JACK

GISELA KLEIN MET John Dennis Profumo for the first time soon after she went up to Oxford University in the autumn of 1933. They were both at a university known throughout the world, alongside Cambridge, for providing the elite of the British Empire. John Profumo was always known as Jack. He had a striking, though not particularly handsome appearance, with dark eyes, a strong nose and receding black hair. In his case, personality took over where his looks left off.

His family made their fortune from the Provident Life Company, which his astute grandfather created. This company allowed people to fund the purchase of their own homes through endowment assurance which paid out at the end of the policy's term. Jack had, by all accounts, an idyllic and privileged childhood accompanied by all the benefits insulating wealth could provide.

His reports from Harrow Public School, quoted in his son David's book, *Bringing the House Down*, suggested he was:

"…an agreeable youth who is not stupid but has little idea of what real work is."

He was clearly not particularly academic and his atrocious spelling, which would remain poor into adulthood, coupled with an obvious appetite for risk in all its forms would probably nowadays mark him out as neuro-diverse, although at that time characteristics like these tended to be regarded as merely part of the upper-class male condition.

Jack Profumo's later wife, the actress Valerie Hobson categorised his interests as: "Politics; girls; horses; parties; holidays in the sun; practical jokes; society gossip; aero planes and above all fun." This list from the 1950s could easily have served as a Who's Who entry, but two decades earlier perhaps, his passion for acting replaced, or was at least interchangeable, with politics.

During Jack's early life the Profumo family started out in some style in Kensington in London and then decamped to Avon Carrow, an impressively odd and faux medieval former hunting lodge in the pretty Warwickshire village of Avon Dasset. Gisela was a guest at Avon Carrow and would become part of the hectic social scene there alongside his younger brother and two sisters.

The house was built in the Victorian gothic school of architecture and is approached up a short drive and through an archway in a barn like building built in the local honey coloured stone. This entrance leads to a quadrangle facing the house. In the 1930s this enclosed area contained stables; quarters for staff and Jack Profumo's own small private cinema complete with flip-up seating, which he built with some assistance in an old laundry.

The carved stone of the armorial shield above the main door to Avon Carrow bears the words:

"God's providence is my inheritance."

The letters look like a later addition and seem to reference the real and rather less divine source of the Profumo family's good fortune.

Today, Avon Carrow has gone the way of many large houses and been subdivided into separate apartments. In the 1930s the main house of two wings was dominated by the square central tower, complete with castellated battlements. Directly beneath the tower, was a high-ceilinged hall. Inside, a large canopied Gothic fireplace in stone would have, in the grand tradition of British country houses, undoubtedly roasted people close to it but failed to dent the chill for anyone further away.

The hall had been created before the Profumos' time by curtaining off the old main entrance to the house, with a series of arched, leaded glass windows. Originally this space was open to the land behind. This allowed the first owner to inspect his horses from a Juliet balcony. The balcony was retained high on the side wall of the hall opposite the fireplace.

To the left and the right-hand side of the central hall, doors led off to the main rooms of Avon Carrow. These included a sprung floored ballroom.

Upstairs some of the windows had stained glass in their leading panes. Gambolling foxes and the pursuit of them being one theme, as this was hunting country. The local hunt was The Warwickshire, whose hounds were kept in kennels not far away in Little Kineton.

The hunting activities during the season from November to March and out of season with Point-to-Point racing to keep the horses in shape, provided much of the social scene in Avon Dasset as elsewhere in the countryside. Jack, who learned to ride as a young boy in Hyde Park while the family were still in London, became an enthusiastic and clearly brave amateur jockey on his horse Decent Fellow even if he was not always successful. He broke his already distinctive nose quite badly.

He was described by *The Daily News* at the time as a "prominent steeplechaser". Local newspaper reports however seem to ascribe rather more places than wins. *The Bucks Herald* records what was probably a typical set of Point-to-Point races on a wet 1930s February day at Somerton in Oxfordshire organised by the Oxford University Air Squadron. Jack managed a 2nd place, and the "wretched weather" saw the last race cancelled altogether.

David Profumo recounts the story of an on-course bookmaker's comments about his father. Pointing to a listing on the race card he was reported to have said that the horse would win:

"If that booger could stay on his back."

A photograph kept by Gisela shows them both at a point-to-point meeting. Jack has presumably been running Decent Fellow. He is wearing a wide brimmed trilby hat and what looks like a jockey's jersey top and boots under a capacious and impresario-like striped double-breasted overcoat. It was obviously a cold day as everyone is wrapped up for the occasion. Tweeds and fur for the English women while Gisela is wearing a dark hat with a Tyrolean air and a dark overcoat and gloves. Her arm is through Jack's as they pose for the photographer. She nearly matches Jack in height. She looks happy with her companion who is smiling as if he has just shared a joke with one of the other people in the party who are identified in a caption on the back as: Miss McMinnis; Mr. McNaulty and Miss Banbury, granddaughter of Lord Banbury.

There is another photograph of Jack she kept. It's a newspaper cutting and shows a moment of public affection, even tenderness. She is tying on his cap before he races Decent Fellow. She is being watched by the second youngest of the sons of MP Nancy Astor, Michael, who would clearly demonstrate that he also admired her, while his companion Miss McMinnis looks on. She later became his second wife.

A passion for horsey activities was shared by Jack's sisters Elizabeth, known as Betty, and Mary, known as Maina, who also appear in a photograph with Gisela which she kept. In this, alongside an unidentified young man, possibly Jack's younger brother, the three women are standing posing for the camera on a summer's day by a river. Gisela has a cigarette in her hand. Smoking was glamorous then and while she didn't really need its supposed allure she was often photographed in the 1930s with a cigarette in her right hand.

There's a family story of how Betty and Maina Profumo, both hunting mad, boarded their first-class compartment at Banbury station on the London train to Marylebone still in muddy hunting clothes from a day spent hurtling across the fields of Warwickshire. They pulled the carriage blinds down so that they could change into evening wear and spend a night out in town.

Gisela later told her daughter she had been fox hunting in England, an activity Hitler banned in Germany a year after she arrived in the UK. He regarded it as unsporting, although it was announced at the same time as the distinctly unsporting Night of the Long Knives where he had senior members of the Nazi SA organization slaughtered because they were suspected of disloyalty.

Gisela didn't ride and so her participation would have been as a "hunt follower": the dubiously enjoyable experience of chasing the hunt as it chased the fox. Hunt followers moved on foot on local footpaths and fields, or in motorcars on local roads trying to spot horses and hounds as they careered around the countryside in the distance, often in the cold and wet. Easily dismissed as the uncomfortable in pursuit of the unspeakable.

The house at Avon Dasset was a clear statement of the Profumos' wealth and status and a desire to cement their position on the social ladder. Jack's father held a Sardinian Baronetcy, not recognised by the British system of peerages, and was a barrister. He'd taken silk, a recognition of his abilities and was therefore a K.C., King's Counsel. Both he and Jack's grandfather had unfulfilled political ambitions. They both stood unsuccessfully for Parliament.

The Profumos, while wealthy and very well connected, would still not have been regarded as from the top drawer of society in the 1930s by the land-owning aristocracy that surrounded them. They were of "foreign descent" as one note in the later MI5 file on Gisela puts it sniffily. Another incorrect file entry betrays its author's leanings with the entry: "Italian Jews", and their money came originally from being in trade. They were nouveaux riche. Although at this point, they were less notorious than a previous owner of Avon Carrow who had inveigled the local postmaster into a betting fraud. He faked the time that bets were placed on horses that had already passed the finishing post.

The fourth Baron Profumo also maintained a connection to his roots. MI5 reported he was a member of the London branch of the Italian Fascist party, which the security service had thoroughly penetrated. He gave generously to various causes, amongst them endowing beds at the Italian Hospital in Queen Square in London. The beds were named in honour of the Italian leader Benito Mussolini. Il Duce apparently gave the Baron a signed photograph in return as a thank you.

The connection between Italian fascism and the UK was strong. Mussolini, the man Hitler copied as he developed his political and particularly presentational strategies, wanted to export his fascism to Italians abroad. Many children of Italian parents in Britain were sent to military style training each summer in Italy or for the rather less fortunate, youth camps set up in Felixstowe and Maidstone. Camp Mussolini in Kent was created in the same year Gisela arrived in Britain. By the mid to late 30s MI5 reported there were active Italian fascist branches in most of the major cities of the UK and Northern Ireland.

But the month after Gisela's arrival that warm summer of 1933 it wasn't the benefits of a fascist youth camp the young Jack Profumo required. He was sent to the Vocational Guidance Department of the National Institute of Industrial Psychology which offered testing to determine suitability for various careers. This suggests the Baron and his wife, Martha, a former actress and dancer from Edinburgh, were not sure what the future held for their son. Jack undoubtedly inherited the divine right of the oldest child but clearly wasn't showing an obvious aptitude for anything.

He was tested and the results suggested he had a marked instinct for self-display. A career in law, like his father, was ruled out, as was the army. It was said that interior design might suit Jack instead. David Profumo wryly calls that one of the "Great Ifs" of history. However, despite this somewhat unpromising assessment, the Baron Profumo seems to have called in a family favour and secured him a place at Brasenose College in Oxford to read law. Proof of the adage that it's not what you know, but who.

The Vocational Guidance Department, however, did get something right, as Jack quickly discovered the law was not for him, and he switched to Agriculture and Political Economy. This had the added advantage of allowing him, as an undergraduate, to officially keep a car for farm visits. The vehicle he chose was no impoverished student's ancient runabout. He drove a Bentley Continental Vanden Plas, a two-door convertible with running boards and space for four people, allowing him to pursue some of his other interests in obvious style.

Jack's instinct for theatricality, the self-display noted by his psychological testing, were given a free rein during his undergraduate years at Brasenose college. He would regularly appear in plays to reasonable reviews and on the 23rd of May 1934 by tuning a valve radio set to 767 kilohertz he could have been heard performing on the wireless as part of an act with his university friend Tom Asher on the BBC Radio Midland region opt out service, broadcast from the BBC's studios in Birmingham.

During his time at Oxford, he also became a member of the Bullingdon club, which had an historic link to Point to Point racing. It was an all-male Oxford dining club infamous for its bad behaviour and tradition of paying immediately for the often-extensive damage to the establishment in which they'd staged a drunken soiree. Later members would include the reputationally damaged British Prime Ministers David Cameron and Boris Johnson.

****

It's not clear exactly how Jack and Gisela's paths crossed. Under later interrogation by French intelligence Gisela would give 2 Keble Road as her initial address in Oxford just half a mile from Brasenose College where Jack was living. There is a photograph in Gisela Klein's papers in California of her dressed for an evening event. The photograph has 1933 written on the back. There are some other marks also in pencil, but they are too faint to decipher. She is seated and looking elegant, with long triangular drop earrings, a sleeveless oriental flowered silk dress and gloveless silk gauntlets on her forearms. There's a stylish bangle on her upper arm. Her pale green eyed gaze is directed at the camera lens.

Strangely, the picture was once part of a much larger photograph and someone, presumably Gisela, has cut out the young men surrounding her. The crop lines on the sides of the picture show the slightly curving marks of someone cutting by eye with scissors. She is seated in what looks like a formal group. She also appears from this to be the only woman, or perhaps one of only a few at a mainly male event. From what can be seen of the man standing behind her, he is wearing a three-button tailcoat that looks remarkably like the ones used by the Bullingdon club. Her reasons for cropping this picture, will never be known, but it does mean that some of her extensive contacts in British society, whom she would later, broadly and vaguely, describe to the British authorities as a "great many friends" remain undiscovered.

David Profumo detailed his father's early amorous adventures with girls with nicknames redolent of the 1930s like *Twinkle* and *Bubbles*, but he would ascribe a rather more special status to the blonde, green-eyed visitor from Dusseldorf.

"The first steady girlfriend was a lovely German blonde named Gisela Klein, who seemed to share his taste for japes."

There is another photograph in Gisela's papers in California that shows her in a white or cream top and high-waisted pale trousers sitting on a large ornamental stone ball, still there in the garden at Avon Carrow. Jack is sitting below her on the balustrade of the steps on the rear terrace of the house. He is wearing what looks like a large beach robe. It would seem they'd been playing tennis on the court in the garden although no rackets are visible. They seem very easy and natural with each other. It's the most relaxed and intimate private record of them together that Gisela kept.

The attraction between them was obvious. She was beautiful, elegant and formal in a traditional German middle-class way of that time. Even 30 years later in the United States she wore gloves and liked to be properly introduced to people. She made her daughter curtsy on return visits to her grandmother in Germany. Her daughter always describes her as "an elegant lady". But it wasn't all just surface. British intelligence, M15 reported she was: "intelligent, witty and companionable." Although in the circles in which she tended to move in Britain, having an interest in anything other than horses and hard partying undoubtedly marked her out as almost an intellectual.

Jack on the other hand had a big personality, and like her was particular about the way he dressed. In his case with a distinct flamboyance. He was rich and clearly fun to be with, a bad boy. That was a type of man for whom she seemed to have a notable weakness, and which later caused her extreme danger.

It seems not impossible that Jack was her first lover, or perhaps, she his. There was certainly a special bond between them that bridged other lovers and friends, and which lasted from the 30s to the 50s before a separation of continents and potentially something darker split them apart.

Gisela and Jack also shared something else together, an interest in flying. During the 1930s and 1940s she was closely associated with Germany's efforts to acquire air intelligence, as both Germany and Britain understood any future war would be dominated from the air. It was at Oxford that Jack began his own love affair with aircraft.

****

The 1930s saw a boom in amateur light aviation with the *Tatler* magazine which recorded the comings and goings of the British fashionable and well born having a regular column, "Air Eddies" devoted to the subject. This was usually accompanied by a photograph of a young male or female aviator in suitable attire just about to set off or having just arrived.

It was a time of the well-heeled in Britain popping over to Le Touquet on the Northern coast of France for lunch. In the 30 plus years following the Wright Brothers' first flight in 1903 the aviation industry still retained its glamorous and slightly pioneering aspect.

Jack already had a nearby example to follow. The Profumos' aristocratic neighbour John Verney, Lord Willoughby de Broke, who was joint master of the Warwickshire hunt and therefore well known to him, was a keen amateur pilot, as was his wife. They had their own private air strip at New Farm at Kineton just down the road from Avon Dasset.

Jack and his sister Maina shared an aircraft between them. He learned to fly with the Oxford University Air Squadron. David Profumo suggests the brother and sister had a Gypsy Moth, a two-seater bi-plane trainer, kept in a hangar at a long-lost airfield on the outskirts of Leamington Spa. However, Jack and Maina certainly progressed to something a little nattier; a 160 horsepower Fairchild, an American make. There were a couple of models from this company available at the time with this power rating: a biplane rather like a Gypsy Moth or probably more to Jack's taste, a side-by-side twin seater monoplane, the Fairchild 24 with an enclosed cockpit. Not dissimilar in looks to the ubiquitous and much later Cessna. Rather more comfortable for longer trips than open to the elements fore and aft cockpits.

The ideal temperament for a civilian pilot is a dislike of unnecessary risks and real attention to detail, particularly in technical matters. These were perhaps not Jack's greatest strengths, and it would catch him out a couple of times. He once nearly ran out of fuel over Mount Etna in Italy with his aunt on board and on another occasion had a very near escape. After a 3,500-mile jaunt with Maina around Mussolini's Italy they were forced to land the aircraft because of bad weather which brought them down at Port Lympne airfield in Kent instead of their intended destination, Heston aerodrome to the west of London. As the aircraft landed people on the ground heard a scraping noise.

An investigation of the plane revealed bolts on the propellor were loose and missing and the propellor itself was cracked, presumably because of the state of the bolts. According to a report in the Warwickshire Advertiser and Leamington Gazette the propellor would only have stayed on the aircraft for a few moments longer. Something a thorough pre-flight check of the aircraft by the pilot or co- pilot might have discovered. The Profumo brother and sister continued their onward journey by train.

Jack's flying career made the local press on other occasions with a social column announcement that he and Maina were setting off to fly to Cannes, a destination that would become a particular focal point in Gisela's life. The Profumos told the newspaper that after their departure in mid-August they were expecting to return in early September. On another occasion, a report records a forced landing well away from their intended destination because of adverse weather conditions.

Jack's love of flying and Gisela's knowledge of this were the subject of a letter which later triggered an investigation of the pair by the security service M15.

But the British authorities usually seem to have been one step behind her. Her file would continue to record the belief that Gisela had gone up to Oxford and had been a "home student." There's a reference to Somerville college. Neither Somerville or the four other Oxford colleges who took female students at this time; St Anne's; Lady Margaret Hall; St Hilda's or St Hugh's seem to have any record of Gisela, and her own curriculum vitae jotted down many years later suggests she may have done some sort of business course, although in the same document she dates her time at Oxford to 1935, conveniently losing a couple of years of age in the process, so its accuracy is probably not of the highest order.

The bare facts of the official notification of resident aliens' records show that while she was in Oxford at the beginning of the Michaelmas term in October of 1933, presumably at Keble Road, only a couple months into the following year she had registered to live in London. There was a request from her to be allowed to take on a job as a Governess with a Mrs Morris of 18 Blackheath Rise in Lewisham. This request was granted.

Then a month later Gisela wrote to the Home Office saying that she wouldn't be able to take up the position of Governess as her mother was ill and she had to return to Germany. Her mother lived into the 1970s, so if she was ill, it clearly wasn't that serious, but after this return to Germany there was a distinct change in the pattern of Gisela's travels. It seems that her continuing freedom from the restraints of Hitler's Germany came along with the increasing burden of other duties. Perhaps revealingly she completely omitted this lengthy return to Germany altogether in a detailed timeline she prepared as an aide memoire in advance of her interrogation by French Intelligence in 1944.

In the meantime, Jack continued to enjoy life to the full.

Brasenose College provided its own entertainments. The lure of free alcohol and fun undoubtedly encouraged him to join in a boisterous ancient tradition.

****

The 10th of May 1934, Ascension Day, saw the annual opening of a small old, planked door at the college. It connects to the adjacent Lincoln college. The undergraduates from Brasenose were assembled and waiting. As soon as the door was opened, they crowded through a narrow passageway to collect free beer on the other side provided by their neighbours.

The history of this is shrouded in the past. Some suggest it was by way of apology for Lincoln not helping a Brasenose man who was pursued and killed by an Oxford town mob or because there was a duel between two undergraduates from the colleges. Whatever the reason Lincoln's generosity is tempered to this day by the addition to the beer of a bitter herb to discourage their guests from consuming too much of it.

Jack also threw his own entertainments. Possibly inspired by this historic adulteration of alcohol, he dyed gin with green food colouring and gave a party, while maintaining that the spirit's colour suggested it was a special strength product. It was an indication deception was part of the fun of having fun in Jack's life.

His friends while he was at Oxford were a raffish set and included remnants of the Russian Romanov imperial family who'd been neighbours when he was a small boy in Kensington. The bespectacled Prince Vsevolod Ivanovich's great-great-great-grandfather was Tsar Nicholas the First. He was a second cousin to Prince Phillip, the late Duke of Edinburgh. Vsevolod was the last male Romanov to be born in Imperial Russia and his father and uncles were murdered in 1918. He escaped as a four-year-old child.

He was said to have a "great heart" and during the early 30s was a major feature of the social scene in Britain. He later attracted the hatred of the novelist Evelyn Waugh, not a very difficult thing to do, by marrying Lady Mary Lygon with whom Waugh was friends, and whose family home, Madresfield Court near Malvern, was reported to have been the real Brideshead.

Prince Vsevolod's sister Catherine appears in a photograph with Jack and Gisela in Gisela's papers. It was presumably taken before 1937 as Catherine married and went to live in Italy after that. The photograph's location seems to be, from the background complete with the glazed mock arrow slit in the wall behind them, at Avon Carrow.

Jack is in a light-coloured, checked, double-breasted suit with a white handkerchief in his breast pocket. He is standing smiling and looking relaxed between the two women with a cigarette in his hand. On his right the dark-haired Princess Catherine Ivanova is wearing a light pleated skirt and belted top with slightly puffed sleeves on the shoulders and buttons down the middle. She looks petite and slightly doll-like in comparison to the statuesque Gisela on Jack's left. She is wearing a dark two-tone calf length skirt, an embroidered belt and dark long-sleeved top with folds of material around the neck and shoulders. There is a large bangle on the arm she's linked with Jack's. She is disguising her height in the photograph by a bend of her knees and a slight swing of her legs away from him. Even so, probably because she is wearing heels, she is only just shorter.

Gisela also kept a photograph of another one of Jack's friends from this time with whom he shared digs while at Oxford. He was called Valerian Wellesley. The picture from what was apparently a social column in a newspaper shows him talking to a young woman who could be Gisela or possibly the youngest of the Mitford sisters, Deborah or Debo as she was known

The photograph is taken at a drinks party, conceivably Jack Profumo's green gin event as Valerian Wellesley's holding a tumbler of some sort of liquid. Wellesley, in a pin striped double-breasted suit, was a junior son of the family that held the hereditary title of the Duke of Wellington. He had no prospects at this time of inheriting. However, the Second World War changed that, and he became the 8th holder of the title. He was described by one of the Mitford sisters as the best looking and nicest of her escorts from this time.

With Gisela away in Germany Jack, who had a continuously roving eye, became associated with another beautiful woman with strongly pro-German tendencies. She was the photographic negative of Gisela. Jeanne Stourton was small with very dark hair and dark eyes. It was alleged she was the illegitimate offspring of a Spanish aristocrat with whom her mother had an affair. She was one of the noted society beauties of her day. She also had a vicious temper and was an enthusiastic supporter of the Nazis. She famously shouted 'Heil Hitler' after kicking her later husband, the gentle and long-suffering Sherman Stonor, Baron Camoys, down the stairs.

She would take as a lover, Hitler's foreign affairs advisor and Ambassador to Britain Joachim von Ribbentrop. According to her own daughter Julia Stonor, she spied for Ribbentrop in the 1930s. She bizarrely held her honeymoon at Ribbentrop's Schloss Fusl near Salzburg, complete with SS guards. Sherman Stonor tried to escape, whether from Jeanne or the Nazis is unclear, and had to be hunted down and brought back to his new bride

Jeanne divided men into two classes. *Boys*, who were lovers and *Guns* who came to shoot at her home at Stonor Park at Henley on Thames. Jack may have fallen into the former class, although a picture of them together at the opening of the Punch Club at the Dorchester Hotel in London shows Jack wearing tails, looking drunk with a cigarette in his mouth, which may be due to an unfortunate click of the camera shutter. He is fumbling for something, presumably a lighter or matches, in his pocket. Jeanne is giving the camera the benefit of a rather fierce stare. They are accompanied by Jack's sisters and the Earl of Mornington, a relative of Jack's friend Valerian.

Although the benchmark was fairly high, perhaps the most exotic of Jack's friends at this time was Man Singh II the Maharaja of Jaipur. He was a successful polo player. Part of the winning World Cup team of 1933, the year that Renee Lacoste introduced the Polo shirt. As well as being the ruler of Rajasthan he already had two wives when Jack first knew him. He would go on to collect a third wife and have an affair with the British socialite Lady Ursula Manners who was close to the Royal family.

Life for Jack was clearly more about intense social activity than conquering the dreaming spires of academe. This was reflected by the formal markers of his progress through university life. He was awarded a half blue for his Point-to-Point activities, an indication of a good performance falling short of the excellence required for a full blue. He also bizarrely gained a half blue for pole vaulting. He had cleverly calculated this sport was massively undersubscribed and therefore the competition would not be too challenging.

However, when it came to his academic efforts as an undergraduate, he was simply awarded a Pass degree in Agriculture and Political economy. This was despite an attempt to gain an advantage by paying someone who claimed to be able to see the final exam paper questions as they were laid out on the desks in the examination room. However, he'd been conned and was clearly in no position to complain about it. He would, however, prove more successful in a different type of deception. This time with the able assistance of Gisela.

4

A "SPY" AT CLIVEDEN

1935

THE YOUNG COUPLE must have looked prosperous to the headmistress of the girls' school. They were both well-groomed and they'd arrived in a Bentley. The plan was for her to take them on a tour of her establishment to see if it was suitable to put their daughter's name down on the waiting list of prospective pupils. This was a regular feature of public schools in Britain at the time where educational establishments were selected and agreed well before children were of school age and often at birth.

There were only a couple of things wrong with this particular scenario. Jack and Gisela weren't married, and they didn't have a daughter. Or at least as far as we know. They were indulging in a strange episode that David Profumo's biography of his father briefly describes as a "*jape*." He doesn't say what names they were using or indicate the school, although there was at least one private educational establishment for girls in Leamington Spa not that far from the Profumo's home, while the prestigious Cheltenham Ladies College was about an hour and a half away from both Oxford and Avon Carrow.

To an outside observer looking back on this event more than 80 years after it took place, it seems rather odd. It's only just possible to see what the attraction of the charade might have been to its two main participants. Headteachers of independent girls' schools tend to be intelligent and tough. This wasn't an am-dram student production, where the audience was prepared to suspend disbelief, or patients at the Warneford Hospital in Leamington Spa, who had no real choice but to watch Jack performing in a Pierrot costume in an entertainment organised by the Profumo's neighbouring aristocrat, Lady Willoughby De Broke.

In this enterprise there was a clear element of risk for Jack and Gisela in trying to pass themselves off as something they weren't. Jack undoubtedly would have enjoyed the acting challenge and Gisela apparently did as well. It points to an enjoyment of deception in her nature, and the love of the thrill of taking risks. A love that helped to bind them together.

It may just have been an indication of Jack's fondness for practical jokes or part of a shared fantasy of a future life together but had they known about this strange escapade, the security services would undoubtedly have interpreted it in a less charitable light than a jape. Was this some sort of test? A practice dry run? Couples are much less suspicious than a single person when doing something or being somewhere that might otherwise give cause for alarm.

German Intelligence understood this already and would use a man and a young woman in 1935 to scout out military installations in Britain, although unlike Gisela and Jack they didn't get away with it.

The young blonde Marianne Emig and her "Uncle" Hermann Goertz were mapping British airfields, while Marianne also used her charms as a rider of a Zundapp motorcycle to inveigle a slightly naive RAF aircraftman into sending her photographs of planes. Marianne, perhaps rather brighter than her "Uncle", had, it was later reported, sensed something was wrong with the operation and insisted on returning to Germany. Their activities were only discovered by chance after they'd gone back, although Herman Goertz returned to Britain to be arrested and jailed for four years.

There was one other "jape" described by Jack's son. The zoologist Solly Zuckerman was a particular expert on the life of primates, and he published a book, The Social Life of Monkeys and Apes, in 1932. He was teaching in Oxford and Jack went to see him accompanied by Gisela and persuaded him to describe the sex life of chimpanzees. Presumably this discussion included the behaviour of the kindly Bonobo chimps who use sex as a way of saying thank you.

The effect on Zuckerman of Gisela during this conversation must have been part of the infantile if cruel fun. Gisela had one of those strange interlinked connections that seemed to follow her, with Zuckerman. She went out with his future brother-in-law who would become the Marquess of Reading. A tip off about that liaison triggered the first true interest in her from the security service M15.

As the bright young things of Oxford continued to enjoy themselves with racing, revelling and "japes", the intense desire to have fun was the other side of the realisation that in the outside world things were not so good and political and military forces were massing in Europe and in Britain.

This was a time when the press baron Lord Rothermere headlined his column in the *Daily Mail* with "Hurrah for the Blackshirts" in praise of Oswald Mosley's British Union of Fascists. Even the chronicle of fashion and social life the *Tatler*, which was more at home photographing well-bred young ladies with their well-bred Borzoi hounds, acknowledged this with a picture and profile in May 1934 of Sir Oswald.

The *Tatler* would hedge its bets with its readers at the end of what was essentially a puff piece: …."whether we are in agreement with the fascist movement or not [...] no one can deny that its founder and leader in this country has the rare gift of political courage."

Gisela may not have seen that issue as she was recorded as being out of the United Kingdom for the rest of 1934 while she tended her "sick mother" in Germany. While she was there a referendum sealed her country's fate. Storm troopers were stationed at polling stations and there was widespread intimidation of any opposition to Hitler's plan to merge the post of Chancellor and President.

The result was a massive 'yes' vote giving the Fuhrer supreme and unchallengeable political power. It was the last vote in which Jews and other minorities were allowed to take part before being stripped of full German citizenship.

Gisela's UK records show she arrived back in Britain a couple of days after New Year in 1935 and a month later wrote seeking an extension to her stay, saying that she was living as a paying guest at 88 Seymour Street in London's Westminster 2 postal district and that she was not working. She was given until December to stay on.

She was lying. She had found work as a professional model with the fashion house to the Royal family, Reville Terry. Founded by William Wallace Terry, the company, as Reville and Rossiter, designed for Queen Mary, providing her dress for the Coronation of her husband George V in 1911 and dressing her and the Ladies of the Court of St James thereafter. After a reorganisation the firm was reborn as Reville Terry and Gisela was earning £4 a week, working as a mannequin at the firm's London showroom at 50 Grosvenor Street in Mayfair.

The Weekly Dispatch ran an article in January 1935 describing a fashion show at Reville Terry in which Gisela could well have modelled. Although from the description by "A London Woman Correspondent" of the event she would probably have passed unrecognised by anyone who knew her.

"I thought I had arrived at Horticultural Hall when I first walked into the show of the new Reville Terry dress collection designed by Madame Elspeth Champcommunal [...] the mannequins were walking flower gardens [...] the biggest flower trimming I have ever seen was used on a black evening gown and consisted of 24 Gardenias in the appropriate foliage. The Mannequin peeped from behind this becoming bush."

As Gisela showed fashions to the women of Britain's elite it was an important time for the relations between Britain and Germany. Hitler still wanted an alliance, although he was quite prepared to back up any negotiations with not-so-subtle threats. He boasted in May 1935 that the Luftwaffe was at parity in aircraft numbers with the RAF. It wasn't, but the inability of British intelligence to confirm or deny this led to an increase in funding for both MI5 the Security Service and M16, the Secret Intelligence Service. MI5 which was responsible for catching foreign spies on British soil, including the colonies, was still operating well under strength since the severe cuts imposed after the end of the First World War. Its counterintelligence operation up until now had been largely composed of a man called Maxwell Knight and his secretary. Knight had right wing and fascist tendencies and largely saw the threat as coming from the Soviet Union, although he was an enthusiastic advocate of the use of female agents at a time when women weren't necessarily seen as reliable in intelligence work.

If the British weren't that well placed to intercept spies in their own backyard, the Abwehr, Germany's military intelligence service, which operated largely despite the Nazis rather than because of them, was on the front foot. An Espionage Training Manual produced in 1934 and preserved in the German National Archives, has a list of information they wanted to know from agents sending information via the British postal service, the favoured method of getting reports out.

The Abwehr office in Hamburg was mostly responsible for

intelligence from England, although a unit in Bremen also had a role as well as an interest in the Middle East. The manual said that all postal reports arriving there and at Abwehr subsections in Kiel and Wilhelmshaven should be forwarded to the Berlin headquarters daily.

Amongst the subjects the Abwehr told its British agents to find out about were plans to use mines and minefields; where fuel supplies were located in coastal cities; the location of aerodromes and bomber aircraft squadrons and where Industrial companies had their headquarters and factories with particular reference to the aircraft industry.

Even while this was going on the diplomatic effort to woo Britain was still underway. In December 1935 Hitler wrote to the *Daily Mail*'s Lord Rothermere:

"…. I want to assure you at the conclusion of this letter I firmly believe that a time will come in which England and Germany will be solid pillars in a worried unstable world."

The Fuhrer was also maintaining his jealous admiration of Britain through the distorting lens of Hollywood. Hitler watched the 1935 Paramount production, the *Lives of a Bengal Lancer* at least three times. Holding screenings at his flat in Munich and his country retreat, the Berghof near Berchtesgaden.

The film starred Gary Cooper and gave the world the phrase "we have ways of making men talk." It was loosely based on a book by a British soldier, Francis Yeats Brown, who was a fan of Hitler and played a part in extreme right wing British politics. He joined the anti-semitic Right Club, whose members sported a silver badge which depicted an eagle killing a snake with the initial PJ under it. PJ stood for Perish Judah.

Around this time Jack Profumo's interest in the politics of the right – or at the very least Conservatism – appears to have become more focussed. He'd been involved with the Junior Imperial league which was an organisation set up by the Conservative party to try to attract young people and especially women, who the party feared might have had an unfortunate tendency to vote socialist. Young women and a strong social scene were more than enough to hold Jack's attention, but it also showed his clear ambition to rise. He later became the Chair of the Rugby branch of the Imps as they were known. He put on performances at local Conservative fundraising fetes around Avon Carrow which would bring him into contact with senior Conservative politicians like the MP David Margesson, a government whip and supporter of the appeasement of Hitler.

In 1935 Jack had been helping an aspiring MP canvas in the London constituency of East Fulham. Bill Astor was a few years older and his mother was the formidable Nancy Astor, the MP for Plymouth Sutton, the first woman to take her seat in the House of Commons.

Bill won for the Conservative party in the General Election of November 1935 and this connection and the friendship of his younger brother Michael saw Gisela and Jack attend a country house weekend at the spiritual epicentre of the dominant British political strand at this time, appeasement of Germany's demands.

The Astor family home in Buckinghamshire, Cliveden is an impressive English mansion. Like a rectangular two-tiered wedding cake in sandstone it dominates a scarp overlooking a beautiful reach of the River Thames near Taplow.

The original house on the site started out in the same vein as the Profumo's Avon Carrow as a hunting lodge, but there the similarity ended. Cliveden showed what could be achieved if money really was no object. First constructed in 1666, the outbreak of a couple of destructive fires and a series of ambitious, titled and rich owners finally resulted in the creation of a magnificent edifice, designed to display wealth, power and art.

A week before Easter, in April 1935, Gisela and Jack travelled to the house to stay as guests together. Jack turned the Bentley off the road to enter the Cliveden estate past the pair of handmade scrolled metal gates. The entrance between pillars topped with carved stone urns was impressive but less magnificent than what was to come. Once through, the way up to the house, took them along a twisting drive past the walled garden and its greenhouses producing fresh fruit and vegetables for the Astors. Because of the history of fires at the house this area also contained the estate's own private fire engine.

The next feature that came into view through the car's windscreen was the Fountain of Love. An imposing sculpture with water rushing away down an enormous, curved scallop shell of carved white Italian marble, surrounded by statues of young women and winged cherubs. It had been commissioned by the father of the current owner Waldorf Astor. Waldorf's father was the richest man in America and he spent his money lavishly on the house and estate he then gifted to his son and daughter-in-law, Nancy.

As Jack turned the car by the fountain, Cliveden house came into focus at the far end of the Grand Avenue, lined with stone Roman sarcophagi, collected during a bulk buy of classical treasures. It was all meant to impress and Gisela would have been in no doubt she had really arrived on the British social and political scene. Jack must have been delighted to have dazzled her with this display of his access to power and wealth.

Their hostess, the American born and raised Nancy Astor had four sons and one daughter by her second husband, Waldorf. The aspiring MP Bill, who Jack had been helping, was the eldest. There was a sister Nancy Phyllis, and then David, a year older than Gisela, with Michael, three years her junior, and the youngest, John Jacob, always known as Jakey. All of Nancy's boys followed her into politics although for most it seems to have been with more of a sense of inevitability than passion.

The social climbing diarist, MP and Hitler enthusiast, Chips Channon described Nancy Astor as an interfering, harsh and overbearing woman, he actually used the word "termagant", who was warm hearted only to those she could patronise. Nancy fortunately had a thick skin and was well used to misogyny of this sort in the House of Commons.

She was very quick, when one male MP in the chamber told her to think before speaking, she retorted.

"How do I know what I think until I've heard what I've said."

She always took particular care her outfits while attending the Commons were plain black and white so that they could not also be used against her.

Others described her as generous with a startling combination of beauty, friendliness, brilliant wit and tremendous energy, but she also possessed a sharp tongue. She shut down one tedious male dinner guest at Cliveden who was droning on about something with "That's interestin', but I'm not interested." This was delivered in her Virginia drawl.

She was a Christian Scientist with strong views against alcohol, Jews and Roman Catholics. Her antisemitism was of the only slightly less virulent "you are alright, it's all the others" variety. She seems almost to have taken a stronger line on Catholics. She refused to attend the marriage of her son Jakey when he wed a Catholic woman. Although she would manage to temper her views enough to remain socially close to the staunchly Catholic Kennedy family.

Gisela and Jack's visit to Cliveden is recorded in the red leather-bound visitors' books covering the social and political comings and goings at the house. They read like a who's who of the establishment and ruling class of the 1930s. Everyone who was anyone stayed at Cliveden, from the author George Bernard Shaw and comedian Joyce Grenfell, a cousin of the Astors, to Neville

Chamberlain, the Kennedys and the young British princesses Elizabeth and Margaret.

It was a genuinely eclectic mix of people with varied views, but there was a political core of associates of Nancy and Waldorf Astor who came to define appeasement of Hitler as a policy. They would be accused of being pro Nazi at the time and afterwards.

These particular visitors to Cliveden and Nancy's London home at 4 St James Square, included Geoffrey Dawson, editor of the *Times*; Viscount Halifax, the future foreign secretary who worked closely with Prime Minister Neville Chamberlain's softly softly approach to Hitler. Halifax favoured a peace deal with Hitler after the defeat of British forces in France and the retreat from Dunkirk. Samuel Hoare, who as Secretary of State for Foreign affairs from June 1935 agreed to Mussolini's expansionist policies in Ethiopia; Neville Henderson, the future British Ambassador to Berlin who had a reputation of being good at dealing with dictators and wasn't particularly, and Lord Lothian, who met Hitler in January of 1935 and as a result was convinced the German leader did not want war "provided he is given real equality" He later changed his views, calling Hitler a "fanatical gangster."

On the first page of the Cliveden visitor's book which covers April 1935 to July 1938 is Gisela's rather scratchy signature in black ink. A plain Gisela Klein. Her entry also identifies her time at the house. She arrived on Saturday the 13th of April and departed on Monday the 15th of April.

Jack's signature, larger and with some flourish is over the page and sits with no dates associated with it.

Gisela would have been awed by the enormous Great Hall of the house. Like the Grand Avenue it was designed to do precisely that. The dark brown wood panelled ceiling and walls were lit rather dimly by draped arched windows to the front looking towards the Fountain of Love. There was a display of art, weapons and suits of armour and three tapestries given to a previous owner, an officer with the Duke of Marlborough at the battle of Blenheim. The tapestries were part of an original series of eight called the Spirit of War.

That wasn't the spirit that Cliveden's hostess was interested in politically, and she also didn't much like the distinctly masculine design of the hall. She attempted to cheer it up with vases of flowers and soft furnishings, including a large red velvet settee in front of the enormous, canopied stone fireplace.

Even while she was snowed under with political work, constant travelling, public speaking and entertaining, Nancy still found time to be in regular and voluminous correspondence with Roma Ltd, an emporium on Exhibition Road in London which specialised in the fabrics she used for the rooms at Cliveden.

Gisela and Jack were assigned guest bedrooms in the East wing of the house. The large numbers of servants required to run Cliveden were accommodated in the West wing, while the Astor children had their rooms on the top floor.

Nancy Astor also kept a close eye on the cost of feeding Jack and Gisela and everyone else at Cliveden. She received a monthly average meal price for guests and staff at the house. That April the servants were costing more than the family and guests because they outnumbered them considerably. The total cost per person for food was two pounds, two shillings and sixpence. The food for the guests was described as superb.

On the Saturday evening Jack and Gisela made their way down dressed for dinner. Jack in white tie and tails, probably the same suit he was photographed in with Jeanne Stourton at the Dorchester Hotel. Gisela undoubtedly had something couture for the weekend from Reville Terry. She would have looked stunning, although whether this would have endeared her to her hostess is debatable. Nancy could be very unfriendly to women she regarded as a threat to her sons. Something of an adventuress herself, she'd managed to marry two very wealthy men one after the other, she could probably detect the underlying pirate in Gisela. Although having competition at dinner from a young, beautiful and intelligent woman may have just irritated her. What is clear is that she definitely spotted something about her weekend houseguest.

That evening Jack and Gisela were led into Cliveden's French dining room, a carved wood and gold leaf confection, yet another treasure bought by Nancy's father-in-law, this time lock stock and barrel from a French Chateau.

At the dining table, as the Astor's butler Mr. Lee presided over the serving of the food, Gisela was presented with private and invaluable intelligence. She listened to an assessment of Britain's position in relation to Germany from the politicians Waldorf and Nancy. Although rather overshadowed by his wife in retrospect, Waldorf was a politically active Conservative member of the House of Lords. Gisela also benefitted from a view from the Foreign Office and the very well informed military perspective of a senior soldier.

Arranged around the table that night were:

Simon Harcourt Smith, a diplomat and author. The social column of the Weekly Dispatch drew a pen picture of him:

"Mr. Simon Harcourt Smith is a foreign office fellow. He has sandy hair, rather lowering brows which lend him an earnest manner and an up and down gait."

He would write a whimsical novel about a country house, The Last of Uptake, which had illustrations by the artist Rex Whistler.

Also dining that night was the aristocratic Margaret Antrim, widow of the 7th Earl of Antrim, who'd died two years before, and her two youngest children: Lady Jean Meriel McDonnell, a year younger than Gisela, and her younger brother James.

There was a relative of Nancy's, Mrs. Ethel B Mallorie who wrote to her frequently calling her "my dear friend" and who lived in St Georges Square in London.

There was also a distinguished man in his 60s who knew Waldorf well. He was the much decorated and now retired General, Spencer Edmund Hollond always known as Tom, formerly of the Rifle Brigade and the Army General Staff. A friend of Winston Churchill he was responsible for training the current top brass in the British Army as Commandant of the Senior Officers school.

As Christian scientists neither Waldorf nor Nancy drank alcohol. Guests were, however, served drinks in relatively generous amounts and the conversation flowed freely. The old-fashioned rule about not talking politics at dinner was not observed here.

Nancy was, as always, the star turn. Debo Mitford described her around this time as: "small, upright and sharp as a needle, often at someone else's expense."

That night she was complaining about having to attend the 12th Conference of the International Woman Suffrage Alliance which was being held on the 18th of April in Istanbul.

Gisela may have told her about what was happening to women in Germany. Nancy was already interested in this subject. She specifically refers to the plight of German women under Hitler in a letter written a week earlier about having to go to the Istanbul conference, which she referred to as a "duty call".

While the elders would have pondered the weighty matter of equality, power and diplomacy with Gisela all ears, it was left to Jack, the McDonell brother and sister and the younger Astor generation to provide the fun. The Astors were particularly good at mocking the more pompous and ponderous guests.

The weather that weekend was only suitable for damp walks in the grounds with drizzle, mist and fog so that the guests had to enjoy the delights of Cliveden House itself. Jack and Gisela must have fallen back on the freedom to indulge in their affair in glamourous and romantic surroundings, as opposed to Gisela's shared flat at 88 Seymour Street in London.

Certainly, Jack seems to have enjoyed himself enormously, writing bouncily to his hostess two days after the visit.

> *"Please let me thank you a thousand times for my most delightful stay at Cliveden. I can't tell you how much I enjoyed myself."*

He undoubtedly couldn't.

> *"I hope one day to have the pleasure again of meeting your charming relation with the false teeth who is such a friend of my charming mother!"*

Presumably Ethel B Mallorie, who must have been the butt of the younger generations jokes and Nancy's famed sharpness. He continued:

> *Hoping your journey to Turkey will anyway turn out interesting and again thanking you very much.*

> *Yours sincerely Jack Profumo.*

It would be a high-water mark for Gisela. Working as a model for a Royal couturier; staying at Cliveden and having a well-connected, enthusiastic and wealthy boyfriend in Jack. But Nancy Astor had formed a strong belief about Gisela during her visit. She and much later her youngest son Jakey, would lead accusations that she was a German spy.

Perhaps Gisela's remit to obtain information, undoubtedly reinforced during her return to Germany in 1934, made her a little too obviously interested in the political, military and diplomatic talk at the dinner table. We'll never know precisely what triggered Nancy's suspicion which she didn't keep to herself. She told Jack his girlfriend was involved in espionage. Something Jack would only reveal to British intelligence in a statement he made about Gisela after the start of the Second World War. It showed that this startling revelation didn't seem to bother him as much as perhaps it might have.

Gisela's thank you letter for her weekend at Cliveden doesn't seem to have survived in Nancy's personal archive alongside Jack's. Gisela was well brought up and always an effective networker. She would undoubtedly have sent one from her London address. Instead, Nancy kept another communication of hers, this one from Dusseldorf.

In December of 1935, Gisela sent a postcard addressed to Viscountess Nancy Astor at Cliveden, Taplow, England. It was posted from abroad.

The message was simple:

A merry Christmas and a Happy New Year to you and the family

Yours sincerely
Gisela Klein

But this apparently innocuous contact from Gisela seemed to trigger an intense interest in Nancy to discover the exact location of the young woman she believed to be engaged in espionage for Germany. Scrawled in pencil across the top of the Christmas greeting was a message to Nancy's personal Secretary.

"Please ask David for Miss Klein's address and send it and this to Suvrata (sic)"

Nancy was staying at the exclusive Suvretta House Hotel near St Moritz in Switzerland. She was recovering with an alpine break after the busy social whirl of Christmas at Cliveden. Her note shows she may have been under the impression that David was the son that had a connection to Gisela, and maybe so, but it was a picture of Michael, his younger brother, that Gisela kept her whole life. Michael had just had his 19th birthday the Thursday before Gisela and Jack's visit to Cliveden. His mother had acknowledged his move out of boyhood earlier that year in a letter which said that he had arrived at the "untouchable age".

The photograph of Michael and the message on its back in Gisela's papers shows he was clearly impressed by her. He sent her a studio portrait taken by T.H. Greville based on the High Street in Maidenhead. He looks young and rather soulfully into the camera. His youth emphasised by a tweed jacket that seems slightly too big. Possibly it had belonged to one of his older brothers.

The message on the back reads:

To Miss Klein from Mr. Astor – an acquaintance!
I hope you have a very good time in Germany and generally speaking enjoy yourself.

Love from Michael.

But it was as Nancy commanded that her secretary forwarded her note to David Astor. David, who later worked in naval intelligence alongside the James Bond author Ian Fleming, showed apparent disdain for his mother's demand, scribbling back to the secretary.

Dear Miss Irvine
Have just turned this up amongst a heap. No, I don't know her address.

Yours David.

The question of addresses, and Nancy Astor's desire to know her whereabouts, may be important; as is the missing thank you letter from Gisela with her London address on it, because at some stage after Jack and Gisela's stay at Cliveden, someone informed on her to the police.

The file on Gisela at the British National Archive at Kew shows that it must have been the Metropolitan police in London who carried out an investigation.

The result was that a month after her visit to Cliveden she was charged with working for Reville Terry as a mannequin in breach of the strict "no paid employment" conditions of her entry visa to the UK.

She appeared in court and was fined £2. Half her weekly wage from the couturier.

The Home office note in her file continues:

"Police sure she knew she was breaking the law. Advise departure at early date."

However, Gisela didn't go straight away but hung on for another two months. In the middle of July Gisela wrote to the Home Office asking for her passport to be returned saying that she intended to leave the UK at the end of the month.

She was heading, not to somewhere where she could advance her career in couture like Paris or Berlin, Vienna or New York, all places she would appear later, but to a country where the British Empire was very worried about its strategic interests against a background of international power politics and a wave of strong anti-British feelings.

5

A POEM FOR A MANNEQUIN

THE DE HAVILLAND Rapide aircraft vibrated as the twin engines pulled it up and away from Cairo airport. All Gisela could see, framed by the struts and wires connecting the aircraft's upper and lower wings, was the clear blue sky and the scrubby desert below interspersed with parched fields and small dwellings. As the machine gained height and made ground, over on the port side there were flashes from below as the sun glinted off the silver body of the river Nile.

She felt the excitement in the bodies of some of the other passengers as they peered constantly out of the large diagonally divided windows bordered by curtains. She was flying on a new route between Cairo and Luxor on El Misr Airworks, a British firm with Egyptian funding. The company would go on to become the national carrier EgyptAir.

The aircraft was making its way to one of the stops on this new route, the small city of Asyut sometimes also spelled Assiut or Assiout. It had once been an important stop on the trade caravan routes but was now largely unremarkable apart from a barrage on the river Nile which carried its name. But it was a centre for linen production and the manufacture of a traditional netting cloth embroidered with metal that made it ripple and shimmer. The material is still known as Assiut and was ideal for the construction of slinky glamorous clothes. Gisela's new role in Egypt was as a "fashionable dressmaker" operating in both Cairo and Alexandria.

Her departure from Britain that summer of 1935 probably coincided with a cooling in her relationship with Jack. He was clearly fun and there was always more than a spark between them as later events would show, but he was never a serious bet as a life partner unless you were prepared to put up with industrial levels of infidelity and by and large Gisela, who could have her pick of anyone, seems to have favoured men who were not cheating on her, at least not in the physical sense. In any event she'd lost her work with the Royal couturiers and had to leave Britain: and these factors initially meant a return to Germany. Michael Astor's note on the back of his photograph which references her going back to her homeland probably dates from this time.

Gisela's departure seems to have triggered something in Jack as well. In the Autumn of 1935 he began his own travels. Ignoring the demands of university life and the run up to his final exams he and a couple of friends set off for the Soviet Union and China via Germany and Poland.

Jack was a keen photographer and cine enthusiast and filmed everything in sight as an official record of the trip. This was despite attempts by the authorities in various places to prevent him from doing so. Jack seems to have found Russia oppressive and its vastness slightly overwhelming. He mused on the fate of the old Russian aristocrats as the train trundled across vast areas of forest and the Siberian steppes. His friendship with Prince Vsevolod and his sister Catherine would certainly have prompted these thoughts. He was relieved when they finally crossed the border into Manchuria. Pleased he could inhale "some non-Soviet air"

Jack seems to have liked China rather better. In Shanghai he visited Jade Street where he bought several mementoes, including a jade ring which he later gave to Gisela, an indication of a continuing closeness, and which although now rather battered by the passage of time, her daughter still possesses.

After leaving Britain Gisela returned to Germany but didn't hang around for long. Within six weeks she was off on her travels to the Middle East. Her destination, Egypt, was occupied by a large British garrison to protect the British Empire's vital trade artery, the Suez canal – and an intelligence target for both Germany and Italy. No wonder Gisela's presence there in retrospect contributed to suspicions of "a high degree espionage", as MI5 pointed out in the latter years of the war to come.

****

In her travelling bag in Egypt Gisela had postcards she'd brought with her from Germany. One of them would go to Nancy Astor with her Christmas greetings.

At this stage, Gisela may well have been carrying another piece of paper. It was amongst the belongings she kept in California and is an item that provides one of the most tantalising clues to an early espionage role. It's a poem about pain and love contained on a sheet that is clearly old and which had been carefully preserved. Not that unusual for a beautiful, intelligent woman to have had such a thing, but this one is not handwritten from an admirer but typed out.

It is on a piece of thin personal memorandum paper from the leading German industrialist Werner Theodor "Teddy" Schaurte. A man with whom she shared local connections in Dusseldorf. The man who'd been so keen to embrace the Nazis he'd used his own workers to create a unit of the SA and who had the ear of Hermann Göring. On the memo sheet the place where the recipient's name should be is blank and there is no date and there's no signature. On the other side of the sheet there is just one word written by hand in pencil. It says Gedicht which means Poem.

Gisela had carefully folded the edges of the paper so Schaurte's printed name at the top wasn't visible. It's possible from the way it was folded just along the sides it may have been in a frame at one stage. If it's an indication of the passion of a considerably older married man for Gisela, it's a remarkably unromantic vehicle. It's clearly not impossible Schaurte was entranced by her, so many were, but a poem like this has another less obvious purpose, spy-craft. The verse is by the German liberal poet Theodor Storm. It reads in translation:

Close both my eyes
With your dear hands
For everything I suffer
Comes to rest under your hand.

And as the pain wave after wave
falls asleep
As the last heartbeat stirs you fill my whole heart.

Short and easily memorised poems like this were the basis for hand encryption of messages by espionage agents. They were used by both Britain and Germany in the 1930s and during the Second World War. The British would later deploy ones specially written by an officer of the Special Operations Executive called Leo Marks, after it was discovered the use of well-known published poetry, like the one Gisela kept, made it easier to crack the messages. He wrote a poem which was used by Special Operations Executive agent Violet Szabo, who was captured and murdered by the Nazis. It's called The Life That I Have and has become famous in its own right. It starts:

The life that I have
Is all that I have
And the life that I have is yours

To encrypt messages, the sender selects several words at random from the poem. A numerical key is created using the position of the chosen words in the poem. This signals the basis for the message. Then each letter in the chosen words is assigned a number. These numbers are put into a grid drawn on a piece of paper to create a letter to number transposition cipher. Further complications could be added at will. But the main advantage is this system is relatively easy to use in the field and doesn't require anything but the knowledge of which poem was being used by sender and receiver.

Werner T Schaurte who gave this poem to Gisela was at the centre of the Nazis' military plans. He was making a fortune out of Germany's rearmament and what his factory produced was so important to the Nazi military machine the Allies would later repeatedly try to destroy it in bombing raids.

Werner, like Gisela, was born in Dusseldorf, and at the age of 24 in 1917 was put in charge of his late father's nut and bolt making business.

He was a prominent member of the Dusseldorf Rotary Club and he undoubtedly knew the successful lawyer and book binder Alfred Klein. It seems possible that the young Gisela worked for him in some capacity before coming to the UK as he had an interest in a textile business.

Schaurte was also a member of the influential Deutsche Herrenklub. The German Gentleman's Club which, at a time when real power often flowed through private networks, put him in touch with many prominent and politically active Germans on the nationalist right. Most of them rabidly anti-communist, not terribly keen on democracy, and many wanted a restoration of the German Kaiser who'd been deposed after the First World War. Members of this influential club included Herbert von Dirksen who would later become Germany's last Ambassador to Britain before the Second World War.

Schaurte was an effective networker just like Gisela. In 1932 he joined the right wing Stallhelm organisation which was also composed of anti-communists who supported the return of the German monarchy.

He also rubbed shoulders with the great and the not necessarily good of the Ruhr's business leaders at the Dusseldorf Industry club. Most of whom like Werner, would later use forced and concentration camp slave labour in their factories.

In 1932 before gaining power, Hitler spoke at the club to try to win support for the Nazis amongst Germany's industrial elite. Werner Schaurte later admitted he was at that meeting and been impressed by the Fuhrer. He claimed to the panel assessing his Nazi culpability post-war that he hadn't hung around to meet Hitler on that occasion but had left.

That neatly ignored his close connection to the man intent on making Germany great again. Werner was later photographed in private conversation with Hitler, who paid a personal visit to his factory in Neuss. There are three pictures of the pair together in the company's mess room where there was some sort of automobile exhibition. In one photograph Schaurte is undoubtedly describing some engineering process while Hitler looks as though he is thinking about something else altogether.

However, Werner's strongest personal link to the Nazi hierarchy was to Hermann Goring. The former First World War fighter ace who took a bullet during the failed Nazi coup attempt in 1923. Göring rose to become the founder of the Gestapo and the leader of the SA. In 1935 he took over the German Airforce and was reported to have authorised the airfield espionage activities in Britain of Marianne Emig and Herman Goertz.

Werner was later a regular guest on Göring's 90ft Motor yacht Carin 11 and Göring who was in charge of all hunting in the Reich, made him Chief Huntsman for the Neuss area, an important indication of his favour.

In the 1930s Göring was regularly using go-betweens for back-channel communications with prominent people in the United Kingdom. Warner, a trained engineer, was a frequent visitor to Britain at the time. His sister and brother-in-law lived in Hertfordshire, and he was undoubtedly keeping abreast of any advances in his field which included aviation engineering and reporting back. He also visited the United States at least four times in the 1930s where the Nazis were targeting intelligence about the aviation industry.

But there was one particular reason for Werner, other than personal advancement, to make himself as useful as he could. He would later admit that one of his great-grandfathers was Jewish, making him in his own words "one eighth jew". Although some of the informants in his Nazi party file claimed his Jewish inheritance was greater. It was still enough to cause him problems with the Nazis. That was something else he may have shared with Gisela and it gave possible leverage to anyone wishing to try to take over his business.

In theory because he was a "mischling" he should have obtained special permission from the Nazis each time he travelled outside Germany. He shakily glosses over this important detail during his questioning in the de-Nazification process after the war, saying that he didn't need these permits because he'd been invited to stay in Britain by his brother-in-law. However, it was undoubtedly his links to the very top of the Nazi party that allowed him to travel with apparent ease to both the United States and Britain during the 1930s. A suspicious freedom of movement also later highlighted about Gisela.

As Hitler gained power in 1933 and just before Gisela arrived in the UK, Warner was keen to ride the wind. He joined the Nazi party as member number 2405526 on the first of May.

He also obtained an SA uniform and wore it in public. His own factory unit of Nazi storm troopers paraded during the May Day celebrations of that year. Hitler personally congratulated him on the dedication of the SA standard at the factory. He was also photographed proudly wearing the uniform when he won the traditional annual shooting competition in the city of Neuss.

Werner also demonstrated his interest in being at the cutting edge of industrial and military developments. At the 1938 Berlin Motor Show, Bauer and Schaurte exhibited a plexi-glass see through engine which showed how their new lightweight bolts could save more than 20 kilogrammes over the standard ones. While components that lightened a motor vehicle were useful, they were utterly essential to the aircraft industry as lightness increased an aircraft's speed and range.

It seems likely the Warner/Göring connection was what linked Gisela to Germany's intelligence organisations and began her long-term association with a series of Luftwaffe officers associated with air war intelligence, although she would prove flexible in her espionage career that spanned social, political; economic and military information gathering.

In the early days she may have been working directly for Warner. It was not unusual for industrialists to run spies at the time. MI5's Maxwell Knight started out in exactly the same way, working for the privately funded Industrial Intelligence Bureau in Britain created by the fervent anti-communist Sir George Makgill. The Swedish industrialist Axel Wenner Grenn would also be suspected by the Americans of running German spies.

Having current British information for his important contact and friend Göring would have been invaluable for Werner. For

Gisela, certainly in the early years, it would have started out as exciting and interesting, with risk she clearly enjoyed. It was also a price she was prepared to pay for a life outside Germany, even if the demands placed on her eventually became wearing and dangerous.

In any case British counterintelligence continued to operate well below par and apart from the astute Nancy Astor's suspicions, all Gisela ever seemed to show herself as was an elegant, if rule breaking, model who was a catwalking advertisement for an apparently Aryan future. Not something that most Britons on the right of the political spectrum had any sort of a problem with at all until very much later.

As the Propaganda Minister Joseph Goebbels remarked to the former head of First World War German military intelligence Count Walter Nicolai:

"Where does propaganda end and espionage begin?"

****

Gisela was certainly playing to her strengths with her new role. She arrived by boat in Port Said in Egypt on the 18th of September 1935. Her German passport came with a visa that only gave her a month in the country. The British Security Office in Cairo, answering a later inquiry about her activities after the outbreak of the Second World War, said that at this stage she was connected to a Mr. and Mrs. J. D. Astley. Mrs. Astley was recorded as Swedish by birth and Gisela went to stay with the couple at Maison Carout in what was recorded as Hazan Assiout Street in Assiut. She would describe them as English friends who invited her to stay.

The British Security Office report also goes on to say a Dr D. Lewis from the Government Secondary School in Assiut busied himself on Gisela's behalf gaining further permission for her to stay beyond her short visa limit, describing her in glowing terms as a

"100 percent German girl" and "respectable". His entreaties worked and she was allowed to remain.

Once again, apparently by chance, Gisela managed to insert herself in a place that was politically interesting and strategically important at just the right time, with lots of posh young British men in uniform to tell her all about it.

On the streets of Alexandria and Cairo though it wasn't English but Arabic, Greek, Italian, French and even German Gisela would have heard. Alexandria was a gateway to and from the Mediterranean. There were large expat communities in Egypt and a numerous and successful Jewish population. Importantly for Gisela there was a wealthy and bustling middle class amongst the many different communities, containing women with the money to buy fashionable clothes.

In 1935 it must have seemed very exotic to the 22-year-old from Dusseldorf, with the street show around her: small boys with donkeys and carts; lemonade sellers; the piled vegetables; food; cloth and metalwork on display in the markets. There was a constant parade of Egyptian men wearing the cylindrical Fez, a reminder of the country's Ottoman past and the covered Muslim women cheek by jowl with the European styles of the immigrants.

Of particular interest to Fraulein Klein was the hectic social life swelled by the ranks of young British Army officers. They were automatically given membership of the exclusive Gezira sports club leased by the British in Cairo. The club was built in an old botanical garden on Gezira Island in the Nile. It had a full-size golf course, tennis courts, a croquet lawn; cricket pitches and polo grounds to stop any Britons feeling too homesick. As Gisela arrived, the club opened its own Lido, with verandahs and poolside umbrellas to keep off the blazing sun. There is a photograph of her taken near some awnings which could have been there. It just says Gisela, Cairo on the back. For night time entertainment there was the Kit Kat Club for dancing and socialising at Cairo's Gezirah Palace Hotel. The club's tables crowding into the square outside in the warm evening air.

Much of Cairo itself away from the old town was deliberately modelled on a sophisticated European city. There were two British army bases complete with young officers and other ranks looking for diversions from the hum-drum military activities of occupation. One on the outskirts at Abbassiaand and one in the centre at Kasr el Nil.

There were further British military bases in Ismailia and Alexandria where there were also plenty of opportunities for nightlife, as well as the beach huts and curving Mediterranean strip of sand at Sidi Bishr. This didn't meet with everyone's approval. One officer of the Gloucester Regiment dispatched there in 1935 described his base less attractively as a "dust hole by the sea". This deployment was, to his evident irritation, denying his regiment its rightful success on the rugby fields and cricket pitches of green and pleasant England.

It's unlikely that Gisela felt negatively about her location. She could dance the night away with young officers and friends at the prestigious Mena House Hotel at Giza with its stunning views of the Pyramids. It was something she must have treasured through what was to come. She would tell her daughter about it and keep a postcard of the hotel amongst her possessions.

But Egypt was not just a multicultural melting pot "protected" by the presence of British troops, there to guard the Suez canal. It was also a wasp's nest of competing ideologies and power plays with Egyptian nationalists, who were winning majorities in elections, being denied power by the King who managed to ensure his supporters still formed the government.

There were strong political undercurrents everywhere. Some Arab nationalists were accused by opposing factions of being bribed by the Italians in an attempt to discredit them. Mussolini's fascists were reported to be trying to create an intelligence network amongst the well-established Italian community and there were Italian propaganda broadcasts aimed at Arabs. Against this backdrop, Mussolini also had strong regional ambitions for his own Empire in North Africa. Italy already controlled Libya and wanted more.

The Germans meanwhile were seeking both military information and economic opportunities to underpin increased influence in the country. The German Military Attache at the London Embassy, Baron Geyr Von Schweppenburg was accused by his British opposite number in Berlin, despite his outraged denials, of liaising with the head of Italian intelligence in Egypt, who was identified as a Signor Falla. He was also accused of trying to supply the Egyptian army with weapons.

1935 was a pivot point in the see-sawing relations between Hitler and the UK. The Prime Minister Stanley Baldwin was beginning the process of rearmament but still in the appeasement camp. Hitler maintained hopes for the diplomatic settlement which would give him the "lebensraum" (room to live) he envisaged in Europe, leaving the Mediterranean and North Africa to his fellow dictator Mussolini.

British counterintelligence in Egypt was led by MI6 and clearly a bit scrappy. To be fair they couldn't predict what was going to happen within the next five years but the official files betray none of the intense interest that would be shown in enterprising young women and other suspected German agents in Egypt only a few years later, as it became more obvious that war was coming.

However just as Gisela was leaving Cairo in September 1936, MI6 identified the man they thought was head of what they described as the Nazi Ausland Organisation.

The spy chief was said to be Herr Friedrich von Homeyer who

was an attaché at the German legation in Cairo. He was clearly an enthusiastic Nazi, or at the very least a man with a keen nose for the future, as he'd joined the Nazi party in June 1931 a couple of years before Hitler seized power.

Homeyer, who'd worked as a journalist, was receiving reports on traffic on the Suez Canal including British warships and troop transports and intelligence from German engineers operating in Egypt, although MI6's main concern seems to have been about the scale of economic intelligence he was collating to send back to Berlin.

"Thanks to this organization Germany is better informed than any other country of the economic matters in Egypt, which greatly facilitates the penetration of German industry and commerce."

Later British attitudes began to harden about military espionage. One woman who attracted attention was journalist, Celine Morriset, also known as Lena or Line Mori, who was apparently asking British officers questions. She was identified as travelling by air to Palestine, Iraq and Iran in 1937 and spending money well beyond what the officials viewed as her "means" as a reporter. She was well connected with Egyptians "of the better class" and she apparently "accosted" a senior British officer at one stage. Most damning in the eyes of MI6 there was a reference to her amongst the papers of an official of the German Siemens company in Egypt with the words alongside "high income for intelligent ladies". Another indication of the role that German industry was already playing in total espionage.

There is also a brief note in the British archives at Kew about another suspected German woman spy, not Gisela, who was thought to have been in the United Kingdom in 1938 or 1939 and worked in Egypt under the control of a Von Borkman, a German based in Greece. The Germans had apparently given her the codename: "Snakeskin". This may have been because she seems to have used at least five identities. She was said to be particularly interested in Air and Naval intelligence. She was also later identified as travelling to the United States on a ship where she spent a lot of time expounding on the benefits of Nazism.

She seems to have lived up to her Snakeskin soubriquet and shed the inquisitive British intelligence officers thereafter.

But by then there would be regular spy scares in Egypt with claims that the entertainments and the nightlife of the Kit Kat club were disguising espionage hidden amongst the swarms of people out enjoying themselves on warm Egyptian evenings. It led one intelligence officer to produce a detailed analysis of the origins of the dancers and entertainers who were employed there to refute the slur on what was presumably his favourite watering hole.

British intelligence however managed to catch one suspected female German agent in Cairo early in the Second World War. Sophie Clapham Kukralova, was a formidable looking blonde woman, a couple of years older than Gisela, who'd also been in the UK. Although she was of Czech origin, she later managed to persuade a British couple to adopt her, presumably for the passport.

Kukralova and her adoptive mother arrived in Cairo in 1941. There, a member of British intelligence personnel was said to have wanted to marry her and there was a further report about another soldier trying to blackmail her into sleeping with him under the threat of exposing her as a spy.

Despite this the British couldn't really work out whether she was a spy or not. Male intelligence officers tended to be a bit diffident about women suspects, something that helped Gisela enormously. However, this time they played safe and judged Kukralova a threat for reasons including her "morbid interest in espionage". She was interned with her mother. It was only after the war that captured German documents identified her as an Abwehr agent.

Hotels in Cairo and Alexandria came under suspicion as well.

One particular "pension" where Josef Goebbels' entourage stayed during his visit in April 1939 was identified as a hotbed of German spying. Photographs of Goebbels from this visit, a clear indication of German interest in the country, show him dressed immaculately in a very well-cut light suit and wearing a trilby style hat. He looked remarkably like the 1930s cinematic ideal of a successful gangster, which of course he was.

Goebbels stayed at the luxurious Mena House Hotel where four years earlier the officially unidentified and undetected Gisela danced the night away with young British soldiers, one of whom, later echoed by the Kukralova case, was reported as wanting to marry the blonde from Dusseldorf.

This was likely to have been Lieutenant Richard Derek Cardiff of the First Battalion of the Scots Guards. He was the second son from a distinguished military family whose home was at Easton Court near Ludlow in Shropshire. This Manor house was bought by his father Colonel Wingfield Cardiff the year he was born. At 24 he was a little bit older than Gisela and had been educated at Eton and the Royal Military College. Gisela used his address as the place she was staying during a later visit to Britain.

Like Jack Profumo, he seems to have enjoyed vigorous motoring, appearing in court after his return to the UK for racing through the streets of Leicester at speeds between 40 and 70 miles an hour apparently oblivious he was being followed by a couple of police officers. He was fined £5 for driving at speeds dangerous to the public and admonished by the Chairman of the Magistrates bench with the words: "You've got to use your brains you know". The impression is that these may not have been his most attractive feature.

****

The James Bond creator Ian Fleming would later place these words in the mouth of his villain Auric Goldfinger:

"Once is happenstance. Twice is coincidence. Three times is enemy action."

Gisela's activities had now gone well beyond coincidence. Her departure from England, via Germany and then to Egypt came as Hitler told Admiral Canaris, the head of German military intelligence, the Abwehr, that he didn't want any spies operating in the UK. This was in case espionage operations came to light and fouled up his diplomatic plans. Hitler unlike Churchill, who loved the intrigue, always had a basic dislike of espionage.

The discovery of the airfield scouting activities of the motorcycle riding Marianne Emig and the hapless Dr Herman Goertz in 1935 therefore had to be passed off to the Fuhrer as a misguided freelance operation, although Goertz later also turned up working for the Abwehr in Ireland and was jailed for a second time.

Gisela admitted to her post-war husband, she was actually recruited to espionage work in 1939 by the senior Wehrmacht officer, Carl Heinrich Von Stulpnagel. But she certainly wasn't averse to giving him, and others who were taking a close interest, an inexact version of her life. She also suggested to him, she'd been a Rhodes scholar at Oxford in the early 30s, as he would go on to tell the British authorities exactly that. She was undoubtedly bright enough, but unfortunately for Gisela and many other women, there were no female Rhodes scholars until the mid-1970s.

Aside from Gisela's fluid relationship with the truth and more to the point, Stulpnagel was actually in charge of German military intelligence for the "Foreign Armies" branch between 1933 and 1936. spanning the time Gisela arrived and then suddenly left the UK to return to her "sick mother" in Germany, before then reappearing to dine with Nancy Astor and setting off on her

Egyptian adventure. Stulpnagel was a senior staff officer with other duties altogether in 1939 when Gisela claimed he recruited her.

Once established in Cairo and Alexandria she was in the ideal position to gather intelligence. The society ladies undoubtedly told the charming couturier the latest news, and young army officers competed with each other to impress the glamorous Fraulein Klein.

The MI5 agent runner, Maxwell Knight, maintained that when women wanted to command attention, they dressed well and when men wanted to impress, they boasted about what they did. He said it made women superior at intelligence work. He also suggested it was far more effective if they didn't sleep with their informants. What better for the Germans than to have a beautiful maker of dresses enjoying the unrequited attentions of young officers far from home.

Gisela's soon to be new friend Lieutenant Derek Cardiff and his Battalion of Scots Guards arrived in Cairo just as things were becoming rather more interesting in North Africa. In October 1935 Mussolini invaded Abyssinia, now Ethiopia, one of the only two independent African countries – the other being Liberia – that hadn't already been grabbed by a great power.

The Italians waged a vicious little war which drew large amounts of public sympathy in Britain and elsewhere for the beleaguered Abyssinians and their leader Haile Selassie. Realpolitik meant the country was doomed, as was the reputation and future of the already floundering League of Nations which failed to take effective action. The Italians were left to get on with attacking spirited but badly armed opponents with modern weaponry, including poison gas which had been prohibited by international convention after the First World War.

There was an ulterior motive for the British and the French in letting Italy's empire building ambitions go unchecked. Politicians and diplomats saw Italy as a useful counterbalance to

Hitler's demands and wanted Mussolini kept on side to help restrict Germany's growth.

Meanwhile Gisela was on hand to witness the unrest triggered in Egypt by British policy. In November the Foreign Secretary Sir Samuel Hoare, who actually recruited Mussolini as a paid agent for MI5 while stationed in Rome in 1917, and who also signed off on the Italian control of Abyssinia, caused public demonstrations by refusing Egyptian student demands for a return to a more liberal constitution.

After previous protests and the repeated closure of Giza University, a crowd of 4000 marched from the university towards Cairo. It was a surprisingly formal looking demonstration to modern eyes. Most of the all-male protestors were in suits with ties and wearing the Fez. They were confronted by British forces at the Abbas Bridge over the Nile. At this point things got out of hand. One student carrying an Egyptian flag, Abdel Hakam Al Garrahy, was gunned down.

It was claimed he was killed by a British officer who told him not to move. The reports of his death quickly became mythologised. It was said he was shot 13 times; each time he'd taken a defiant step. This coupled with the story the young man used his own blood to write a damning condemnation of the British occupation was a clear indication of how fevered things had become. His funeral was a focus of national protest and his name was still being chanted at student demonstrations 40 years later.

****

As 1935 turned into 1936 and Gisela was busy with her double career, Britain was facing problems on multiple diplomatic and military fronts. In March 1936 Hitler's troops reoccupied the Rhineland including Gisela's home city Dusseldorf, which had been demilitarised since the First World War. It was the first of the high stakes gambles that would help to convince Hitler of the essential weakness of the British and their Empire.

Gisela was observing and reporting on events that must have helped to confirm his developing views. A month later Arabs in the British Palestine Mandate bordering Egypt went into armed revolt. The 2nd Battalion of the Scots Guards was promptly dispatched to Egypt to reinforce the 1st battalion and bolster the local forces.

The revolt involved Palestinian Arabs demanding independence from British control and the blocking of Jewish immigration to the area in pursuit of a permanent Jewish homeland in line with the Balfour Declaration. This declaration by the British Foreign Secretary Arthur Balfour came during the latter stages of the First World War and the location it identified covered a section of the old Turkish Ottoman empire which had fallen under British control.

Quite a few Arab nationalists were naively keen on the Nazis' anti-Jewish measures and made efforts to get German backing, and even form their own Nazi party sections, but the National Socialists who regarded all semitic peoples as inferior wouldn't become involved or authorise an Arab Nazi party.

A German diplomat in Baghdad received requests for weaponry for the Palestinian Arabs as soon as the revolt broke out, but this was refused. However, the Germans kept an eye on what was happening and encouraged Arab nationalists, while seeking intelligence about economic and military activity in the area.

Some of this intelligence was also provided by someone who would have the closest possible personal and espionage connection to Gisela. He was a young German man who appeared in Cairo just as the Arab revolt broke out. His sharp blue eyes missed nothing and he was already noting the numbers of military aircraft being deployed and the "tough" Scottish soldiers who were filling the Egyptian trains with their kilted bodies and heavy kitbags.

He was tall with dark hair and was on a round-the-world espionage spree for the German Foreign Office. His travels taking him through the United States from coast to coast, onwards to South America and Japan and then back through the Suez Canal.

There's no direct evidence he and Gisela met in Cairo, apart from a faint hint in something he wrote later, and his suggestion under later interrogation she had been in Palestine, which disguised the fact that both of them were in the same place at the same time. In a travelogue written during the war he deliberately chooses not to describe his time in Cairo and amongst the Pyramids because he said it had been done before. There's also an oblique reference to a "honeymoon".

He had a self-admitted eye for blonde women, and prior to this he and Gisela had both been in Britain in 1933 and later when he went to university. She was in Oxford while he was at Cambridge. The pair would also appear in Paris at the same time in the mid to late thirties, where she would be identified as his mistress, and yet again during the German occupation of the French capital. They both had close links to the book trade and printing in Germany through their families. These multiple connections in both time and place would certainly pass Ian Fleming's Goldfinger test, something that would only be revealed partially to British Intelligence with the benefit of hindsight.

This young man would go on to change the course of Gisela's life in ways that she could never have believed as she danced to Fred Astaire's hit of that year, "Cheek to Cheek" with the young British officers in the ballroom of the Mena House Hotel as the moon rose and shadows lengthened over the Pyramids of Giza.

6

THE BRANDSTETTER INHERITANCE

THE TALL, DARK, handsome man whose life and travels were already intertwined with Gisela Klein was called Wolfgang Krause-Brandstetter. She kept several black and white photographs of him all seemingly taken at the same time and showing a good looking determined face and capturing the pale gaze of his eyes. He was intelligent, duplicitous and charming, what could possibly go wrong?

His father, Ernst Krause was killed in the first year of the First World War while fighting for Germany, and Wolfgang's mother, Suzanne, a formidable motorcycle riding woman, if a family picture of her is anything to go by, then married Justus Brandstetter. He was the rather austere but respected co-owner of a printing firm in Leipzig who chose to cycle to work like his 900 plus employees rather than use the expensive motor vehicle he owned.

Oscar Brandstetter was a thriving and well-connected business in Germany and much further afield. Wolfgang and his younger brother Rudi added their stepfather's name to their own. Justus already had a son, Horst, and the three boys all developed a passion for fast cars which saw Horst killed in a racing accident and Wolfgang also injured in a car accident.

The young Wolfgang was raised in Leipzig and after attending the university there he was groomed for the business of his adoptive father. The same year Gisela arrived in the UK he came to Britain on a visit and then returned the following year to Cambridge University where he studied English literature at Gonville and Caius college. This was part of a programme devised for him by the British publisher John Holroyd Reece who at this early stage clearly recognised his potential and perhaps more importantly was involved in business with Justus Brandstetter, so was doing him a favour.

Wolfgang spent about a year studying. He was in good company. Cambridge in the 1930s, was a breeding ground for spies. The Soviet agents Kim Philby, Guy Burgess, Donald Maclean, Antony Blunt and John Cairncross were educated there. At Peterhouse college was a man called Ronald Sidney Seth. Seth later became a double if not triple agent during his rackety espionage career. He started with Britain's SOE during the Second World War before being captured and going over to the Germans. Seth then volunteered to be sent back to the UK as a double agent before finally apparently returning to the British side. For the Germans he became SD agent 22d.

Like many agents he was a stranger to the truth and in his case possibly reality. Seth met Wolfgang and Gisela much later in occupied Paris, but back in 1935, Cambridge seems to have reinforced Wolfgang's high estimation of his own abilities. He described in an article in a Leipzig newspaper how to win friends and get on with the British:

"Nothing is worse than to engage oneself as an active propagandist and go like a bull at a gate [...] The more one conforms to their ways on the surface [...] the better the chance one has to leave behind an effective and positive impression"

It seems, like Gisela, he was a natural dissembler and also something of a proselytiser for the new Germany, a role he later made official in such extensive propaganda and espionage work aimed at Britain, that he became known as "The English Expert".

He was an ambitious young man who tended to divide opinions rather starkly. To his mentor and business associate in the 1930s, John Holroyd Reece, the young man behaved "badly" and in a personally "treacherous" manner. Wolfgang had hidden his support for the Nazi party in the mid 1930's from the Jewish Reece and his instructions from the Germans for espionage activity while travelling around the world on business.

The business trip where Wolfgang ended up in Cairo at the same time as Gisela was, on the surface, a joint venture between the Brandstetter company and Holroyd Reece. It seems to have involved both the Tauchnitz book series, which published English language books on the continent printed by Brandstetter, and the paperback Albatross series, set up by Holroyd Reece.

Albatross books were the role model for the later Penguin paperbacks with different coloured dust jackets for different genres. Albatross used silver covers for anthologies; red for adventure and crime; blue for love stories and purple for biographies and historical novels.

Holroyd Reece, had adopted Britain, despite his German heritage. He was himself no stranger to concealment and was also suspected of espionage. The French thought him a spy for the Germans. The British seemed to think he was working for them. He actually fought on the British side as a cavalry officer in the First World War despite not having become a naturalised Briton and still possessing German citizenship. It would have been surprising if they had not put his background to good use during the war with an intelligence role.

Holroyd Reece also used, by default or design, numerous aliases in his business dealings. They were all similar to his adopted English one of Reece, including his father's original German name Reiss. In the end, like his protege Wolfgang, he was probably mainly working for himself. He was, according to his own daughter, quoted in the book, Strange Bird, a fascinating study of Albatross publishing, an "embobiner," a French word for spooling thread onto a bobbin, as he slowly and naturally drew other people into his complex plans. These involved multiple companies owning parts of each other in smoke and mirror operations that always made it hard to follow the money and the power. An example of these complexities resulted during the Second World War in Wolfgang being able to disguise the origins of the Albatross book business originally funded by British Jewish finance so that he could sell the books for his personal profit, although they were meant to generate desperately needed hard currency for the war enfeebled economy of the Third Reich.

While Holroyd Reece turned against Wolfgang and later worked with British intelligence to interrogate him, superior German officers during the war were more impressed by the young man. They variously described Wolfgang in his official soldier's record held by the German Military Archive at Freiberg as:

"Popular among colleagues. Always correct towards superiors. He is confident in all areas of responsibility," and…. "Thanks to years spent abroad we always have a good overview".

He was also a "convinced National Socialist" and elsewhere "rooted in National Socialism and knows how to pass on good ideas."

Although he only officially joined the Nazi Party in 1940 – which seems to suggest that he saw it as an opportunistic route to success rather than a particularly attractive ideology – he clearly possessed of a certain degree of toughness.

"He faces obstacles that suddenly arise with absolute certainty and firmness and is able to overcome all the difficulties that arise with his own strength."

British intelligence were less charitable than Wolfgang's German commanding officers. The Security Service's Lieutenant Colonel Vivian Home Seymer later dismissed him as: "A calculating Nazi only suitable for close confinement"

****

More than a decade before that view of him, Wolfgang set off for America on business and in his intelligence gathering role. According to Holroyd Reece, he actually volunteered his services to spy for Germany. However, as is likely with Gisela, being told to spy would have been an integral part of the process of obtaining the relevant permission to travel outside the borders of the Third Reich as the Nazis increased their grip on their own population.

Wolfgang's first target was the United States. He recorded a censored version of his adventures in a travelogue produced during the Second World War.

Wolfgang didn't have to look very far for a publisher. The German Tauchnitz imprint had been taken over pre-war by the Brandstetter firm with help from Holroyd Reece. The green covered paperback book, one of three he would write about his life, was marked as not being for sale outside Greater Germany which by this time encompassed most of Europe and large sections of the east. As Wolfgang was producing the book in 1943, the Germans were fighting a desperate battle in the Soviet Union and suffered the loss of General Paulus' 6th army at Stalingrad. The writing for those who cared to see it was clearly on the wall, and in this book Wolfgang, with an eye to the future, was at pains to portray himself as an intelligent and internationally minded young man, certainly not an inward looking Nazi.

The paperback was called *Welt Im Wurfelbecher*, World in a Dice Cup. He published under an alias, one of many. He used his genetic father's first name for a surname, Wolfgang Ernst. The book is dedicated to his parents. He sets out his aim at the very beginning of the book, describing it as the result of a foray out into the world by him in 1935 and 1936:

"It is intended to give the reader a colourful picture of all the experiences and encounters and the lighthearted perspective of a young man[...]Some of the names of the people and ships have been changed. The events took place in the order that they happened."

It seems likely that he kept notes or a diary of his travels because Welt im Wurfelbecher contains quite detailed passages, including large chunks of reported speech. This had the double benefit of allowing him to record any useful intelligence he discovered. He was accurate about certain things that would have been of interest to Berlin, less so about more minor matters such as misquoting the words to the 1933 Bing Crosby song "Home on the Range" which he recalls as Home on the Ranch.

Blonde women seem to feature quite heavily in the pages, and there was at least one ship board romance on the way to America, with a "straw blonde" or "blonde angel" called Sylvie, which although he doesn't claim for himself, it's fairly clear he was the man he describes in a clinch with her, leaving his companion and competitor Moritz apparently to "cry in the dark".

In California he also seems to have enjoyed himself.

"An alcohol-fuelled blue wall enveloped me immediately and it was only with difficulty that I could see where to turn. The party was already in full swing. In the haze of the opposite corner of the room stood a piano, which was compelled to utter a howling note of jubilation under the barbarous hands of a tousle-headed giant."

In the book Wolfgang was clearly not going to fall foul of the Nazis' hatred of "degenerate" music and, by his description, its African American pianist, by suggesting in this entry that he really enjoyed what he was hearing.

Wolfgang then left California and headed for South America and Japan as part of his tour. If his statement at the beginning of the book is true about the events he covers happening in the correct order, it was his return to Germany via the Indian Ocean that places him in Cairo and Alexandria at the same time as Gisela.

Arriving in Egypt he mentions the presence of 500 British aircraft, and describes members of a Scottish regiment who he encounters on a train on the railway line that runs alongside the Suez Canal.

"We had the windows open and enjoyed the view of the canal. At a station the train suddenly filled up to capacity with kilted Scotsmen carrying heavy kit bags on their backs, tanned and looking tough."

Wolfgang quoted a railway official:

"Everybody goes to Palestine" says the brown express train conductor as he checks our tickets. "Big fight there, Arabs excitedly shoot at everyone: Jews, English and foreigners. Every evening the train's full with troops coming from England."

The soldiers were the 2nd Battalion of the Scots Guards who were sent out to deal with the Arab revolt in Palestine. This puts Wolfgang there just after April 1936 when the revolt began and Gisela had firmly established herself as beautiful couturier and a favourite of the British Officers stationed in Egypt. Even in the unlikely event it was their first connection it certainly wouldn't be the last.

****

Jack Profumo's return to Britain in October 1935 from his round the world trip became a newspaper story. Along with the Jade ring for Gisela he also used his time in China to purchase a coffin decorated in imperial yellow. Newspaper reports from the time show him standing alongside the coffin at the railway station at Plymouth where his ship had docked from America. The clear thrust of the reporting was he brought it back specially for his father. The Baron Profumo was quoted by the Evening News as saying: "I was certainly not expecting such a gift from my son" Jack hastened to reassure reporters that it was not for his father's personal use.

A month after Jack graduated from Oxford, Gisela reappeared in Britain from Egypt. She did not head for Avon Carrow this time, although she and Jack must have met up for him to give her the Jade ring. The official entry in the Home Office list of her travels merely notes: "8.9.36. Alien lands." Gisela told the authorities she was going to stay with her new Guardsman, Lieutenant Derek Cardiff at his family home near Ludlow in Shropshire.

As the leaves began to turn on the trees that autumn the attraction of Easton Court and the young Derek Cardiff seem to have palled. Gisela was once again busy and on the move. She applied for a further extension of her stay and within eight weeks she was off to spend a weekend in Paris with a different Guards officer.

The name of her sponsor for the extension of her leave to stay in Britain would be proof of her well placed contacts. He was Lord Mount Temple, the Chairman of the Anglo-German Fellowship, a pro-German and some would claim pro-Nazi organisation. He'd only just returned from attending the annual Nazi rally at Nuremberg, held between the 8th and the 14th of the month.

The year before the Nazis used the event, which Lord Mount Temple declined to attend, to announce the Nuremberg race laws ensuring Jews were no longer Germans but merely subjects of the Reich who could not marry Aryan Germans. The Anglo-German fellowship made it clear in a letter to the Nazis that the organisation didn't want to be seen to be associating itself with such measures.

Mount Temple's late first wife had been a member of a prominent British Jewish family

The Fellowship only came into being in 1935. It was formed first in Parliament following a speech by the then Prince of Wales, later Edward VIII, that called for a better understanding with Germany. The prince was obsessed by his German ancestry and the insight he believed it gave him into Anglo-German affairs. The family name of Saxe-Coburg-Gotha only having been replaced by Windsor in 1917, and Edward always displayed a marked and some would say a treacherous affinity for Nazi Germany.

Those who joined the Anglo-German Fellowship were an interesting group, including Sir Barry Domville, an Admiral and former Director of Naval Intelligence, later locked up for his pro-Nazi stance; Cliveden set member and *Times* editor Geoffrey Dawson; some of the fox hunting mad Mitford pack: the father and mother, Lord and Lady Redesdale and their daughter: Unity Valkyrie Mitford, who physically stalked Hitler in Germany. She was described by the Fellowship's Secretary Ernest Tennant as "the young and beautiful Unity Mitford who believes Hitler is divine in the biblical sense". She was accompanied by her sister Diana who would marry Sir Oswald Mosley, leader of the British Union of Fascists. Duncan Sandys, a "friend" of the glamorous Nazi lover Jeanne Stourton, and son-in-law to Winston Churchill was on the scene which also included William Joyce, a fascist friend of MI5's Maxwell Knight, who possibly tipped him off about his impending arrest at the beginning of the war, allowing him to escape to Germany and become well known as the Nazi propaganda broadcaster Lord Haw Haw.

Bizarrely, the Soviet spy Guy Burgess was brought in to do publicity for the Fellowship. He was followed by Kim Philby, whose father St John Philby had converted to Islam in 1930 and was known for his antisemitic and fascist tendencies. The British intelligence services also had their own agent within the Fellowship who went by the codename M3.

The route for Gisela to Lord Mount Temple is interesting. Ever the successful networker, she knew his mistress who called this former Government minister, member of the House of Lords and also Chairman of the Anti-Socialist and Anti-Communist Union, by the somewhat unlikely nickname "Rabbits" or sometimes "My own darling Rabbits" or "Darling Wilfy." Lord Mount Temple's mistress kept the signet ring he'd given her as a mark of his affection and the loving bond between them.

It is unlikely however that Gisela was actually aware of the precise nature of this connection although on meeting Lord Mount Temple she undoubtedly realised his strong interest in the opposite sex, amply demonstrated by the fact that the archive at Southampton University holding his papers, catalogues several bundles of photographs of his friends with the words "especially women" in brackets. His address book also holds more than a few female names and the details of the jewellers Faberge.

One of Wilfy's daughters was married to Lord Louis Mountbatten, later Viceroy of India and she would inherit her father's flair for amorous adventures allegedly taking the Indian politician and prime minister Jawaharlal Nehru as a lover.

With the help of Lord Mount Temple, Gisela obtained permission to stay in Britain until the end of 1936. She then became involved in a more open war than espionage that the Nazis were already waging against Britain and France. There were plans for a concerted invasion of Nazi fashion.

7

HEIL HITLER HIGH FASHION

TODAY THE SPRAWL of Gatwick airport to the south-east of London can be an industrial abattoir of dreams of the exotic and soul enriching nature of travel, as anyone who has watched an ominously still baggage carousel at midnight can testify.

On the 17th of November 1936 the aerodrome still held an allure for the well off and adventurous. It was then home of the "beehive", the world's first circular terminal building, officially opened earlier that year, and more importantly it was the aerial gateway to Paris Le Bourget airport and other destinations on the continent.

Gisela presumably bought her combined rail and air ticket at Victoria railway station in London and once at the airport she was able, via a specially built tunnel, to board the plane from the train without stepping outside. Boarding happened in under 20 minutes and Gisela was on a De Havilland aircraft, heading to the fashion capital of the world. Beside her was a young Guards officer, the very handsome and well heeled, Hanmer Cecil Hanbury, three years her junior.

Hanmer and Gisela's enterprise in flying to Paris together wasn't entirely risk free. Two months earlier a De Havilland 86 like the one they were taking to the French capital, crashed after take-off for Hanover. The co-pilot got his foot stuck between a fire extinguisher and the rudder bar preventing the pilot from maintaining control. While the young couple were enjoying their holiday, another aircraft, this time a German Fokker, crashed on approach to the airport. Gatwick wasn't exactly a runaway success, only a year later it was closed because of severe flooding.

This particular trip to Paris was for the "weekend" according to the official British file on Gisela, although the 17th was actually a Tuesday, so they had four or five days to enjoy the delights of the French capital.

If Gisela's companion had any apparent and publicly known fault it was that he owned a wire-haired Terrier he couldn't control and was a menace. This dog landed him in court after it went into battle with a pair of Dachshunds near his London home in Smith Square in Westminster.

The Westminster and Pimlico News reported the Dachshunds' female owner was bitten. Only throwing a jug of water over the scuffle allowed the dogs to be separated. The potential metaphor of this struggle for canine dominance between England and Germany undoubtedly escaped everyone involved. The magistrates, despite a plea of not guilty, fined Hanmer £2.10 shillings and ordered the terrier kept under control.

Hanmer Cecil Hanbury was always known as Pat, or Patsy by his doting mother, and was in the Grenadier Guards. He met Gisela in Egypt, where like Derek Cardiff, he was stationed. The Grenadier Guards were based in Alexandria, although he was brought home in the summer of 1936 after a head injury rendered him unconscious and put him in hospital for a month, so possibly he'd sustained a fractured skull. His mother had set off from the United Kingdom on a P&O liner to Port Said in Egypt to collect him. It's not clear whether his injuries were as a result of action during the Arab revolt or given the general nature of the British occupation of

Egypt, playing polo. Whatever the cause, he carried a scar on his forehead ever after.

He was the second son of Sir Cecil and Lady Dorothy Hanbury. The family had homes in both Italy and the UK. The British residence was Kingston Maurward House, near Dorchester in Dorset, a Georgian mansion in Portland stone surrounded by a large estate.

While at La Mortola near Ventimiglia in Northern Italy, not far from the French Italian border, Pat's grandfather Thomas, who made a fortune in property in Shanghai, had a house and created spectacular gardens which supplied seeds and plants to botanical collections all over the world, including Kew Gardens in London. Pat's mother later gave Mortola to the Italian government and the gardens remain a tourist attraction.

Gisela was certainly on form with Pat. In an echo of Jack Profumo's family background, one of his parents was an Italian fascist. In this case it was his mother Dorothy, or sometimes Dods or Dodo, who had the distinction of being the first English woman to be enrolled in the fascist party of Benito Mussolini. She also had the distinction of being very much in love with Lord "Rabbits" Mount Temple, "Darling Wilfy" as she also called him, the good-looking Chairman of the Anti-Socialist and anti-Communist Union, and the Anglo-German Fellowship, who vouched for Gisela to British immigration. Dorothy maintained a devoted and passionate correspondence with him for years.

As the aircraft took off from Gatwick the pair of younger lovers were possibly unaware that Dorothy Hanbury had contacted the British authorities about Gisela three weeks previously. This was now the second time her activities had been brought to their attention. The letter informed them that Gisela had a good job as a designer and was also in receipt of a "private" income of £2 10 shillings a week. Dodo Hanbury had been in the clothing business herself, running a boutique premises on New Bond Street with a Lady Peacock in the 1920s. Lady Peacock's husband was the Secretary and Treasurer to Edward, the Prince of Wales who was a driving force in the foundation of the Anglo-German Fellowship. Gisela was operating in such a small world.

The letter to the authorities may not have been sent with malice aforethought. Although British mamas seem not to have been as keen on Gisela as their boys. The letter could have been in unwitting support of her application to stay in the UK. Whatever Lady Hanbury's motives, the outcome was the same as following the visit to Cliveden and the interest that Nancy Astor had taken in her. Four days before the "weekend" trip to France the immigration authorities issued a notice to Gisela to leave without delay, for once again being in breach of the no employment restriction on her visa.

Today Gisela's movements and associates would set alarm bells ringing almost immediately in the security services. Her activities were an almost textbook example of someone acting as scout for intelligence sources, a "forscher" in Abwehr parlance, as well as gathering military and political intelligence herself and probably acting as a courier for information from other sources as well. The Abwehr made much use of in and out agents like Gisela at this time. Its failure to create much longer term penetration networks along the lines used by the Soviets hampered its operations massively in the future.

Gisela's life of continuous travel was neatly analysed by Malcolm Muggeridge, who was in the espionage business in the 1930s, as being part and parcel of the life of a spy. He maintained that constant movement was the defining feature of someone engaged in espionage.

"A stationary intelligence officer is a contradiction in terms like a sedentary eagle; he (she) moves therefore he (she) is."

A female member of the intelligence service whose name has

been redacted in Gisela's British dossier made exactly that observation after meeting her.

In a handwritten note from the counterintelligence B division of MI5, dated 10th October 1940, an officer who just uses the initials G.R. makes a reference to the female staff member as being based in Room 312 and says:

"She tells me that she met Gisela Klein in Germany and was suspicious of her – largely on account of the way she popped backwards and forwards between London Paris Germany etc with no apparent difficulty."

Gisela was heading towards a new phase of her life as she sat next to Hanmer Hanbury on the flight to Paris. The city would come to play an increasingly important role in her life.

****

Paris was always the subject of a love/hate fascination for the Nazis. Hitler loathed the arrogance of the French capital's establishment after the Treaty of Versailles. In a 10-page rambling personal letter to Lord Rothermere, the owner of the *Daily Mail*, Der Fuhrer described Versailles, with what was unusual succinctness for him, as "a more than stupid treaty".

He also hated the dominance of the Paris couture industry whose fashion shows effectively drove the international fashion trade. He was very interested, in a controlling way, in women's fashion and engaged personally in the design of the uniform of the female arm of the Hitler Youth, the BDM, the Bundes Deutscher Madel. At least part of Hitler's concern with German fashion coincided with one of his other fanatical obsessions, the hatred of Jews, who were highly represented in the German fashion business.

In May 1933 after Gisela first arrived in Britain, Goebbels told the organiser of a Berlin fashion show to drop the French elements in it completely, while a month later Hitler declared in an interview that Berlin women must become the best dressed in Europe while also stating: "No more Paris Models".

By that he was referring to the slim, tall and handsome women on whom French couture hung so well. Gisela in other words. The Nazis regarded this look as decadent, with its suggestion of what they saw as the "degenerate" jazz age morals of the Weimar Republic, and its direct challenge to the party-ordained and severely limited role for women in Hitler's Germany.

In 1933 the official Nazi policy on couture saw the creation of the German Fashion Institute. This was designed to underpin an Aryan fashion industry and destroy the influence of Jewish couturiers, and the dominance of Paris in the world of fashionable clothing.

The Honorary President of this organization was the Jewish designer wearing fashionista, Magda Goebbels who had a taste for handmade Italian Ferragamo shoes and was the wife of Propaganda Minister Joseph.

Magda was a blonde with icy blue eyes, and a drive and ambition distinctly at odds with the Nazi ideology about the role of women. She smoked cigarettes, although never in front of the Fuhrer, (who hated smoking as well as despising make-up on women), and her beauty regime apparently included the strangely precise 42 strokes of the hairbrush, a complete re-application of her make-up before appearing in public and different outfits for lunch and dinner. She was, in competition with Göring's wife Emmy, keen to be presented as the first lady of the Third Reich. Hitler always wanted to promote the idea he was only married to Germany, hiding both his sinister controlling relationship with his half-niece Geli Raubal, who killed herself with his gun in 1931, and his long-term mistress Eva Braun.

Goebbels however, sacked Magda from the German Fashion Institute later in 1933, probably because of an interview she gave to a newspaper reporter in which she announced the "Gretchen" image of German women was dead and said that:

"...the German woman of the future should be stylish beautiful and intelligent."

Given the male Nazi love of "Tracht," the traditional and historic style of costume, and their projection of how women should dress and behave, this didn't go down well. Goebbels' propaganda ministry let it be known that anything she had to say on fashion in the future was not to be reported.

However as with anything to do with the Nazis there were double standards. The reality was that high fashion never went away despite the constantly broadcast fantasy of blonde Rhine maidens with fresh scrubbed faces producing the next generation of little Hitler worshippers.

Both Magda Goebbels and Eva Braun led the charge for indigenous German Haute Couture. Previously this and the ready to wear sector in Germany were largely driven by knockoffs of the Paris catwalks, with designs being smuggled out from the shows as sketches. Both Magda and Eva favoured the Berlin couture salon Annemarie Heise, who also dressed German film stars of the time.

Eva loved Heise so much she ordered a dress from the couturier to marry Hitler shortly before their suicide in the Berlin bunker in April 1945. Russian soldiers were so close to the centre of Berlin at the time that it was reportedly impossible to deliver the dress normally and a courier from the bunker had to undertake a hazardous journey to collect it. Eva also ordered all her bills from Heise were to be destroyed to hide her expensive couture addiction paid for by Hitler via his personal photographer and Eva's former boss Heinrich Hoffman.

A photograph of a Heise design held by the Vasiliev Foundation in Paris shows that Gisela modelled for this designer which places her both in Berlin and at the centre of Nazi high society.

In the black and white photograph Gisela is wearing a dark slim fitting mid-calf length dress with long sleeves and gathered folds in a V neck at the chest and embroidery in a curved panel below, typical of German efforts at the time to promote its own struggling embroidery industry. An embroidered motif is also featured on the front of the skirt. Her thick hair is tied with a dark bow..

The nearly full-length framing with a side profile shows her with one knee on a chaise longue and she's holding a wide brimmed dark shiny straw hat with ribbon around the rim.

The Vasiliev Foundation dates the photograph to around 1940. Gisela kept a cropped version of it which presumably removed the stamp or marks on the back that linked it to the Heise salon.

Gisela later made a pencil note on the back of a piece of paper listing her career highlights. The list included "learned service in the best haute couture salon in West Germany". Strangely although perhaps understandably she doesn't give its name, but it was undoubtedly Heise. This link may have led to a throwaway line that Gisela's later husband Edward made to their daughter Lisl:

"Hitler had her picture on his wall," he told her.

Lisl was too young to make much sense of it, she couldn't tell if he was joking or not:

"I thought what a stupid thing to say."

But the phrase always stuck with her and worried her. The connection to Heise put Gisela, who would have served in and shown fashions at the Berlin shop itself, in direct contact with the women of the Nazi elite and it's perfectly possible that her natural blonde looks gained Hitler's attention.

He loved the presence of good-looking women despite his complete lack of small talk. It's possible that she modelled a series of female uniform designs submitted to the German High Command which came to his attention.

She admitted years later to having seen Hitler speak at a rally and found him "captivating". The contact was probably more direct than that.

Gisela also seems to have modelled for a very similar name, Anneliese Heise. In Lisl's collection of her mother's papers in California is a picture of Gisela modelling an outfit for the photo-atelier Deutscher Verlag. The caption reads: Modele Anneliese Heise Cliché.

The Deutscher Verlag was created when the Jewish Ullstein family of the liberal Ullstein publishing house were forced to sell up in 1937. The Deutscher Verlag was closely associated with Nazi party publishing and one suspected female Abwehr agent, Ingeburg Berta, who came to Britain in virtually identical circumstances and at around the same time as Gisela, was last heard of by British Intelligence working for the Deutscher Verlag in Paris. Throughout Gisela's life there would be an unusual and continuous link between couture, publishing and espionage.

While individual elements of the German fashion industry proved relatively successful, the German Fashion Institute ended up as an ineffectual organization achieving virtually nothing, but others carried the flag for Nazi fashion forward. One of these was the Frankfurt Fashion Centre created by the Mayor of Frankfurt who saw his city as becoming the leading light of the industry in Germany.

The Fashion Centre was designed to educate a new generation in design and techniques as well as promoting German inspired fashion abroad. The Centre put on shows with student models in Austria, Hungary, and Italy before advancing on London.

Lord Mount Temple and the Anglo-German Fellowship were planning an exclusive fashion show with young German models wearing the latest designs from Frankfurt.

The Frankfurt Centre was run by Frau Margarethe Klimt. She was Austrian by birth, educated in Art and Design at the

University of London and her devotion to the cause of National Socialist fashion was underlined by Joseph Goebbels awarding her the special status of "cultural icon" as the war began to go badly for Germany. This was meant to protect her and her work from any of the other demands of "total war" as by 1943 the German fashion industry was effectively defunct as it was turned over to war production.

But in 1936 if the Germans thought their fashion blitz on London would storm in without opposition they hadn't factored in Her Majesty's Customs and Excise. The customs officers became obsessed with the idea that because the outfits to be worn by the student models were in theory for sale they should attract import tariffs levied on anything made of silk.

A bureaucratic correspondence between the Anglo-German Fellowship and Customs followed. This involved Frank Tiarks who was a Governor of the Bank of England, a member of the Fellowship and incidentally of the British Union of Fascists as well, offering to provide a deposit until the dresses left the country again.

The Fellowship attempted to outflank Customs by protesting that the whole affair was "purely cultural [...] The girls will move about among the guests and the secretary will explain the special features of the dress's materials used, etc."

The Customs officers continued to maintain an unenthusiastic eye on everything, even insisting on inspecting individual dresses on arrival and again on packing for departure.

The Daily Mail, ever eager to promote friendship with Germany, covered the arrival of the fashion models from Frankfurt. The show was due to be held at Claridge's Hotel on the 27th of November 1936. The headline ran:

"Student Mannequins to show us German Fashions".

The paper pictured a group of the young models on a cultural visit to Windsor Castle. The reporter assigned to the job clearly had difficulty reading back their own handwriting, or the Pitman's shorthand outline for Frau Klimt, actually rendering her name as Klunt, an easy enough, if unfortunate mistake.

The models were photographed in front of Windsor Castle. Gisela doesn't seem to be amongst them, she must have by then received her notice to leave the UK for working without permission. She however later played a leading part in organising and modelling for the Nazi fashion front in Europe.

A programme for the Claridge's Hotel show still exists in the Bodleian Library Collection of Trade Ephemera in Oxford. Her Majesty's Customs and Revenue won a small if largely pointless victory. The three-page programme notes sternly:

"This display is not in any sense a mannequin parade. Nor has it any commercial object whatever."

It then went on to outline the apparent objectives:

> *The work of the FRANKFURT FASHION CENTRE is purely artistic and its objects are cultural and social.*
>
> *Throughout history fashion has always been a facet of culture: and just as culture formerly was the monopoly of the few, so fashion also has tended to be the luxury of the few.*
>
> *It is because today that fashion is no longer the monopoly of the few and because the spread of culture is bound up so closely and vitally with peace and progress and the very life of civilization, that the task of the Frankfurt Fashion Centre in Germany is to draw together all that is best at home and abroad.*
>
> *The Frankfurt Fashion Centre is anxious to take this opportunity of explaining and illustrating their work to a British audience, and they hope that it may become a bond of constructive artistic and social interest between the two countries.*

It was couture propaganda and an invitation to appeasement,

all in one delicious package, delivered by the attractive young models of the Frankfurt Fashion Centre circulating amongst the appreciative and invite only guests of the Anglo-German Fellowship at Claridge's. The leaflet then goes on to conjure a vision of the National Socialist education of the students at the Centre:

> *"A striking example of what is known in Germany as gemeinschaftsgeist or community spirit. Pupils from every stratum – daughters of workmen and the well to do- give mutual expression to the love of grace and beauty in their work on designing, on material production and fashion handicrafts.*
> *A remarkably cheery and happy atmosphere pervades the classrooms in an old-world building of noble architecture where the ideals of today show constant inspiration from the traditions of yesterday."*

It must have been music to the Anglo-German Fellowship's ears, although the idea that there was no commercial underpinning to this fashion show was not in any way true. Germany wanted foreign exchange to help pay for the massive rearmament taking place and the Nazis decreed fashion must play its part. Frau Klimt was later berated by the Mayor of Frankfurt for not producing enough commercial designs. She acerbically replied that most women couldn't afford what they were offering anyway and the exhibitions they staged were more about propaganda than fashion. Gisela's later role was in organising and appearing in similar shows for yet another Nazi fashion competitor to Berlin and Frankfurt, Vienna's Haus der Mode.

In the next few months Gisela would disappear from British official view as Paris became a focus for her activities, but the French authorities also became interested in what Mademoiselle Klein was doing. MI5's French counterpart the Deuxieme Bureau compiled files on her. These identify her as located in the French capital in the New Year of 1937, What's more these files do not display quite the same restrained understatement of their British counterparts, and French Military Intelligence had people spying on her directly.

8

CHERCHEZ LA FEMME

WITH THE BRITISH authorities curtailing her activities in the UK for the time being, Gisela created a new life for herself in Paris that was much as it had been in London, if, in line with the general ethos of the City of Light, rather more chic. The different language presented no problem to her at all. She spoke French and carried the internationally recognised visa of youth, beauty and fashion.

Her vitality and capacity for hard work while leading a hectic social life were once again in evidence. She was working as a model for French magazines like Votre Bonheure where she made the front cover, draped across the French flag, and for another magazine identified in the French secret files on her as "Vig", although this was most likely the French edition of *Vogue*.

She also got her own four page spread, which she kept, in an unidentified French language magazine whose gossip column seemed to have an English slant. The feature detailed the process of dressing a model, creating the set and taking a colour photograph of her. The headline in French said: "One photo that demands 10 hours of work."

The strapline reads: "All this work just for a colour photograph!"

The photographs chart the process from the initial call to Gisela at her Parisian home. It shows her answering the phone in a checked outfit sitting on a brushed velvet overstuffed armchair with her legs up on the telephone table. But once again it was not quite as straightforward as it seemed. In these photos she has a new identity. She is called Karin. Oddly a version of the name of Hermann Göring's much beloved late wife, Carin. He named both a house and yacht after her.

"Karin's type seems to everyone (at the photographic studio) to be the best one for the projected photo, it's really lucky she's at home and able to come here."

Under the other photographs of Gisela are captions describing her doing her make-up, curling her eyelashes, having her hair styled and putting on the clothes. She's also shown in various decorous states of underclothing and corsetry while she prepares for the shoot.

In the meantime, the French authorities seem to have thought, naively, that Gisela or Karin was not paid for this modelling work and was in an echo of her time in the UK being supported by her family with "money orders" which their watchers spotted being sent to the place she was staying at 19 Rue Copernic, in Paris' 16th arrondissement.

The photographic essay however makes it abundantly clear that she is being "well paid."

Her new home, maybe the location for the telephone call shot in the feature, was in an Art Deco building on the Rue Copernic with decorative iron railings outside the upper windows. Just along the road was the towering stone wall of the Reservoir de Plassy which supplied water to the city. It was a short walk to the Victor Hugo station of the Paris Metro. This was an area where French high society chose to live, the London equivalent of Kensington and Chelsea. Not bad for an impecunious model.

Her income seems to have more than doubled. A report for French military intelligence, the Deuxieme Bureau says she was in receipt of 4,000 francs a month, worth more than £2,000 (2025) now. If Pat Hanbury's mother Dorothy had been correct only a year or so before, her income from "home" of £2 pounds 10 shillings a week was the equivalent of £870 a month.

The British file on Gisela said she had been receiving money from her mother living in Holland. Gisela may have provided this detail to the immigration authorities in pursuit of a visa application or the French surveillance of her would have been the source.

The archives in Dusseldorf show this wasn't true. Gisela's mother Henriette, although Dutch by birth, was living with Gisela's father Alfred at an address in Kapellerstrasse in the city in 1937 and the evidence suggests she only left Dusseldorf after his death in 1941 as she was living in Beuel, a borough of Bonn in 1943.

So, who was "Mother" in Holland who was obligingly sending the money orders to Gisela?

One candidate was Hilmar Dierks, from the Abwehr unit in Hamburg, which along with its substation Bremen, was targeting the UK. Importantly, Bremen also had an interest in intelligence from Egypt.

Dierks had a long pedigree in espionage. He was a German spy in the First World War operating from Holland against Britain. According to research published by the Netherlands Intelligence Studies Association and largely based on British intelligence reports, at one stage in the 1920s he even offered his services to the British claiming things weren't going well for him financially as an arms dealer. This was possibly an attempt to work as a double agent. He was again very active in the 1930s and importantly he used money orders to pay agents. These originated from a number of different cut outs he was using in Holland.

The British eventually became aware of several of these spy financial support lines, including a securities broker in Amsterdam housed in a beautiful double fronted merchant's house facing the Herengracht canal. One of the directors of this company was

Gustav Adolf Heubel whose daughter later married the leader of the Dutch equivalent of the Nazi party. The firm had an account with the Midland Bank in London and several German agents in the UK were paid via this route.

Dierks also had form running female agents in various roles. The Hungarian military historian Lladislas Farago in his 1971 book on the Abwehr, Game of the Foxes, claimed to have found an overlooked treasure trove of German intelligence documents seized by the Americans. He was always a bit vague about them, which has led some to dismiss his accuracy. However, he said Dierks was one of three Abwehr officers running a handful of female agents, the others, Nikolaus Ritter and Johannes Bischoff were also out of the Hamburg and Bremen Abwehr stations.

Dierks was reported to have married one of these women agents, described by her later handler Nikolaus Ritter as "the most beautiful spy". She was called Vera Erikson, amongst other names. Like Gisela there was something about her. Unlike Gisela she had dark hair and dark eyes and was of Russian extraction. She also operated for the Germans in Britain in the 1930s.

In September 1940 she was captured after landing in Scotland from a small boat. It was planned that she would travel to London to link up with a female Nazi sympathiser and provide intelligence. Suspicious railway staff tipped off the police. Her two male companions were hanged after capture and trial, but she survived to disappear mysteriously after the war, either dying shortly after her return to Germany or, of more interest to the romantically and conspiratorially inclined, living out her days on the Isle of Wight with another ex-spy.

There is a further tantalizing mirror flash of a connection between Gisela and the Abwehr female agent runners Dierks and Ritter. According to the KV series of intelligence records held by the British National Archives at Kew, Dierks transferred three of his agents to Ritter in 1937. In the summer of 1937 one of Ritter's agents was known as "Frau Krause" who was being used as a link to other intelligence sources. It may of course just be yet a further coincidence that Wolfgang Brandstetter would use his genetic father's name, Krause, as his passport identity for a later spying trip to America. Mrs. Krause could have been something of a joke about Gisela's status because someone was about to identify her as his mistress.

This first official link between Gisela and Wolfgang, as opposed to their previous "coincidental" appearances in the UK and Egypt and their family backgrounds, was the reason the French began to take such an interest in her. It was because of a nosey British journalist based in the French capital. Thomas Cadett was appointed the Paris Correspondent for the *Times* in 1937. He attended Sandhurst Military College and was in the army during the First World War. He went on to report on the German invasion of France and work for the SOE and the BBC.

In June 1938 he wrote to M16 on *Times* headed notepaper with the subtitle "Office of the Paris Correspondent. 9 Rue Halevy". The letter begins "Dear Frank" who was probably Frank Foley, who'd been head of the Berlin MI6 station. The handwritten note goes on to tell a story that Thomas was clearly not going to follow up in the newspaper himself:

"I hear that the eldest son of Lord Erleigh has picked up a pro-Nazi mannequin called Klein who is the mistress of the German military attaché here and is taking her to stay in England if he has not already done so. Your friends in M15 might like to know this."

Cadett's close connection to the MI6 man is confirmed by his friendly sign off:

"Here's to August, yours ever Thomas."

Possibly a reference to the August start of the great exodus from Paris when anyone who was anyone left the capital for the country or the South of France. Cadett's letter meant there was now a known direct link between Gisela and German military intelligence.

A request stamped Secret in red capital letters was sent by M15 B2b, the German counterintelligence section of M15, to Colonel Valentine Vivian of MI6, on the 5th of July 1938. The request gives a reprise of the information provided by Thomas Cadett and adds:

> *"...a Home Office circular of the 2nd of October 1937 was issued against her [...] for taking up unauthorised employment as a photographer's model. She appears to have received her visa owing to an oversight.*
>
> *We should be very grateful for any information which the Deuxieme Bureau can give about Fraulein Gisela Henrina(sic) Klein and we enclose two photographs."*

Gisela's repeated episodes of unauthorised modelling work in Britain had really caught up with her. After previously being told to leave around the time of her trip to Paris with Pat Hanbury she'd been back to the UK again in March 1937 when she'd landed at Croydon airport. On this occasion she was going to stay with "Baron Profumo", i.e. Jack, at Avon Carrow. She'd also rented accommodation in Clarges Street, not that far from Buckingham Palace and the Ritz.

She was working for British *Vogue* and Harper's Bazaar and kept an advert for the department store Debenham & Freebody showing her modelling a flowing floor length coat in white fur.

She then left the UK in July 1937, officially for Dusseldorf, but not before being caught breaching her no work visa conditions yet again. This was the third time and her expulsion was due to last for a year.

Her further visit to the Britain noted by the *Times* man Thomas Cadett in 1938 happened despite that ban remaining in force. The row over how she managed to get a visa this time rumbled on for a while in her official dossier, before the bureaucratically convenient conclusion it was just one of those things caused by the limited system of immigration alerts and no one was really to blame.

Gisela used this mistakenly issued visa at British immigration on the dockside at the south coast port of Newhaven, after arriving on the ferry from Dieppe. This was the fastest sea route from France to Britain. Her landing card, a copy of which still exists in her file at Kew, states she was going to stay care of Lord Erleigh, 65 Rutland Gate, London.

The young man who got her into the UK this time was Michael Isaacs. He was three years younger than Gisela, and the eldest son of the second Marquess of Reading who also carried the title, Lord Erleigh; Thomas Cadett had that wrong as was noted in pencil on the bottom of his letter by an intelligence officer. The Isaacs were the highest profile Jewish family in the British aristocracy. This link with Gisela was a further indication, if needed, of the incredibly small upper-class world in which she moved. Michael Isaacs's sister Joan married the primate expert Solly Zuckerman who was teased by Jack Profumo and Gisela at Oxford.

Gisela was playing an increasingly complex and dangerous game. The pressure on her to be in Britain, despite having successfully established herself in Paris, clearly overrode the knowledge that she was officially banned by the British authorities and that she'd obtained entry by outflanking the system. Following the letter from the *Times* man in Paris and this first connection to German Intelligence there were now men on the streets of London actively hunting her down.

Gisela took what could easily be interpreted as a counter measure to throw them off the scent. Towards the end of June 1938, she made an unusual request to a young British socialite and friend, Diana Russell Clark. Diana was the owner of a dashing red Alvis speed 20 sports car and like Jack Profumo's sisters was keen on fox hunting.

She lived in a large London townhouse with her widowed mother at 74 Onslow Gardens in South Kensington nearly three miles from Gisela's usual residence in Clarges Street. The two young women who were the same age got to know each other because Diana's cousin and another friend served in the British army in Egypt and after their return to the UK "a very beautiful German girl" materialised as well.

Gisela told Diana the lease on her flat was ending and asked if she could come to stay with her. Diana asked permission from her mother Frances who wasn't that keen on the idea. She was planning to shut the Onslow Gardens house as usual in the summer so they could decamp to the other family home, Penbidwl, a few miles from Abergavenny in Wales. This large stone built house overlooked beautiful countryside and the black mountain, Skirrid Fawr.

However, Diana's mother did give her consent and said Gisela could stay for a couple of weeks before they left. Diana would later recall the lots of "very nice young men" who called at 74 Onslow Gardens to take Gisela out. She also referred to one in particular who she said went to prison after becoming involved with a "very strange lady". Diana was in her mid 70s when she told this story and this may have been a reference to the much later Profumo affair, although Jack didn't go to prison.

On a warm and pleasant Friday, the 8th of July, Diana and Gisela were both planning to spend time with friends for the weekend:

"…. anyway Gisela Klein and I both went away for the weekend on the Friday morning. Soon after lunch on the Friday afternoon the front doorbell rang and our old butler Christie went down to answer it and there were two men there and they said 'we understand that you have a young lady called Gisela Klein staying here, we have a warrant for her arrest."

Apparently by sheer luck Gisela had got out in the nick of time. Her clothes and belongings were left in the spare bedroom. she never collected them and the Russell Clarkes never saw her again. Diana's mother was apparently given a "terrific doing over" by these men although what they revealed to her isn't recorded. It seems likely they were Metropolitan Police Special Branch officers tasked with catching Gisela by MI5.

From the British archive evidence Gisela bolted via Dover on a ferry to Calais. She didn't return to Paris for any length of time but escaped back to Berlin. Jakey Astor, Nancy's youngest son described meeting her in the German capital that summer while he was staying with a family in Mecklenberg.

Tellingly she introduced him to a man he described in a later letter to Military intelligence as a "low grade agent" called Rudolf Goldschmidt. He was suspicious enough about him to forward his details to MI5 at the end of the war when Goldschmidt got in touch with him again.

After making the introduction Gisela told Jakey she was off to Cairo. This would have placed her in Egypt once again in 1938, although given her incredibly full diary for that year it seems a squeeze even for her.

There is a reference in the Dusseldorf archives which suggests officials in Germany also thought she was heading to Cairo in 1937 and British intelligence thought she might have been there again in 1940. It seems when things got too hot for her in England, she and more probably the Bremen Abwehr unit saw Egypt and potentially Palestine as a good fallback for her activities.

The *Times* correspondent, Cadett, did not however, provide one vital piece of information in his letter that set the whole investigation in train and helped to trigger the abortive attempt to arrest

Gisela by the British. He only identified her alleged lover as the "military attaché" at the German embassy in Paris.

It is pretty typical of the time and much later that Cadett would only view Gisela as mistress material. The French did the same later. It was a complacent and chauvinistic pigeonholing of an intelligent woman because she was also beautiful and enjoyed a busy social life. It meant investigations weren't pursued as vigorously as they should have been.

According to a published summary by an archivist at Kew the military attaché in question was none other than Wolfgang Krause Brandstetter, publisher and spy. This assertion raises questions.

Wolfgang was probably in Paris when Gisela flew in from Gatwick accompanied by Guards Officer Pat Hanbury in November 1936. In early 1937 he was learning the ropes of the publishing business in Paris on behalf of his stepfather's firm Oscar Brandstetter, along with a sideline in Nazi intelligence and propaganda work. But he isn't listed as a military attaché at the German's Paris embassy during this period. It seems Brandstetter, whose later army record in 1940 shows him as working in Paris for The German Foreign Office Unit B IV, propaganda and intelligence targeting the UK, was however running round in diplomatic circles in Paris and would have been known to Cadett.

There is, however, one military attaché at the Embassy at the relevant time who later cropped up connected to both Wolfgang and Gisela. He was Oberst De Luftwaffe Friedrich Carl Hanesse. He and Wolfgang, along with Gisela, were also in Paris during the German occupation. Wolfgang and Hanesse both worked in the same building that was commandeered by the Germans. Wolfgang was involved in aviation intelligence gathering and Hannesse was in charge of the Luftwaffe, and was at one stage apparently trying to place sabotage agents in Britain. He also ran a sideline in looting art and treasures on behalf of Göring.

The files held in the archive of the Paris Prefecture of Police who were instructed by French Military Intelligence to investigate Gisela, show a surprising and what must have been for her a highly expensive level of travel.

She'd officially been in France in October 1937, then again between December 1937 and April 1938. As well as the UK she'd also been in Germany, then Switzerland where she'd stayed in Lausanne, Geneva and St Moritz, apparently for "reasons of her health" then Germany once more before returning to France. What this meant in practice was that her activities and contacts were always largely unexamined. Neither the British nor French intelligence services ever got anything but a partial shot of the constantly moving model.

The connection to Wolfgang and or Hannesse were however, the first real spotlight on Gisela's activities and the French not only followed her in Paris but identified her in Cannes where according to a report by French intelligence provided to MI5 officers, she was also on "good terms" with a couple of French army officers on leave. Her magnetic attraction for men in uniform never deserted her, and there was also, the Deuxieme Bureau said, a French Prince whose name unfortunately was not known at the time.

The South of France was the location for another important source for Gisela, someone who could provide top level insider knowledge of the British establishment, especially air and defence capabilities, as well as an understanding of the Prince of Wales in whom the Nazis had a special interest.

George Sutherland-Leveson-Gower was the 5th Duke of Sutherland and a politician belonging to the Conservative party. He worked with Winston Churchill and had an expertise in British aircraft as former government Under Secretary for Air. He'd also been Under Secretary of State for War and was a senior member of the British Royal Household.

He was floating, lonely as a cloud, on a lilo in a swimming pool surrounded by a low sun-bleached wall. His body was noticeably pale and thin, and he was wearing dark swimming trunks and a pair of rounded sunglasses to protect his pale eyes from the bright sunlight flickering off the ripples in the water. With his red gold hair brushed back off his forehead, the way he tended to wear it, he is looking straight into the lens of the camera which Gisela is using to take his picture. The Duke is in his mid to late 40s and the photograph doesn't show anyone else present. It's the sort of snapshot that lovers or a couple on holiday alone together might take. He'd been married the year before Gisela was born.

The swimming pool is on the coast with the sea just behind it. The background to the black and white photograph suggests they were in the South of France or possibly Monte Carlo. This was an area that entranced Gisela so much she lived there after the war and years later made her husband and young children drive across the United States to escape from the bitterly cold winters of Ohio to the warmth of California, searching the Pacific shoreline until she found somewhere that reminded her of her beloved Cote D'Azur.

George Sutherland-Leveson-Gower was always known as Geordie or "Geordy" as Gisela writes it on the back of the picture which she kept alongside those of the men she'd clearly liked or loved. He was a friend and companion of David, better known to the British public as Edward Prince of Wales who became the short-lived Edward VIII. In 1936 Geordie was appointed to the post of Lord Steward of the Royal Household by David's father King George V. This position came with the full backing of the British Prime Minister Stanley Baldwin. Only a decade or so before, the post had only ever been given to a current member of the government.

He was exactly the sort of person that Germany in the mid to late 1930s either wanted to do business with or know what they knew. His understanding and intimate knowledge of the highest levels of the British establishment and as Under Secretary of State for War until 1929, military planning, were a potential goldmine for someone blonde, intelligent and witty who had an attractive interest in current affairs.

Apart from the intelligence angle, aristocrats like Geordie held a special importance for Germany and were deliberately targeted because Hitler didn't trust his own foreign office to deliver his policy goals.

Hitler left much of his real foreign policy to one of the few Nazis who had any real experience abroad. The lover of Jack Profumo's friend Jeanne Stourton, Joachim von Ribbentrop. As a younger man he'd spent a year in the UK and later developed a passion for Cornwall, identifying St Michael's Mount near Penzance as his preferred headquarters after a successful German invasion. He also worked in Canada and the United States although Geyr Von Schweppenburg, Military Attache to the German London embassy who juggled the roles of spy and diplomat in the 1930s, claimed that Ribbentrop was not even of average intelligence.

Ribbentrop's drive, a far more important factor in success than talent or brains, however had seen him wriggle himself into a position close to Hitler, mainly by echoing and amplifying what he knew the Fuhrer already wanted, much to the disgust of other senior Nazis who didn't rate his abilities at all.

Ribbentrop's approach to dealing with Britain, shared by his master and Göring, was to believe they could bypass the traditional and formal mechanisms by which nation states talked to, and did business with, each other. The Germans thought that Britain at this time was a nation really run by the upper classes whether they were in government or not.

Ribbentrop however, would commit so many social faux pas during his tenure as Ambassador to the Court of St James, between

1936 and 1938 that he was christened "Herr Brickendrop". Many of the British upper classes he wooed were immediately able to identify him as man on the make. He'd effectively bought the 'von' bit of his name from an aunt by marriage. He also attracted another nickname and pun "Londonderry Herr" because of his devotion to the appeaser and pro-German, Marquess of Londonderry, Charles Vane-Tempest-Stewart. Ribbentrop was also initially very keen on the Anglo-German Fellowship of which Londonderry was a member.

It was Ribbentrop's lack of real understanding of where the levers of power lay in Britain or indeed how far Germany would be able to push the coutnry to concede to its demands that led him to believe it was through organizations like the Anglo-German Fellowship, that he could bring enough pressure to bear on the Government to obtain what Hitler wanted. This belief in the power of the upper class quite literally went all the way to the top.

In 1935 at Hitler's command, Ribbentrop even approached Princess Victoria Louise, the only daughter of the ex-Kaiser Willhelm II, to see if she would marry her daughter Frederica off to Edward, the Prince of Wales. Frederica's father was the pro-Nazi Duke of Brunswick. There was however a large gap in age between the pair, Edward was only two years younger than Frederica's mother who'd been discussed herself as a possible match for him.

The marriage didn't happen, but it was an indication of the Nazi interest in Edward as an important link in their plans. An interest which would continue during the 1930s and into the war years. Geordie Sutherland was a very useful source in the Royal Household. His wife also held a senior position there and both of them would be on hand to observe the effect of the American divorcee Wallis Simpson, who Ribbentrop described in an intercepted communication as a "Germanophile", on the man who would become Edward VIII and then abdicate.

Geordie undoubtedly found Gisela not only personally attractive but was in sympathy with the outlook of many Germans like her. Anti-communism was one of the major selling points the Nazis used to promote themselves in Britain and particularly to the landowners and the wealthy who had more to fear than most. The industrialist Werner Schaurte, who sent Gisela the memo with the poem on it, was a strong anti-communist and Geordie echoed him. Geordie's abiding hatred of the Communist revolution in Russia was evident from the early 1920s. In the spring of 1921 he was, as a senior Scottish aristocrat, appointed Lord High Commissioner of the General Assembly of the Church of Scotland. His speech to the assembly Hall wouldn't pull any punches:

"... our country has been the object of a secret international propaganda to undermine that British moral stability in which is perceived the greatest hindrance to the propagation of anarchical and un-Christian doctrine all over the world."

He thundered on:

".... this great tide of irreligious savagery and agnostic paganism linked with every description of brutality has been sweeping from Russia."

But like most of his class Geordie wasn't a man for all work and no play. He was a member of the Riveria set based on the South of France where the rich and famous came to relax. The area was traditionally dominated by wealthy Britons but by the mid 1930s it attracted artists, writers and wealthy Americans. It was the sort of destination where the Duke of Westminster paid to furnish the villa of his lover Coco Chanel, who befriended Winston Churchill, a frequent visitor. Her friendship with Winston was claimed to be one of the reasons she wasn't later prosecuted for "collaboration horizontale" with an Abwehr officer during the German occupation of Paris, although Coco's other French contacts probably played the key role.

"As long as you know men are like children, you know everything" Coco apparently remarked. It could have been a female spy's motto.

British visitors to the area crossed the Channel and piled on to the Blue Train's sleeping cars at the Gare Maritime Calais, calling at two stations in Paris before heading south to reach Marseilles the following morning. Some of the more adventurous, like Jack Profumo, flew themselves. Others drove and the train would attract the attention of racing enthusiasts who attempted to outpace the 20 hours it took from Calais to Marseilles.

It was a glamorous time, the Riviera a glamorous place and Geordie took refuge there. His marriage to his first wife Lady Eileen, who was the senior Lady in the Royal Household, was reported to be unhappy. His autobiography *Looking Back* reveals a life in which a considerable part was spent shooting large animals in Africa and smaller birds elsewhere. He was also keen on yachting, taking long cruises and had a house in Montego Bay in Jamaica. Gisela kept another picture of him sitting in a chair near a palm tree which was probably taken there. A note on the back says, "Guess Who?"

His wife Eileen had shot a lion, and drove a van for the *Times* newspaper during the General Strike of 1921, so was a woman of some character if not completely to his taste. Like Jack Profumo, Geordie was a film fan visiting Hollywood and having film stars like Douglas Fairbanks and Mary Pickford to stay with him in the UK. The British Film Institute of which he was the founding Chairman still presents a prize in his name.

He was a source of Royal gossip amongst the people he knew well and would have been far more open with Gisela than he was in the uncontentious *Looking Back*. In this he claims, astonishingly, not to have known anything about Edward's intentions regarding Wallis Simpson or anything about her really.

He was either intensely stupid, or, of course, a liar. His insider position within the Royal Household, not least via his wife who was close to Queen Mary, who loathed Wallis Simpson with a passion, and his connection to Prime Minister Baldwin under whom he'd served as a minister, ensured he knew what was coming. When it did and the Abdication crisis blew up in 1937, he arranged to be on his yacht well out of the way. He was also clearly no stranger to having mistresses of his own. The writer Barbara Cartland maintained he was one of two possible fathers of her daughter, Countess Raine Spencer, Princess Diana's stepmother.

Maxine Elliott, the owner of an art deco villa near Cannes, at one stage described Geordie as:

"At Monte Carlo with a bad throat and more or less surrounded by his little bits of fluff."

It would be rather more accurate to describe Geordie as one of Gisela's little bits of fluff. In Cannes and the surrounding area where style was almost as important as money, she was as successful at the social whirl as she had been in London and Cairo and was in Paris.

And it was in the French capital city while her frequent comings and goings were under surveillance, French Intelligence unknowingly spotted a diplomatically important connection that would provide some of the evidence for Gisela's greatest intelligence coup of all.

9

THE NAMELESS FIANCÉ

GISELA WASN'T THE only German to make Paris a base. There was an influx of Jews who'd fled. Amongst them was a young man called Herschel Grynszpan, living illegally in the city with relatives. His actions triggered an event that would lay bare the terrible final destination of the Jews under the Nazis. That was a year in the future but in 1937 the city authorities in Paris were running an event that illustrated the coming conflict at an altogether more cerebral level.

Gisela visited the Paris Exposition Internationale des Arts et Techniques dans la Vie Moderne, one of an estimated 30 million people at six francs a ticket. She had a personal reason to do so. The Ruhr industrialist and poem sender, Werner Schaurte was there with his company to show off machine screws, nuts and bolts. She told her daughter years later, with only a certain exaggeration, she parachuted off the Eiffel Tower. The Exposition actually had its own 243 foot tall parachute jump tower specially constructed, so she could certainly add physical bravery to her attributes as well as the ever present delight in risk.

Werner also naturally attended the competing exhibition being run by the Nazis in Dusseldorf where he was photographed with his protector Hermann Göring examining one of the exhibits. Göring is looking directly at the camera while Werner explains something.

The eyes of the fleshy Göring clearly tell of the morphine addiction he'd had ever since his treatment for the bullet wound received in the abortive Nazi putsch in 1923. It seems highly unlikely Gisela wouldn't also have taken the opportunity of visiting such a prestigious gathering in her home city.

The Paris event, unsurprisingly, was more celebrated and dwarfed the six million visitors of its Dusseldorf rival. The Eiffel Tower was the visual centre. It had been built for the exhibition's 1889 predecessor. The tower was even scheduled for demolition and replacement with an even bigger structure christened The Lighthouse of the World, but there wasn't enough money for the project.

There were pavilions from many countries. The brutalist German design was by Hitler's pet architect Albert Speer who described it as a "nouveau riche architecture of prestige". A massive tower composed of rectangular columns surmounted by a golden eagle with spread wings whose claws clutched a swastika, provided the entrance to the pavilion. Outside bronze uplighters spread around the base of the tower illuminated the edifice at night. Alongside the entrance were a pair of nude male statues holding hands, apparently meant to symbolise Aryan racial brotherhood. It was the Watchtower on the Rhine from the traditional German song. A bulwark against the communism of the Soviet pavilion opposite.

The Russian structure was in keeping with the grandiose totalitarian theme. It was also massive, although not as tall as the German offering due to some espionage on behalf of Speer who claimed he saw the Soviet plans and made the German pavilion taller.

Onlookers likened the Soviet pavilion to a cathedral although architectural historians have linked it to the Rockefeller Centre in New York, completed four years before, and which had received much publicity in the Soviet Union. Unlike the Germans the Soviets opted for an Art Deco form with the tower at the front like a ship's bow or possibly a charging locomotive. The design suggested forward momentum. On top statues of a man and woman in classic Soviet worker poses.

Further away the box-like British pavilion didn't exhibit the grandiosity of the Germans or the Russians. It was rather like British foreign policy of the time, a design that wasn't going to really impress or upset anyone.

As the workers whose strikes delayed the start of the exposition finally cleared the last remnants the following year, the secret watchers of the French intelligence services, undoubtedly aided by the all-seeing concierge lurking on the ground floor of Gisela's appartment building in the 16th arrondissement, were finalising a detailed, yet still incomplete picture of the life she was leading.

On the 28th of November 1938 a letter from the Paris Prefect of Police enclosed a report on her for the President of the Council and the Minister of Defense. It was copied to the Deuxieme Bureau who liaised with British intelligence. The letter described her as a national security suspect.

The report that resulted from this surveillance didn't spot any obvious nefarious activities, but it did highlight a mystery man.

> *Gisela Klein's fiancé is the American owner of a Packard motorcar with American plates who is staying in Paris. He is currently in Lausanne in Switzerland where he is staying for a fortnight. No identifying information (for this man) has been collected.*
>
> *During her fiancé's absence from Paris, Klein has been receiving phone calls inviting her to dinner and quite frequently the callers come to collect her by car. These invitations are renewed almost every evening and these people sometimes come to visit her at home, all of them are people of a certain social standing. Sometimes a car with Diplomatic Corps identification comes to visit her.*

It's almost possible to see the informant's eyes widening with a significant pause as the details were relayed, but all it amounted to was that Gisela's social life was clearly flourishing amongst the upper echelons of Paris and its embassies. Paris was a city for parties and she was well enough known about town for her close connection to Wolfgang Brandstetter or Carl Hanesse to have been noted by the *Times* man Thomas Cadett. As before in Britain she had plugged herself seamlessly into a well-heeled set with a busy social life. She was also in the epicentre of the fashion world where her looks and love of haute couture commended her to many and did not run contrary to the prevailing culture as they did in Germany.

But while the cafés, restaurants and social events were her playground and gave an appearance of business as usual in the capital, France itself was politically rickety. The government was relying on thin political coalitions and there were, particularly in the 1930s, very sharp divisions between the left and right, exacerbated by the continuing effects of the Great Depression.

As Gisela charmed and glittered through Paris, the country was suffering the after effects of a series of strikes involving two million workers. The French coalition government, with the socialist Leon Blum as Prime Minister, enacted a series of measures to pacify the workforce. These included immediate 12 percent wage increases, general collective bargaining with the unions, a 40-hour week and paid holidays.

It was socialism in action, but the economy did not perform as the Government hoped as a result of its measures. Industrial production did not increase and inflation negated the pay rises and hurt savers. The coalition with Blum at its head collapsed after just over a year in June 1937. His successor was the apparently hawkish Edouard Daladier, who wanted to nationalise the French arms industry to meet the threat from Germany, but who later sided with Chamberlain's appeasement.

It was a political situation of intense interest to Germany whose leaders really needed to know whether the French would go to war and perhaps invade just as they had done in the Rhineland in 1923. A question that was on Hitler's mind as he planned his series of high stakes gambles.

The attitudes of France and Britain were therefore a priority to both military intelligence and the organisation set up by Joachim von Ribbentrop, the Dienstelle Ribbentrop. In February 1938 he would become the Reich minister of Foreign Affairs.

What the surveillance of Gisela didn't reveal at the time was that the American they'd connected to her had the highest level diplomatic and political contacts. He gave her a direct route to information from inside the two main Embassies of the United States of America in Europe. One of them was France, the other Britain. A connection her "military attaché" at the German embassy would be only too happy to exploit it to its full extent.

In Paris the US Ambassadorship was in the hands of the talented but egotistical William C Bullitt. He spoke fluent French and German. He'd been in post since 1936 and he liked the French and his knowledge of the continually shifting alliances and views of the politicians that made up the French government was undoubtedly second to none.

But while the French security services never got round to identifying the young American man in the Packard motorcar, someone else would. Many years later Gisela was driving across the United States in a yellow VW beetle as she took her daughter all the way from California to University in Georgia. During the long journey she revealed his identity. She said she had "dated" the eldest son of a very prominent American family.

At first there was no direct evidence to support this claim but then the discovery of a picture in an old photograph album in the US put Gisela and the owner of the Packard together.

What the French watchers and informants didn't realise was that Gisela's supposed fiancé and the driver of the American car was Joe Kennedy Jr, aged 23, the eldest son of the American ambassador to Great Britain Joseph Patrick Kennedy, the controversial banker, prohibition booze runner, stock market share ramper, Hollywood executive and patriarch of the Kennedy family whose political legacy still endures and fascinates to this day.

Joe Kennedy Jr was working as a political intern in the Paris Embassy for Ambassador Bullitt who he met back in 1934 as he toured the continent and the Soviet Union where Bullitt was then Ambassador. Joe was accompanied in the French capital and all its earthly delights on several occasions by his younger brother Jack, who became US President John F. Kennedy. They both stayed with Bullitt's right-hand man and fixer Carmel Offie at his Paris apartment. Offie was described as close to openly gay, as was permissible in 1930s America. Ambassador Bullitt described him as the power behind the throne and he, like Gisela, was a favourite with the upper class French. Gisela was now the best connected she'd ever been and as a result so was the "military attaché" at the German Embassy.

10

A MAN FOR ALL LIAISONS

IN 1938 JOSEPH Kennedy Jr was the chosen one of his father, not just the favourite, but the Kennedy golden boy with everything ahead of him, and a driving ambition planted and nurtured in him. Unlike the young Jack Profumo it wasn't just a pursuit of excitement and display that drove him. He certainly took his pleasure where he could find it, but in the morning the senses of duty and above all of destiny reasserted themselves. Even though he was only in his early 20s he accepted his future role was to be President of the United States of America.

Joe was a couple of years younger than Gisela and born into a very different world. He was the first of the nine children of Joseph Patrick Kennedy and Rose Fitzgerald, the daughter of an old school Boston Irish politician. Joe Sr had a particular talent alongside his capacity to make money; he had a long-term vision of where he and most importantly his family were going to end up. It took him nearly a decade to get himself into a position where Rose's father accepted him as suitor but after he achieved that he set his eye on higher prizes, immense wealth and political power.

Joe Jr provided the perfect clay for a model son. He was physically robust, tall and strong.

One contemporary described him as:

"...a good-looking clean-cut chap; good head of hair and broad shoulders, athletic, all-American type, with a wonderful smile [...] I think he could meet people and make friends quickly and keep them."

As far as Joe Kennedy Sr was concerned it was his sacred duty to turn Joe Jr into a serious political player. Make him the first Catholic President of the United States, a fate already predicted for the boy at birth by his maternal grandfather, John F "Honey Fitz" Fitzgerald, who served in the House of Representatives and twice as the Mayor of Boston.

Joe Jr's father's plans for his political education were well in train just as Gisela first arrived in the UK in that warm summer of 1933. That was the year that Joe Jr graduated from school in America and his father, after canvassing various opinions, decided to send him to England to study. Not to Oxford or Cambridge, which would have seemed an obvious and traditional choice, but instead to the London School of Economics. Joe Sr apparently believed his son needed to understand the policies of socialism with which he would deal as a politician.

Joe Jr won the prize at school for the student who was the best at both sport and academic work, but he wasn't an intellectual by any means. He was naturally rather inflexible and conservative in his views, an apparently devout Catholic who sinned whenever he could. In many ways he was far more like his father than his younger brother Jack, who struggled with regular bouts of ill health, and was in his older brother's good looking and physically robust shadow.

At Joe Sr's command his eldest son studied with the left-wing political theorist and economist Professor Harold Laski at the LSE. Joe Jr, it seems, understood he wasn't as quick as some of Laski's other young firebrands, but he was determined to learn and calmly put up with any sniping that came his way from his fellow students.

"He has often sat in my study and submitted with that smile that was pure magic to relentless teasing about his determination to be nothing less than President of the United States," Laski said.

Joe Jr spent a year studying and socialising in the UK. He lived in a flat in a block in Earls Court in London which he shared with a friend Aubrey Whitelaw, who later spoke about the film starlets they entertained and Joe's humour and poor attempts at mimicking the English accent. He always smiled when he spoke of his ambition to be President, Whitelaw said, but the smile didn't reach his eyes.

Joe always seemed to prefer the company of actresses and models to the British debutantes on offer and given his propensity to head for the most glamorous woman at any social event, it seems more than possible that he met Gisela for the first time then or at the very least they had acquaintances in common.

His time at the LSE wasn't wasted and Joe Jr certainly took on board some of Laski's teachings as, like many other young people, he zigzagged through ideas and influences seeking to develop a personal path. Material in the Kennedy archive in Boston suggests at one stage members of his family were slightly alarmed by his enthusiastic espousal of leftist sentiments.

In 1934 Joe Jr was touring Italy, Germany and elsewhere at the wheel of a convertible he bought in London. His father sent him £200 for the trip, warning him it was coming out of his million-dollar trust fund, but still cabling American ambassadors in Berlin and Moscow, to tell them the anointed son was on his way. Joe Jr also visited Munich, the spiritual capital of the Nazi movement, where Hitler ranted in the beer cellars and attempted his abortive coup in 1923. Joe Jr kept postcards in his scrapbooks from the Oberammergau Passion Play in Bavaria. which was celebrating its 300th anniversary. Hitler also attended a performance that August.

Gisela left the UK in March and was officially back in Germany at this time, although whether at home is another matter. Joe liked what he saw in Germany as did so many others at the time. In that he may have been influenced by an intelligent young woman from Dusseldorf. He does mention in a letter to his mother Rose meeting a beautiful German woman who spoke four languages and was a granddaughter of the composer Robert Schumann. Although Schumann did have a Dusseldorf connection, unless Gisela's sometimes vivid imagination was in overdrive it doesn't appear to be her. However, as with Jack Profumo, she maintained a relationship with Joe Jr that would last. There is evidence he told her of secret British war plans.

But back in 1934 in assessing Germany in letters home and to friends, Joe echoed his father's noted antisemitism.

"Hitler's dislike of the Jews was well founded," he said.

He drank the Nazi vitriol that Jews dominated the Weimar republic and needed to be driven out. He went further than his father, suggesting it was probably necessary some blood would need to be spilt. Joe Sr, with better political intuition than his son, warned him that Hitler had already gone too far.

Joe Jr was also in favour of eugenics, supporting the Nazi sterilisation of people to prevent "many of the disgusting specimens of men who inhabit the earth".

He doesn't seem to have made the connection to his own intellectually disabled sister Rosemary to whom he showed particular kindness and attention. Rosemary suffered a seizure at the age of seven. She had brain damage and as a result, violent mood swings. Her father later subjected her to brain surgery in an attempt to cure her. The operation went terribly wrong leaving her completely disabled. Joe Sr never went to visit her in the care home where she spent the rest of her life.

Joe Jr arrived back in the UK after graduating from Harvard in

1938 just as his father was settling into his new position in Britain. It was to be a honeymoon period for the US Ambassador to the Court of St James and his family as they were subjected to much self-sought and approving press coverage.

Joe Jr then set out for Paris where he worked as an attaché for two months for the American Ambassador Bullitt, who was yet another friend of Nancy Astor. Both Joe and his younger brother Jack were in Paris on a number of occasions in 1938.

It was during this time the French security service unknowingly picked up on the relationship between Joe Jr and Gisela. Joe Jr's approach to women was informed by his father's example. Joe Sr had a long and very public affair with the actress Gloria Swanson. He was also a serial philanderer with a weakness for blondes, reportedly even showing an interest in his son's girlfriends much to the boy's wry if presumably embarrassed amusement.

Joe Jr's approach was similar, but Gisela was not just going to be a "What happens in Paris stays in Paris" for the 23-year-old Kennedy. After his stint as an attaché at the Paris Embassy he set off on travels across Europe, visiting Warsaw, Leningrad and the Sudetenland in Czechoslovakia, with its majority German speaking population. The Sudetenland was next on the list of Hitler's acquisitions after the unopposed march into Austria earlier in 1938. Joe undoubtedly mirrored his father's view that the integrity of the border of Czechoslovakia wasn't worth a drop of blood to defend.

The relationship with Gisela would endure through this time. The intelligent and resourceful young woman therefore had a conduit through Joe Jr to people whose views were of great interest to Germany. Joe Jr understood and supported his father's position on keeping America out of European arguments and he was privy to the views and gossip of the United States Paris embassy about the vacillating state of French politics. Information she gained from him went into the Paris German Embassy information gathering network and the Abwehr either via Wolfgang Brandstetter or Carl Hannesse.

Her espionage activities don't necessarily mean that she wasn't sincere in her attachment to Joe Jr, although according to her family she didn't keep a photograph of him as she did of others like Jack and the Duke of Sutherland, which may be significant. There was in any case the unavoidable if heavy price that had to be paid to maintain herself as an independent young woman outside Germany.

However, what she learned from Joe Jr would dovetail neatly with the continuing attempts by the British Prime Minister Neville Chamberlain and others to appease Hitler.

The complex brew of German nationalism, mixed signals, intelligence and weakness by the big European powers over Hitler's demand to be given the Sudetenland with its German speaking population was a death sentence for Czechoslovakia. The Munich agreement signed by Britain's Prime Minister Neville Chamberlain alongside France and Italy in September 1938 gave Hitler the green light to take what he wanted.

Hitler was advancing his plans even while Neville Chamberlain was filmed at Heston airport by the cinema newsreels to cheers, waving his document signed by Herr Hitler, that wasn't worth the paper it was written on, and suggesting the agreement was "to assure the peace of Europe." The German annexation of the Sudetenland was followed by the effective takeover of the whole of Czechoslovakia early in 1939.

Evidence Gisela was with Joe Kennedy for at least some if not all of his 1938 continental tour, lay hidden in the records in the John Fitzgerald Kennedy Presidential Archive and Museum at Columbia Point in Boston, Massachusetts.

The archive contains a photograph album and scrap book belonging to Joe Jr from the 1930s. It's a poignant record of the life of the charismatic and privileged young man with a bright future. Although most of the photographs are not particularly well framed and amateurish, the whole thing, with its press cuttings, invitations, menus of important dinners, telegrams and black and white pictures, is brushed with the Kennedy mystique, placing it in that compelling world where none of the people contained in its pages knew then what we know now.

Three pictures on one page of the album are of special interest. They are captioned in pencil:

"During German occupation of Czechoslovakia 1938."

This caption seems to date these pictures to the first ten days of October. One photograph shows seven men, who could be Sudeten German supporters of the takeover, at least one has an indistinct armband of some kind, hanging around outside a large Czechoslovak municipal building.

The other photograph shows what must be Joe Jr's large touring car stopped on an unidentified road lined with telegraph poles stretching away into the distance. It seems to be on the Czechoslovakian border. It looks as though the party's papers are being examined by a German army officer who is peering down at a sheaf of documents in his hands. The driver in a chauffeur's peaked cap and dark uniform is standing by the door of the car while a trio of not terribly interested German soldiers look on. They are armed with rifles, typical coal scuttle helmets and jack boots, a uniform that in under a year would become a much more recognisable sight elsewhere. Joe was witnessing history, and he would develop a taste for it, later travelling to the Spanish civil war to observe events.

The most important picture sits above these photographs on the same page of the album, presumably predating the ones in Sudetenland. It seems to contain evidence of the Gisela connection. The photograph is captioned Copenhagen 1938. It is not taken by Joe himself, but contains him and a group of four others, two men and two women. They are posing outside the entrance to a theatre. The frames for posters that flank them, the lamps and the shape of the door behind them identify it as the front entrance to the Royal Danish Theatre in Copenhagen, which is famous for its ornate and gilded baroque interior.

The party are all smiling at the camera lens. With her arm intertwined through Joe's is a blonde woman wearing a dark dress with a plunging cowled top and either a costume jewellery necklace filling the neckline, or perhaps a colourful silk blouse. Joe is wearing a dark double-breasted suit, white shirt and dark knotted tie with a white handkerchief showing in his breast pocket.

The woman looks like Gisela, but her daughter did not think it was her mother because the woman's hair in the photograph was too blonde and she was not tall enough.

But the woman has dropped a shoulder and bent her legs so that she would appear to be smaller than her male companion. Joe Jr was 6ft tall; Gisela was 5ft 10ins and the woman in the photograph is wearing low heels. The bend at the knees appeared to be a tall model's familiar trick. A trawl through other pictures of Gisela shows a very similar pose, this time alongside Jack Profumo at Avon Dasset when he was flanked by Gisela on one side and on the other by the petite Romanov Princess, Catherine.

The Kennedy image was compared with some of Gisela's own collection of photographs by a commercial firm that employs "super recognisers". These are people used by the police and security agencies to help identify people on CCTV and in still photographs because of their particularly enhanced powers of face recognition. They are still, in certain conditions, more effective than Artificial Intelligence computer recognition programmes.

The company Super Recognisers International was created by former Detective Chief Inspector Mike Neville. He formed the world's first unit of this sort at the headquarters of the Metropolitan Police, New Scotland Yard. He emailed the result:

"The super recogniser states that she believes that they are the same person, so a Yes."

So, had Gisela dyed her naturally blonde hair an even lighter shade for some reason? It's not impossible. There are modelling photographs of her where her hair is clearly dyed, but what is also possible is that the photograph was slightly overexposed, bleaching out both Gisela's hair and that of the blonde woman in a tight-fitting dark dress, heavily embroidered in a contrasting colour, possibly gold, who was on the other end of the group. An expert photographer of models also suggested that very shiny hair can reflect bright light back from other sources. In this case from the two large lamps on either side of the group or perhaps from a photographer's flash gun.

The blonde woman on the other end of the party from Gisela is the former Miss Denmark, actress and journalist Inga Arvad and the man next to her with whom she has linked arms, her second husband, the film director Paul Fejos who she married in 1936. Inga was also believed to be a German spy. She used her beauty and charm to further her career in journalism by interviewing all the leading Nazis including Hitler. He was so taken with her he gave her a signed photograph and apparently invited her to his box for the 1936 Berlin Olympics.

In the 1940s after separating from Fejos and moving to the United States with her mother, she was suspected of espionage by the FBI, who watched her and bugged her telephone calls. She was linked to the Swedish industrialist and millionaire Axel Wenner Gren, himself a suspected German spy runner.

Wenner Gren who made part of his massive fortune from Electrolux domestic vacuum cleaners, was later, during the war, associated with the Duke of Windsor then in exile as Governor of the Bahamas. Wenner Gren's activities led both the Americans and the British to place him on an economic blacklist.

The FBI intercepts of Inga Arvad's phone calls detailed part of her affair with a young United States Naval Ensign in the early 1940s. The man was Joe Jr's younger brother Jack Kennedy who fell for Inga rather spectacularly. His biographers have suggested that it was the one time in his life that he didn't really control his relationship with a woman. His letters to her show a candour and vulnerability his normally armour-plated persona did not usually allow, even with close confidants.

It has been claimed that Inga met Jack after working with his sister Kathleen "Kick" Kennedy on the *Washington Times Herald*, but the photograph of her with Joe Jr shows she was already in the Kennedys' orbit in 1938. The affair with Jack and the suspicions about her role led to him being moved out of his position with US Naval Intelligence.

The FBI was never able to prove Inga was anything more than the "adventuress" she called herself. A word also used about Gisela. However, her connection with Gisela and the Kennedys and the highest echelons of the Third Reich only adds further proof, of Fraulein Klein's networking abilities and well-informed contacts.

****

Paris and the Copenhagen trip were not the only times Gisela was with Joe. On that 2,500-mile journey in the US to Georgia in the 1960s she also told her daughter she'd sailed with the Kennedys and met the youngest son, Teddy when he was just a little boy.

While Joe Sr was Ambassador to Great Britain in the late 1930s the Kennedys took holidays near Cannes. In August of 1938 he rented a villa for them a 15-minute drive from the town.

The word villa doesn't really do the Domaine de Beaumont, as it was called, justice. It had 15 bedrooms, a swimming pool and tennis courts and its own wine cellar. In 2023 it was on the market boasting of its Kennedy heritage for more than $33 million.

Joe Sr assembled the whole tribe including all the children: 23-year-old Joe Jr; Jack who was then aged 21; Rosemary, 19; Kathleen, 18; Eunice, 17; Pat, 14; Bobby, 12; Jean, 10 and Teddy who was the youngest at six.

The Riviera at this time seems the most likely location for Gisela to have sailed with the Kennedy clan although there would be other opportunities the following year. Both Joe Jr and Jack were committed sailors and never missed an opportunity.

During this holiday Joe Sr proved himself to be especially enamoured of one particular glamorous blonde German woman who spoke good English with a pronounced and attractive accent.

Not far from the Villa Domaine de Beaumont was the luxurious Hotel Du Cap. It was a favourite with the Duke of Windsor and Wallis Simpson and boasted guests ranging from Noel Coward and Ernest Hemingway to Picasso and Matisse. A description of it forms the first lines of F Scott Fitzgerald's last complete book, *Tender is the Night.*

"Deferential palms cool its flushed façade and before it stretches a short dazzling beach. Lately it has become a summer resort of notable and fashionable people."

The actress Marlene Dietrich was staying at the hotel along with her husband and his mistress. She also had her daughter in tow and her current lover Erich Maria Remarque, author of *All Quiet on the Western Front.* His writing were declared "unpatriotic" by Goebbels in 1933 and his most famous work ended up being burnt in public by the Nazis. His German citizenship would be revoked in 1939. Dietrich has been quoted as saying:

"What a man notices first about a woman is whether she notices him".

Dietrich noticed Joe Kennedy Sr and he her. He was a regular visitor to her chic cabin on the hotel beach while Remarque worked on his latest book.

It seems that both father and sons had very similar tastes in women. Both Marlene and Gisela were good looking, strong willed and knew what they wanted.

But Gisela's stay in France was coming to a close for the time being. By the end of September 1938 she'd quit Paris and headed for Rome where she stayed for two months. Jack Profumo and his sister Maina were also, according to one newspaper report, touring Mussolini's Italy in their light aircraft at this time.

Her departure from Paris for Italy came quite suddenly and the watchers for the French security services recorded it. The explanation they received pointed in one direction. That she was fearful about the imminent possibility of war between France and Germany following the Sudeten crisis and the steadily increasing tensions in Europe.

A report titled Secret and dated the 25th of November 1938 from the Chief of Police in Paris was sent to the President of the Council, the Minister of National Defence and the Headquarters of the Deuxieme Bureaux. It stated:

"On leaving Number 19 Rue Copernic she said she was going because of her fear of hostilities and the concentration camps".

However, there was conflicting evidence. Gisela, according to the French, originally gave notice on her apartment at 19 Rue Copernic because she was due to get married and alternatively, she also implied she would return to Paris after a visit to America.

She would later tell French Intelligence interrogators yet another story, that she'd actually left because she'd lost the papers that allowed her to stay in France. Which perhaps suggests she didn't possess them in the first place or that she was under pressure from the German authorities over her documentation. The difficulties around renewing her passport mentioned in her British file.

The reference to the concentration camps also takes us back to Gisela's heritage and the leverage that could be applied to her to keep her supplying information. Even if she didn't carry any significant Jewish ancestry, her potentially Jewish surname would have been enough to cause her problems with the Nazis. Working as an agent for the Abwehr would not provide real protection. The organisation was regarded as suspect by the Nazis and there were several attempts to take it over completely. These would only succeed after the Abwehr was thoroughly implicated in the attempt to blow up Hitler in 1944.

And there are other question raised by Gisela's departure for Rome and her conflicting explanations. French intelligence had already assumed Joe Kennedy was her fiancé. Was he the man Gisela was giving up her apartment to marry?

Perhaps she hoped so. He was good looking and there was his ambition for the future his father had mapped out for him. An attractive proposition for a beautiful young woman making her way in the world. However her religion as a professed protestant Lutheran would have counted against her with the staunchly Roman Catholic Kennedys. It led to intense trouble for Joe Jr's younger sister Kathleen when she decided to marry the British protestant aristocrat Billy Cavendish. Her father sent her off to the United States to try to break them up. He was unsuccessful and she married with the support of her eldest brother Joe.

Another female friend of Joe Jnr, the former Ziegfeld Follies dancer and foreign correspondent Lorelle Hearst was clear about the difference in Joe's mind between lovers and the woman he would marry:

"He was terribly sweet and immediately made you feel very close to him and that you'd known him forever. He had tremendous physical attraction and also there was a tough side to him. I don't know what would bring it out in him, but sometimes he could be cruel. He preferred girls who were a little older than himself because they had a little more sense. He never would have married anyone who wasn't socially prominent, mostly virginal and Catholic I think."

In any case Gisela was an intelligent worldly woman, and she would have known what she had in Joe Jr. The photographs he kept show several very good-looking women who may have had hopes of him, not least the American ice skater Pat Wilson with whom he was linked romantically by the newspapers during this time.

As a result, it may have just been easier for Gisela to pass the handsome American off as her fiancé with the concierge and neighbours. The French were far more liberal in matters of love. This was a culture that accepted the principle called Cing a Sept, indicating the late afternoon early evening time a man would visit his mistress, but Gisela was living in a fashionable neighbourhood where things like that would have to be handled with a certain discretion.

There is potentially another explanation for her leaving Paris. That she'd spotted someone watching her or been tipped off that she was of interest to the French security service. Perhaps the concierge had let something slip.

Whatever the reason, Gisela was on the move yet again and her horizons were broader than ever before.

11

THE LAST YEAR

THE LINER AQUITANIA wasn't the fastest of the Cunard transatlantic fleet in December 1938, but she was the most luxurious and stylishly fitted out. The first-class lounge had a working marble fireplace at one end, there were fluted columns with scrolled capitals, heavily upholstered furniture, semi-circular fan lights with intricate metalwork and painted ceilings. The overall design and craftsmanship surrounding the passengers led to the vessel's nickname: "The ship beautiful."

Early that month the Aquitania carried the former British Foreign Secretary Antony Eden on a goodwill visit to the United States. Eden split with Neville Chamberlain over the Prime Minister's weak foreign policy, and he claimed the visit was of no "political significance" but to encourage friendship with the United States, while cinema newsreel Gaumont British News described him a Britain's "unofficial envoy".

He met President Roosevelt who spent some time pointing out Britain and France's inferiority in airpower compared to Germany. He told Eden that America was rearming.

Eden's visit was promoted by Joe Kennedy Sr, who seems to have ignored that Eden was more closely aligned to Winston Churchill's anti-appeasers than to Joe's political friend and confidant Neville Chamberlain.

The British politician wasn't the only person to head to the United States that month at the call of a Kennedy. It's likely that another passenger on board the Aquitania later in December 1938 was also travelling on a similar basis. Whether she received a case of champagne from Joe Jr like the one Joe Sr put on board for Eden we don't know.

Gisela had, according to the Paris police report on her, gone back briefly to Germany after her time in Italy before setting out for a new venture. She would have enjoyed the social life and the distractions of the ship's entertainments: a cinema; swimming pool and gymnasium as she spent a week on board heading for a new country.

She was leaving behind a continent wracked with violence. In Paris that November a German diplomat died of gunshot wounds, killed by the young Jewish refugee Herschel Grynszpan, who was furious because the Germans marooned his parents and thousands of other Jews on the border with Poland. The ever-opportunistic Nazis channelled this attack into the hysterical and vicious outburst of violence against Germany's Jewish population. The pogrom Kristallnacht, the night of broken glass.

In Britain Lord "Rabbits" Mount Temple resigned as Chairman of the Anglo-German Fellowship in protest over Kristallnacht but stayed as a member. The Fellowship lost nearly half of its members because of the appalling scenes in Germany and Austria.

America must have seemed an obvious choice for Gisela personally, as well as to her contacts with German military intelligence. Britain had banned her from entering. The French surveillance meant she was under suspicion there. She was also, because of the difficulty in renewing her documents in France, apparently under pressure from the Nazi authorities which is presumably why she chose to go to Italy and Rome to get a renewed German passport instead of doing so in Paris.

The day before Christmas Eve 1938, New York looked the way Hollywood has always believed it should. Snow was falling lightly and lying thinly on the ground, steam was rising from manhole covers and vents in the freezing air. People were hurrying about on their errands before the holiday.

Men were buying last minute presents for their children at Schwarz's toy store on 5th Avenue, the home of American Santa Claus. The Lord and Taylor Department Store further along 5th Avenue had a window display with a row of swinging golden bells synchronised to a recording of sleigh bells.

In Lower Manhattan at one of the piers on the dark freezing viscous water of the Hudson River the passengers were well wrapped up as they disembarked from the Aquitania. As she presented her documents in the cold air of the arrival hall on the pier, Gisela's papers showed her as being 25 years of age with no profession and she'd begun her journey across the Atlantic at the French Port of Cherbourg.

While many of her fellow passengers queuing up to face US immigration officers described themselves as of German origin and Jewish or Hebrew, Gisela answered German to both questions. The Americans were imposing strict quotas on the German Jews desperate to leave their persecution behind. Gisela's passport visa showed she was just planning to visit the United States. But given that she had no officially recorded profession, seemingly not to work.

She was following in the footsteps of Wolfgang Krause Brandstetter who was already in the United States.

Not quite three months before Gisela's arrival in New York, the Hamburg America line freighter, the SS Vancouver docked in Los Angeles. It also carried passengers and one of them was a 6ft 2in tall German man with dark hair and blue eyes, using his birth name, Wolfgang Krause with a passport in that name issued in Leipzig that August.

Wolfgang was being accompanied by the man who married his mother and adopted him, the successful Leipzig printer Justus Brandstetter. The pair officially came from the Panamanian west coast port city of Cristobal, after passage through the Panama Canal. Their destination was Pasadena in California.

Wolfgang later admitted to Allied intelligence interrogators he'd been in Brazil, Argentina and Chile before arriving in California. All countries with expatriate German populations and places where German intelligence was developing operations for espionage on the United States. Some of these intelligence units would continue their activities until the end of the Second World War.

Wolfgang was always looking for business opportunities and the cover for the trip would have been publishing. Wolfgang though always liked to multi-task, and his espionage mission was to obtain information about aircraft technology. A fake ID he was carrying on his capture in Paris five years later gave Pasadena in California as his supposed birthplace. Pasadena was a convenient car ride away from plants and manufacturing sites belonging to both the Douglas Aircraft corporation and Lockheed. He later pretended he'd worked for Lockheed in California.

The German intelligence effort in the United States was heavily focused on anything to do with air warfare. Germany's spying was relatively successful and amongst other American innovations it stole details of the accurate Norden bomb sight. This device was meant to be a highly guarded secret. Ironically the Americans refused to give the Norden bombsight to the British because of the Neutrality Acts, designed to keep the United States out of any European war. In the meantime, the Germans produced a similar bomb aiming device with the help of their espionage.

United States immigration officials reduced Wolfgang and Justus's stay in the country to 30 days. They'd wanted 60 and it's not clear why they weren't given it. Their visit didn't pass without incident. The ship that brought the two men to Los Angeles became the target of hostile action while still in American waters. The SS Vancouver was trying to leave San Francisco Bay after loading cargo and more passengers when there was an explosion. The captain immediately steered for shallow water. His desperate act to save the ship was successful because the boat settled by the stern but did not sink. The ship's departure had been delayed by a snagged anchor. If it had been on schedule, it would have gone down in deep water.

Initially the captain denied anybody was hurt but it led to headlines in the Oakland Tribune:

"Nazi Ship Explodes in Estuary. Many Endangered. Sabotage Suspected".

A 25ft hole was blown in the side of the ship near the engine room. An investigation recovered the shattered remains of an explosive device attached to the ship's metal hull with magnets. Four crew members were injured. Nazi officials blamed communists for the attack. At one stage a Nazi-hating dock stevedore was held by police but later released. The investigation into the sabotage was finally dropped after the United States entered the war.

Meanwhile in late December 1938 as Gisela arrived in New York, Wolfgang was probably there to greet her. He later said he left the US from New York that same month. He may have stayed even later. He clearly hadn't abided by the restriction on his visit imposed on his October arrival. Whether Gisela and Wolfgang met or passed as ships in the night isn't clear, but it's a fair bet they met. His name or any of the several aliases he was known to have used don't appear in the departure lists, but once again the pair were in the same city in the same country at the same time.

Joe Kennedy Jr had also been in New York for a couple of weeks.

He accompanied his father across the Atlantic in the second week of December on the liner Queen Mary from Southampton.

Joe Sr returned to try to patch up his rocky relationship with President Roosevelt who needed Kennedy, and the Catholic vote he represented, for the 1940 Presidential election but didn't particularly like or certainly trust his isolationist British Ambassador. After a trip to Washington DC, where Joe Sr apparently did little to mend fences with the administration, father, and eldest son along with Jack, took off for the Kennedy House in Palm Beach, Florida for Christmas.

That December the temperature in Florida didn't get anywhere near the cold of New York maintaining a relatively balmy 7C. The Kennedy's "Mediterranean revival" villa was right on the sea at Palm Beach with steps from the garden down to the shore, although the water lapped against the garden wall at high tide. The house was surrounded by palm trees and there was a swimming pool. Inside the low building there were exposed beams in the sunny and light main rooms with their tiled floors. During Jack Kennedy's Presidency the place became known as the "Winter White House" but in the later 1930s Kennedy "fun house" would possibly seem more appropriate.

In her book about Joe Kennedy Sr, The Ambassador, author Susan Ronald reports the older Kennedy men spent that Christmas of 1938 without the female members of their family or the younger sons. The other children were spending Christmas with Rose Kennedy in Switzerland. Joe Sr took the opportunity of surrounding himself with his cronies and playing golf, while Joe Jr and Jack had "friends" to stay. Gisela certainly counted as a friend – after all she knew Joe very well and indeed both brothers from their time in Paris.

Gisela never really had the ability to be anonymous; she hid very effectively in plain sight. As with many women, she could also clearly switch off the part of herself that encouraged the attentions of men, but she went especially high profile in New York. She appeared in a full-page advertisement in the prestigious magazine, *The New Yorker*. She was modelling for the famous Bergdorf Goodman Department store on 5th Avenue.

Early the previous year Bergdorf Goodman created a surrealist fashion window display. It was composed of three faceless artificial mannequins wearing dresses. One was apparently kneeling; one was standing and the third was floating. The display also incorporated the internal metal frame for the strings of a grand piano. In another version one of the mannequins is holding a fencing rapier and the other two mannequins are floating and have their backs to the public viewing through the window, while the piano frame is propped up beneath them. The effect is mildly sinister.

Gisela's later photograph for the store also has a surrealist element. She is seated on an upholstered stool which resembles a distorted and disturbing version of a bird with a pheasant's head. She is wearing a dark dress with a shallow V neck, with extensive Venise lace trim and short puffed sleeves of the style made famous in the original Disney Snow White. There is a triple twisted rope of pearls around her neck and a cuff of eight strands of pearls on her right arm and another smaller bracelet or cuff on her left wrist. She is looking slightly to one side and is holding a cigarette. She is heavily made up and her nails are painted. The caption running underneath which is partially lost by damage states:

"Venise lace makes a beauty frame".

It's a late 1930s sophisticated woman about town look – one officially despised by the Nazis.

The Bergdorf Goodman advert in *the New Yorker* appeared sometime around the second week in May 1939 because on the back of the page there is a calendar for "events worthwhile" happening between the 11th of May and the 20th. *The New Yorker* was roughly fortnightly. Possible entertainments included "Stars in Your Eyes" with Ethel Merman and Jimmy Durante at the Majestic on West 44th and dancing to Happy Felton's orchestra at the Biltmore Hotel on Madison.

Bergdorf Goodman was famous for dressing the beautiful, fashionable, and rich including Joe Jr's mother Rose Kennedy. The store's Spider Dress of that year, a slinky number in black, complete with its own web cape would be photographed by German-American Horst P Horst, who brought the Avant Garde and an architectural approach to fashion photography. The photograph of this dress appeared in Paris *Vogue* in 1939 just before he fled to the United States from the French capital.

Gisela told French intelligence, during her later interrogation, she'd stayed in the United States for about seven months and as all the Kennedys left in February, she clearly found plenty to occupy herself.

****

New York was home to the enormous World Trade Fair from April, with art deco pavilions, funfair rides and a major fashion exhibition including a competition to win dresses worn by models. Germany, however, did not attend. The Bergdorf Goodman advert shows she was, in her usual style, well connected to the world of fashion on east coast America. She would, in a later and age-reducing resume she kept, only mention the prestigious store.

Although she wouldn't mention Bergdorf Goodman at all to the later interrogators of French intelligence but say she'd worked for some fashion magazines, without naming them. As always when questioned about her life by people with a real interest in her intelligence activities she tended towards the non-specific, a sometimes-inconsistent vagueness also noted by the later interrogators of Wolfgang Brandstetter.

In fact, she'd clearly had some designs on a Hollywood career as she had her photograph taken by the John Robert Powers Agency in New York which specialised in promoting models into the film world. It's likely Joe Kennedy Sr via his son helped with these contacts. He founded RKO pictures in 1928 and made a fortune from the silver screen.

One photograph for the agency shows her spotlit against a wall alongside a large candelabra on a column. She's wearing a high-necked dress, possibly in jersey and a long draped soft jacket. It looks like a film set. There's also one other picture she kept where she is clearly channelling Marlene Dietrich. It's a harder look than she usually portrayed, and her figure is clothed in a tight shiny satin or leather dress with straps, a low back and a sculpted bodice. Her daughter's later clear-eyed verdict was that Gisela couldn't act at all so the Hollywood foray seems to have come to nothing. However, in real life, like all big film stars, she was only ever portraying a thinly disguised version of herself, and with that she'd already created a substantial fan base and the skill only to reveal what she wished.

She left the United States in July 1939. Three months later the Abwehr sent another photographer's model and spy to New York, Lily Stein. Stein was Jewish and from Vienna. She probably had, because of her background, less choice than Gisela about the nature of her work. She was friends with a German woman who was living in the US with the brother of senior Abwehr officer Nikolaus Ritter.

Stein was, from contemporary pictures, dark haired with a strong face, although not in Gisela's league as a fashion model. Stein arrived via Sweden in October and became part of the biggest Nazi spy network the Americans ever discovered. She was later damned, typically for a woman at the time, and ideally for newspaper headlines, as a "nymphomaniac" who slept with men for secrets. In fact, she seems to have had a coordinating role in the movement of intelligence from the US for transmission to Germany.

The espionage ring with which Lily Stein was connected was named by the Americans after its leading member, Fritz Duquesne, an Abwehr colonel. He led one of those bizarre lives that reads like fiction. He claimed to have killed Lord Kitchener, famous for the First World War British recruitment poster featuring him with the caption "Your Country Needs You". In 1916 the battleship with the British Secretary of State for War on board was sunk. Duquesne maintained, probably falsely, he directed a German submarine to do the job. Duquesne coincidentally also worked on publicity for one of Joe Kennedy Sr's Hollywood operations, FBO Pictures which he would merge to form RKO.

Gisela later maintained she did have permission to work and stay in the US, where she said she'd been invited by an American friend, noted by French intelligence as a Mrs Kay Spaulding-Kirkbride, who has proved elusive in the records. She may have been Catherine Kay Spaulding-Kerr, who married Clark Kerr in 1934, a Californian academic. She later helped to create the first coastal protection agency on the US west coast. So, it's possible Gisela also travelled from New York to California during her 1939 visit in pursuit of her Hollywood dream. However, if she did have permission to work, it would have been something of a first for her. In both her intelligence work and her modelling, she was generally guided by the 11th commandment: Thou shalt not get caught.

In the box in California, there is also a photograph she received in 1939 which has something rather odd about it. It seems to contain a potentially unexplained number.

The photograph was sent to her from someone calling himself Leo, and it's a studio portrait of him. The self-deprecating or jokey message in German suggests the photograph is a mechanical reproduction that hasn't done its job very well. Having highlighted the fact the picture is a copy, on the front underneath Leo's picture written on the negative of the print there are a series of what could be Roman numerals, presumably a reproduction number.

The numerals cannot be Roman, as a zero is used and the Romans didn't have a figure for zero. If on the other hand the numerals and the zeros are expressed in binary it is possible to come up with the base 10 number 279332. Was it for use with a poem code or something completely innocent?

Photographic archivists in the UK, including at the National Archives at Kew, who have seen the picture and the numerals beneath it are unsure as to whether this is just a photographic copy numbering system or something different altogether. There is no studio stamp or marking on the back of the photograph which is unusual for a formal portrait like this. Attempts to identify Leo – Gisela kept two pictures of him – have so far proved fruitless.

There is another detail about Gisela from this time that also remains in doubt. British intelligence maintained she first met a handsome man, Edward Winegard, who she would later marry, in New York in 1939. Gisela's family don't believe they met at that time and accept Ed and Gisela later maintained this fiction too to disguise the strange, and for Gisela dangerous, circumstances in which they did first meet.

By apparent chance someone else that Gisela knew arrived in New York shortly before her departure. Werner Teddy Schaurte. He arrived on the 22nd of July 1939. He was no stranger to the country. He was educated at the Massachusetts Institute of Technology and made regular visits in February 1934, March 1936 and April 1938. America was undoubtedly a land of opportunity for someone so interested in engineering with a specialisation in aviation technology and with the ear of the man in charge of the Luftwaffe.

On the passenger roster of the SS Europa which set out from

Southampton, he described himself as a manufacturer and said he spoke English and German.

There was just enough time for there to have been a brief crossover between Gisela and Werner before she headed for her favourite place in the world.

****

In August 1939 the rich and famous were gathering like clamorous seagulls on the French Mediterranean coast for their annual enjoyment of the social swirl and the hot sun. Gisela was back on the Cote d'Azure as well. The Kennedy tribe were there in force. This time at the Villa de Ranguin with views out to sea over the Baie de Cannes.

Like the Villa Domaine De Beaumont from the year before, Ranguin was less a villa and more a Chateau. It had been extensively remodelled by Sir Edwin Lutyens who was regarded at the time of the refurbishment as the leading British architect. Lutyens designed country houses and public buildings, including those of New Delhi for the British Raj.

The Kennedy holiday home had a double height entrance hall with chequered black and white marble flooring laid on the diagonal and vaulted ceilings. There was ornate plasterwork and the main rooms had marble fireplaces. The house came with its own panelled library and 19 bedrooms, allowing the family to spread out. The gardens were originally designed by horticulturalist and gardener Gertrude Jekyll. The Villa Ranguin later ended up as the Regional Headquarters of the Gestapo.

According to Laurence Leamer's book "The Kennedy Men", on this holiday the Kennedy matriarch Rose would take the children swimming at the Hotel du Cap Roc. He recounts an episode where Joe Jr and Jack spent a while diving from a very high rock before then persuading the seven-year-old Teddy to do the same. The youngest Kennedy said:

"I could barely swim at that point. I would jump in the water and grab hold of them. I did this several times. I think I was scared".

While the Kennedy boys were competitively proving their manhood, Joe Sr was demonstrating his by resuming the romance with Marlene Dietrich, who was once again staying at the Hotel. She somewhat spoiled things for him by going off with a different lover altogether, a woman called Jo, which may have rubbed salt into any emotional wounds he might have felt, although the odds on that are not high. He was reportedly able to console himself, in his rather transactional way, with a young French woman who carried his golf clubs.

As well as renewing her friendship with Joe Jr and meeting the family and sailing with the Kennedy boys, Gisela caught up once again with Jack Profumo who was visiting Cannes as part of another air adventure with his sister Maina. They left Britain in their light aircraft in mid-August and were planning to stay in Cannes until September according to one of the regular local newspaper gossip column entries charting their activities. There is an undated photograph kept by Gisela, possibly from this time, taken near an aircraft hanger which shows Gisela next to Geordie Sutherland and alongside him Jack Profumo in a group of others. She is wearing an outfit complete with what looks like real leopard or ocelot skin trimmings to the shoulders and cuffs, possibly the result of one Geordie's big game hunting forays.

The Riviera that year was even more glamorous than usual, a cruise liner chartered by the Hollywood Studio Metro Goldwyn Meyer anchored in Cannes containing a constellation of 1930s film stars including Tyrone Power, Gary Cooper, Douglas Fairbanks and Norma Shearer.

They were there to walk the red carpet at the first ever Cannes film festival, created in response to the previous year's Venice Biennale event which ended in a furore. The result of the Biennale was a deliberate fix by Germany and Italy. Hitler's favourite cinematographer Leni Riefenstahl won joint first prize, the Mussolini Cup, for her stylised documentary about the 1936 Olympics. The other joint winner was, "Luciano Serra, Pilot", a film that involved Mussolini's son and was set against a backdrop of the controversial Italian invasion of Abyssinia.

In Cannes everyone was looking forward to the receptions and parties, including a sparkling star-studded event at the Hotel Du Cap. A cardboard replica of Notre Dame Cathedral was erected on the beach in the town to mark the showing of The Hunchback of Notre Dame starring Charles Laughton and Maureen O'Hara.

It was the only film to get a screening, other entrants like the Wizard of Oz were not seen at all as the continent hurtled towards war. The announcement of a peace pact between Russia and Germany in late August cast a long shadow over the sunny playground and that was swiftly followed by Hitler's invasion of Poland on the 1st of September. According to the official Cannes festival history, this calamitous event was marked by a suitably filmic metaphor, a stupendous storm in the area which can't have done the cardboard Notre Dame Cathedral any favours.

America's Ambassador to Britain had already returned to the UK on the announcement of the Russia Germany peace deal, which secretly allowed Stalin to take a chunk out of Poland for the Soviet Union while Hitler got the rest. Joe Kennedy's personal closeness to Neville Chamberlain saw him meeting the Prime Minister and reading through the speech Chamberlain was planning to deliver to Parliament on the 3rd of September, two days after the Germans marched into Poland.

Ever alert to a photo opportunity, the Kennedy children appeared in the newspapers walking into the House of Commons to hear the speech from the visitors' gallery, Joe Jr in a serious, dark, striped, double-breasted suit and diagonally striped tie and Jack in a slightly more louche lighter grey, double breasted suit with diamond pattern tie. They were flanking their sister Kathleen. She was looking suitably sombre in a dark high-necked dress with white piping around the neck and short sleeves, dark heels, white gloves, and fedora style hat with a light band around it.

Gisela told French intelligence she was surprised by the outbreak of war while she was still on the Riviera. The fact she used the word surprised is surprising in itself.

Her contacts with the Kennedys, Geordie Sutherland and Jack Profumo must have provided enough political background to see the way things were heading and she was an intelligent woman. Only the year before she claimed she was leaving Paris because of the danger of hostilities and ending up in a concentration camp. However, with the interrogators of French intelligence she was undoubtedly happier playing her role as an innocent and beautiful socialite. It was a role that would serve her so very well, even in the face of incontrovertible evidence.

She was also in exalted company among those who didn't really expect Britain and France to declare war. The Kennedys, both Joes, father and son, thought and hoped the British would funk it, and they weren't alone.

When the British declaration of war over Poland was delivered to Hitler by his translator Paul Schmidt, the Fuhrer apparently sat still and unmoving before uttering the words "Was nun?" (What now?). This was coupled with a look at Joachim Von Ribbentrop, as if to suggest that Ribbentrop had misled him as to the British reaction. Hitler successfully rolled the dice with the occupation of the Rhineland, the annexation of Austria and the march into the Sudetenland followed by the subjugation of the whole of Czechoslovakia. Like most gamblers he didn't quit while he was ahead, although at the time the strenuous efforts to appease him seemed the final proof that Britain and its Empire was decadent and finished. Couple this with the various intelligence streams including Gisela's about the United States' and the Kennedys' attitude, and it was easy to see how Ribbentrop and Hitler could have felt secure about crossing the Polish border on the 1st of September.

Neville Chamberlain had weakly accepted Hitler's protestations during their talks that he respected him. It was, in the terrible clarity of hindsight, the very least of his miscalculations. Privately Hitler called him an "arschloch" (arsehole).

Gisela told French intelligence interrogators that on the outbreak of war she left the Riviera and went to Italy as she had done in September 1938. She didn't specify where, Jack had family connections and she knew the Hanbury family with their estate at La Mortola and Princess Catherine Ivanova, with whom she'd been photographed with Jack Profumo. Catherine was married to an Italian diplomat. Wherever she went, Italy seems to have provided temporary sanctuary before she returned to the one place that she'd spent the best part of the last six years seemingly trying to avoid for any length of time, Germany. Her return to her homeland attracted the unwelcome interest of the Nazi secret police, the Gestapo.

12

JOE SAVED MY LIFE

ON A SPRING day a distinctive vehicle drew up outside Gisela Klein's family home on Goltsteinstrasse in Dusseldorf. Nicknamed the people's car or Volkswagen, it was designed by the famous e ngineer Ferdinand Porsche at Hitler's behest and post war would become the VW Beetle. Werner Schaurte's company made parts for the vehicle. A scheme was originally set up so ordinary German citizens could buy this, their first car, by saving special stamps in a booklet. At the outbreak of war no one had actually managed to accumulate enough stamps to do so. The Kraft durch Freude Wagen, Strength through Joy vehicle, was now only available to those with very good contacts indeed. Gisela and one of her brothers began to load up the car with belongings and valuables from the house. They seemed to be in a hurry to leave.

That evening at RAF Marham in Norfolk, a 26-year-old pilot, Alec Pringle, hauled on the controls of a bomb laden Wellington aircraft to get it off the runway. It was the 15th of May 1940. The twin engines of the plane strained and roared as it gained height over the dark shrouded fields around the airbase. They were heading for the British coast. The navigator's map, lit by a shrouded lamp on the chart table, showed that they were en-route for the Ruhr in Germany.

The Wellington was from 115 Squadron and it was part of a

much larger formation of 99 other medium bombers, from various RAF units, with multiple targets in the industrial powerhouse of Germany.

What set Alec Pringle and his young crew apart from the other aerial raiders, was that it was their second attempt to join in with the attack. They'd taken off from RAF Marham earlier that night but been forced back because of the failure of one of their two engines. They could have used it as an excuse to abort their part in the mission but instead. leaving a sick crewman behind, Alec and the rest of his companions took off once again in another Wellington bomber.

Amazingly, Gisela knew they were on the way. Years later she told her daughter Joe Kennedy Jr had saved her life. He apparently sent a telegram, presumably to her home in Goltsteinstrasse in Dusseldorf warning her. We will never know what words this startling communication used but the message was apparently clear. The British bombers are coming. Get out.

At this time Gisela was stuck in Germany, although in touch with both Jack Profumo and Joe Jr. Her country-hopping activities were, she would later claim, brought to an abrupt halt by the Nazi secret police, the Gestapo.

Gisela wrote in French for the benefit of the intelligence officers of the Services Speciaux who later interrogated her in Paris. She told them about her intentions at the beginning of the war during questioning in 1944 at their headquarters on the prestigious Boulevard Suchet.

"Before definitely returning to America I planned to spend a couple of months in Germany with my family. Immediately after my arrival I had great difficulties with the Gestapo because of my time abroad and my anti-Nazi attitude."

Wolfgang Brandstetter also displayed a similar knowledge of this time in her life, during his interrogation by the British after his capture in Paris. He initially maintained he only met Gisela in 1944 in the city but later after further questioning he made a further statement about her.

"After amplifying his statement of yesterday PW (prisoner of war) states that before the war she (Gisela) was in Palestine as well as England. In 1939 she returned to Germany where she was interrogated by the Gestapo and then took up a job as a mannequin for a Viennese fashion firm, name unknown."

The Germany Gisela returned to following the outbreak of hostilities was fully in the grip of the Nazis and on a war footing. There was rationing of basic items and on the streets of Dusseldorf work parties regularly collected raw materials like rags and scrap. There was even a special collection of metal in the city to celebrate the Fuhrer' birthday that April. The population was swamped with a constant stream of lies from Goebbels' propaganda ministry.

Military activity formed the largest part of the economy with state attempts to directly control industry and business in all spheres. Göring was in charge of Germany's economic plans. Sugar, coffee, chocolate and cotton were now extremely scarce for everyone because of a British naval blockade of German imports and exports.

Petrol was also hard to come by although Germany was way behind France in terms of private car ownership. The German army was still largely horse drawn, despite all the propaganda films showing armoured vehicles at full speed. The Nazis were however reluctant to increase taxes on their population to pay for the war so instead they relied on plundering the wealth of Jewish Germans and later stripping the countries they'd invaded of anything that could be moved.

Children's education in Dusseldorf and elsewhere consisted of plenty of sports and physical activity with militaristic overtones. The Nazis ensured that the remaining part of the curriculum didn't encourage intellectual curiosity or argument. All teachers were members of the Nazi party and children, except the excluded Jewish ones, were enrolled in official uniformed youth groups.

Internal surveillance and repression of German dissidents was carried out by the Gestapo. In Dusseldorf the secret police were originally based in the old police headquarters in a four-storey house on Muhlenstrasse. In March 1939, because of their continually expanding role, the Gestapo moved to 94-98 Prinz George Strasser in the Pempelfort district.

The series of art nouveau buildings, stone clad at street level, were knocked through and connected together. Prison cells were built in the basement. It was from here Gestapo officers organised the shipment of Dusseldorf's Jews to their deaths in the camps, ghettoes or killing grounds, and it was here in one of the building's interrogation rooms it seems Gisela faced questioning about her activities.

The Gestapo had a remit to investigate and maltreat a wide range of Germans. Former members of opposition political parties, especially communists and even members of the Esperanto society were targets. They were particularly interested in people who had been outside the borders of Germany and who reappeared. This category was called "ruckwanderer" which literally means hiker or backpacker, and Gisela's return via France appears in a brief reference from the Nazis foreign organization which tracked and registered German citizens abroad.

The Dusseldorf archives do still have some of the Gestapo's files from the war, although a search of them has produced no reference to her. This is not particularly surprising as many files were scattered or destroyed, some even burned after their capture by the Allies before they realised their significance.

It is of course possible a reported brush with the Gestapo and her apparent stance as an anti-Nazi were ways of enhancing Gisela's legend to maintain useful intelligence contacts outside Germany, but what seems likely is that even with her impeccable connections she was in a difficult position. She was a woman with a potentially Jewish name who had been out of Germany for long periods and wasn't showing the required Nazi interest in being a child-producing housewife. The archives of the Mettmann district near Dusseldorf record that between 1936 and 1942 the region's Gestapo interrogated many returnees to Germany and at least four died in concentration camps.

Gisela must have been able to call in support from the Abwehr or other high-level contacts, without an existing Gestapo file, we cannot know for certain. She couldn't however rely on the industrialist Werner Schaurte to intervene. Not only would his Jewish ancestry cut no ice with the Dusseldorf Gestapo, who already had more than one file on him, but he had been arrested in 1939 after crossing into Canada following his trip to New York. He was with an aristocratic German companion on a "hunting trip" at the outbreak of war and was imprisoned by the British authorities.

Gisela however clearly escaped this apparent brush with the Nazis' feared secret police. She told French intelligence interrogators Gestapo officers had confiscated her passport, frustrating her stated ambition of returning to the United States.

The lack of a passport placed her at home in Dusseldorf just as the "phony war" or "sitzkrieg" lasting between the invasion of Poland in 1939 and the invasion of Norway in April 1940 turned into a hot war between Britain and Germany. Allied aircraft had previously only dropped propaganda leaflets over the German heartland in raids codenamed "Nickel". People on both sides still clung on to the hope that peace would be possible.

One British propaganda leaflet warned German citizens:

"Hitler cannot retreat but are you willing for his madness to bleed to death."

Another said:

"Germany has forced a war on Britain which promises to involve mankind in a greater calamity than the First World War."

These leaflets were packed into large bundles in the bombers that dropped them. A full load actually weighed more than the bombs they were designed to carry, making the aircraft delivering them particularly sluggish during take-off from their airfields in Britain.

While Gisela was adjusting to her restricted life in Germany, in London, Joe Jr's father was closely following the problems of his fellow appeaser PM Neville Chamberlain. On the 8th of May 1940, Chamberlain faced a concerted political attack in parliament which damaged his position fatally.

Jack Profumo was part of the opposition to Chamberlain. He was now a Member of Parliament after winning a by-election in Kettering in March. He was one of the 33 conservatives including the future Prime Minister Harold MacMillan, who voted against Chamberlain in a motion of no confidence. This was over the Government's withdrawal of support for the Norwegians who were fighting an invasion by Hitler's forces. It was Jack's first vote in Parliament.

Feelings were running high. A government minister spat on Jack's shoe as he waited to go into the opposition lobby to vote against his own party and the government. It also earned him the vicious personal condemnation of the Conservative Chief Whip, David Margesson who was quoted as saying:

"I can tell you this, you utterly contemptible little shit. On every morning that you wake up for the rest of your life, you will be ashamed of what you did last night"

Although Jack was later partly blamed for the fall of the Conservative government after the "Profumo Affair" in the 1960s, his part in this 1940 vote, and the subsequent resignation of

Chamberlain, was of far greater consequence for Britain. Winston Churchill became Prime Minister on the 10th of May.

Just five days later at RAF Marham in Norfolk, the Wellington bombers of 115 RAF squadron including Alec Pringle and his determined crew took off from Norfolk to bomb the Ruhr. The reality was that although their targets were industrial and strategic, bombing technology was so inaccurate that everyone in Dusseldorf and the surrounding areas was in danger that night.

The 99 British bombers hit targets all over the Ruhr. Dusseldorf received its first bombs of the war. The closest were over a mile away from Gisela's family home although the house on Goltsteinstrasse would be destroyed in a raid the following year.

The question remains as to how Joe Jr could possibly have known details of a British bomber raid even before it was launched so that he could warn a woman on a different continent.

He was back in the United States, studying intensively for a series of exams at Harvard Law School in Massachusetts. Even with the Kennedy drive, Joe described how hard he was finding the effort. He told his father in a letter preserved in the Kennedy archive.

"I don't know how the dickens I am going to learn all this stuff in the next three weeks but I suppose everyone else is in the same position"

Joe Jr was also negotiating the beginning of his political career by putting himself up for election as a delegate for the 1940 Democrat Convention which was due later in the year in Chicago. It was the first step in his father's plans and schemes designed to take Joe Jr to the top of the Democratic Party and then the United States of America.

The Massachusetts Delegation, of which Joe was part, pledged support to James Farley, a former campaign manager for Roosevelt. President Roosevelt was facing challenges from four other candidates from within his own party, although in the end he swept the board.

With all this going on in his life Joe Jr still took time to concern himself with the safety of a young blonde woman thousands of miles away in a war neither he nor his father wanted any part in.

There are compelling clues that point directly as to how Joe Jr could have had information for her about this specific attack on the 15th of May 1940. That's because this was the first strategic raid of its kind by the British during the war and was the subject of intense political controversy at the highest levels of the British Government.

As the French faced the onslaught of the German blitzkrieg, they only wanted British air power to be used in tactical support of ground forces. The concern that had steadily developed during the 1930s, further fuelled by the Spanish Civil war activities of the German Condor Legion, was of vast bomber fleets razing cities to the ground. One of the reasons why Paris was later declared an open city allowing the Germans to march in unopposed.

The Royal Air Force high command was tasked with selecting targets in Germany and had plans in place to erode the Germans' industrial capacity to wage war. Even then Churchill was in two minds about the issue. His doubts increased when the British received intelligence that Luftwaffe bomber numbers were far higher than the British had realised.

Would bombing targets like synthetic oil plants and rail heads in the heart of Germany by the British trigger an overwhelming and devastating retaliation on British and French cities? The French certainly thought that would be the case and urged their British allies to refrain from this type of attack.

The former Prime Minister Neville Chamberlain was still at the heart of this debate as Churchill had included his predecessor in his war cabinet. Sir Samuel Hoare, another arch appeaser, as

Secretary of State for Air had previously given a presentation about strategic bombing that managed to sit on the fence and either side of it at the same time. He was removed from office five days before the raid as part of the deal Churchill did with the opposition to form a coalition government, but it took the German bombing of Rotterdam with the loss of thousands of lives beginning on the 10th of May for Churchill to finally give the green light for the 99-bomber raid.

Chamberlain always confided in his ally Joe Kennedy Sr and this seems the most likely route for information about the prospect of this particular raid being passed onto Joe Jr. Chamberlain and Joe Sr were so close that even with a war going on Chamberlain, soon to be diagnosed as terminally ill with cancer, agreed to Joe Sr's request to read Jack Kennedy's University thesis on appeasement which Joe Sr was getting licked into shape for publication.

There would have been no problem in sending the warning telegram from Harvard to Dusseldorf as the United States was not at war with Germany, and from the regular letters between the father and eldest Kennedy son at the relevant time it's clear the pair spoke on the telephone on many issues that were not committed to paper for posterity.

That Joe Kennedy Jr would betray a British military secret to a German citizen is an indication of the 'one standard for the Kennedy's another for everyone else' view of the whole clan. Gisela clearly contacted him, as she had Jack Profumo, about her apparent position, marooned by the Gestapo in Germany, ensuring he knew where to send the alert.

It's also an indication of the overall Kennedy view of the situation. As Joe Jr readied himself for the 1940 Democratic convention, he like his father was still keen for the United States to stay out of the war and was deeply suspicious of Roosevelt. The conflict in Europe was not America's war. His father had summed it up neatly:

"There's no place in the fight for us. It's going to be bad enough as it is."

Back in 1939 Joe Sr had even told his close friend and employee Bill Hinton, a former Correspondent of the America Internal News Service:

"Bill, I'd sell a 100 Polands down the river any day rather than risk the life of a British soldier.... (and of perhaps more importance to the astute stock market player Kennedy) ...or the loss of a British pound."

There is another possible explanation for Gisela's claim to have been warned about a British bombing raid on Dusseldorf. She wasn't always a reliable witness to her own story and in wanting to tell her daughter about an exciting and important event in her life it was easy enough to change the identity of the informant. By the time she revealed this version, Joe Jr was long dead and nobody but her and the person who warned her knew the truth of the matter

However, it was Jack Profumo who admitted to British Intelligence she'd been in touch with him after the start of the war. As the youngest Conservative MP, he was officially the baby of the House of Commons, Jack's love of political gossip ensured he was aware of the politics surrounding the decision to mount the raid on the Ruhr and the war cabinet's decision to go ahead after the German bombing of Rotterdam. Unfortunately, the diary he kept during this time has been unavailable to help to throw any light on this question.

Alternatively, Joe Sr, the American Ambassador to the Court of St James may have knowingly helped to pass sensitive and secret British military information to someone in Germany. It wouldn't be his last brush with the betrayal of secrets. Five days after the Ruhr raid, he was caught up in another serious breach of security, once again involving high fashion and espionage, which directly resulted in top secret United States embassy material ending up in

German hands. He was forced to lift diplomatic immunity for one of his staff at the Embassy in London's Grosvenor Square and allow the British to arrest them.

Tyler Kent, a code clerk at the Embassy, a fervent isolationist, and anti-communist, had been copying documents and making summaries of Winston Churchill's communications to President Roosevelt. These proved the pair were in touch behind the back of Neville Chamberlain while he was Prime Minister, a major breach of the diplomatic rules.

The documents showed Roosevelt was prepared to allow Britain to break America's neutrality by allowing the British navy to capture German shipping in US waters and to intercept mail sent to the United States. Kent's motivation seems to have been to highlight these attempts to help Britain in direct violation of the United States Neutrality Acts. Joe Sr was caught between having to protect the President who appointed him and undoubtedly largely agreeing with Tyler Kent's viewpoint.

The espionage conduit to Germany for Kent's stolen information was Anna Wolkoff, a white Russian émigré. She was involved in the fashion world in Britain in the 1930s offering ball gowns under the name Anna de Wolkoff, Haute Couture Modes from premises at 37 Conduit Street, in London's Westminster 1.

She was filmed in 1937 while designing on a model at her salon. Ripping pieces of fine fabric by hand to drape over the young woman. That same year she was advertising ball gowns for women attending events connected to the coronation of Edward VIII. She was mentioned in some newspaper reports as in the same league as Schiaparelli and Molyneaux and had the Duchess of Windsor and the Duchess of Gloucester as clients, although her business wouldn't survive. She was the daughter of a Russian admiral of the Imperial Navy, a staunch anti-communist and a member of the antisemitic, Hitler supporting Right Club.

The founder of that club, the MP Archibald Ramsay even entrusted Tyler Kent with the membership list of the organization which was found along with the copies and summaries of hundreds of secret communications handled by the United States Embassy.

Luckily for both Kent and Wolkoff, who were tried in secret at the Central Criminal Court at the Old Bailey in London, they were not subject to the death penalty because the offences happened before the 1940 Treachery Act. Both were imprisoned. The MP Archibald Ramsay would be interned during the war.

In the meantime, the first strategic bomber attack on the Ruhr heralded the later terrible destruction for Germany, although this would be obscured by the rapid advance of Hitler's forces through Scandinavia and Europe. Wolfgang Brandstetter was operating as an intelligence officer and involved with a Luftwaffe unit making propaganda films as the Germans swept through Poland and later France.

There's no obvious evidence that Gisela passed on the warning she'd received about the arrival of the British bombers to anyone else other than her family. If she did it had no practical effect on the course of the raid itself.

For the young Alec Pringle and his crew on board the Wellington bomber of 115 Squadron, the return journey to their airbase in Norfolk from the Ruhr saw strong winds blow them massively off course. Their aircraft collided with high ground in Normandy, many miles to the south of where they should have been crossing the coast of Europe. There were no survivors. It was the only loss of the raid.

The story promoted later by both Gisela and Wolfgang about her activities following the raid was that she began working for a Viennese based fashion organization.

The actual evidence points in a different direction. One that would put her at the centre of fashion in the Third Reich.

The picture of her modelling for the Berlin couturier Annemarie Heise places her in the German capital in 1940, the location that had already seen her linked two years previously to the suspected German agent Rudolf Goldschmidt.

At this time the Annemarie Heise fashion house as well as dressing Hitler's lover and Magda Goebbels was also favoured by German film stars like the dancer singer and actress Marika Rokk, who was the same age as Gisela. That year Rokk would appear as herself in the successful Nazi propaganda drama, Request Concert about a couple who fall in love at the 1936 Olympics but are separated by the outbreak of war and then finally reunited.

Gisela's espionage career was seemingly on hold as her main interest in couture reasserted itself, but she wasn't the only spy to work for Heise. One of the other models was working for the other side. Ina Lautenschlager was a dark-haired former seamstress who was denied a proper education because of her communist father's anti-Nazi activities. She was spotted by a prominent photographer Hans Hubbers because of her long legs and was pursuing a modelling career in the same way as Gisela.

It was via the communist cell to which she was connected and later via the famous Rote Kapelle, (the Red Orchestra – a loose network of resistance groups), that she was able to tip off the Russians about a planned attack on Moscow in 1941 from the gossip provided by Eva Braun as she attended the salon for private shows of the latest couture on offer, shown by Gisela and the other models.

"I asked why she needed the winter clothes," she recalled, as it was the middle of summer then.

Eva Braun replied, "Moscow is to be taken on November the 7th."

Braun was expecting to travel to a big reception held in the city to mark the event.

Lautenschlager also used her ability to travel as a model to help establish a communist courier link between Berlin and Brussels. Gisela's constant travel in the 1930s points to a similar role, however Ina Lautenschlager didn't escape the Gestapo in the same way as Gisela. She was caught and imprisoned for distributing anti-Nazi leaflets, although her courier work was never discovered. Post-war she rose to become the head of the Criminal Police in Dresden in East Germany, investigating sabotage activities and Nazi crimes.

Gisela was also definitely in Berlin in July of 1941 as the German archives have her de-registering from Bavaria to go to the capital. Also in Berlin at the same time as Gisela, according to his Nazi party records, was an aristocratic intelligence officer 14 years her senior with whom she became closely associated. He had links to the banking industry and family connections to both Vienna and to a publishing business based in Konigswinter not far from Bonn where Gisela also had family connections. Once again Gisela's espionage work was both partly obscured and partly defined by the men she knew.

13

OH VIENNA

THEY WERE AN elite unit of sorts. Gisela and the other young women arrived by train in the main railway stations of the capital cities of Europe like so many German troops. Some of them were carrying loot from occupied Norway in the form of silver fox fur coats and almost impossible to find silk stockings seized following the fall of Paris. Their munitions were carefully packed in layers of tissue paper in suitcases, boxes and trunks. Gisela was back doing two of the things she did best, travelling and modelling. She was selling the finest clothes that Germany and Austria could offer to those women who could still afford them.

She was now partly based amongst the elegant palaces, opera houses and culture in the former Hapsburg Imperial capital of Vienna. She later called this the happiest time of her life.

There was no more running from the increasing interest of the intelligence agencies in Britain and France. No more men turning up with warrants for her arrest, at least for the time being, or having to please her German espionage handlers in order to retain her ability to move about. She could give free rein to her drive and ambition. As before, her social contacts were very good indeed and her networking abilities were in no way diminished.

The enterprise she now worked for had planted its roots in Vienna before the outbreak of war. In 1938 the Nazi mayor of the city implemented plans for a direct competitor to the Frankfurt Design Centre and the aryanised industry in Berlin. This fashion operation was to be called the Haus der Mode.

The Austrian Nazis were particularly keen to keep their semi-independence and to see off any attempts at control from the capital. There were a series of meetings about a role for the German Fashion Institute, which once had Joseph Goebbel's wife Magda at its helm. The Viennese managed to rebuff efforts to get them to cede power.

The man chosen to lead the Haus der Mode was Alfred Kunz. He was another Dusseldorf link for Gisela. He was a student at the Academy of Fine Arts in the city, before pursuing a career as a costume designer and stage and set designer at theatres in Vienna and in the film industry.

Kunz also turned the women's academy in Vienna into a fashion school along the lines of the Frankfurt school whose students had modelled in Claridge's in London for the Anglo-German Fellowship back in 1936.

With the Nazified Ullstein Press takeover of the prominent Austrian fashion magazine Wiener Mode, Vienna was ready to flex its design and couture muscles, but without the previously important contribution from the city's Jewish fashion sector.

In December 1940 Hitler gave the go ahead to make Vienna Jew free. Many thousands had already fled abroad and between February 1941 and October 1942, more than 45,000 Jewish men, women and children were deported to the east for murder from the city's Aspang station.

In stark contrast to the terrible daily reality for some of those on Vienna's streets, the baroque 17th Century Lobkowitz Palace, a magnificent town house, where Beethoven performed on a number of occasions and where his Eroica Symphony had its premiere, was the glamorous headquarters of the Haus der Mode.

This was Gisela's workplace when she wasn't travelling or back in Berlin. There was an exhibition office specially created in the building where designs intended for foreign shows were collected. The man tasked with remodelling the interior of the palace for its new role described the changing room for the mannequins as "exemplary". They were on the first floor near a "small comfortable restaurant". The official opening was at the beginning of 1939, while Gisela was still in the United States.

As war broke out and intensified it was easy to see couture and fashion as an essentially frivolous enterprise. It wasn't. Fashion was still regarded as a desperately needed source of foreign currency to pay for the raw materials that Germany required to fight. Robert Ley, the man in charge of the German Labour Front, the Nazi-run trade union organisation, claimed fashion was worth more to Germany than iron and coal put together.

Gisela, according to the official records, spent the next couple of years touring the continent with fashion shows for the Haus Der Mode, her travels taking her to countries including Hungary, Sweden, Denmark and Switzerland.

The pictures she kept for her modelling portfolio show that a sort of internal exile in Vienna with added travel wasn't the whole story. She was still regularly modelling for Berlin photographers. There are numerous modelling shots in a variety of styles taken in the German capital up until about 1942.

The fashion collection of the Vienna Museum though has a picture of her modelling what could be beach or leisure wear, a cloth-belted, ruched tunic with a long flowing headscarf, in the same material as the belt, worn beneath a wide brimmed straw hat, for the Haus Der Mode, which dates to the middle of this period in 1941

She clearly had feet firmly in both camps. She was once again very busy – as well as the travelling model shows there were two Vienna

Fashion Weeks a year as well as exhibitions in Berlin attended by the women of the Nazi elite.

But espionage always walked hand in glove with her fashion work. She was linked in Austria around this time to two brothers: Friedrich Siegler von Eberswald, and in particular his younger sibling Heinrich. They, like her, were partly based in Berlin and Vienna and the brothers once again connected her to the world of publishing and espionage. They somehow acquired an economic research publication in Vienna which had been owned by a Jewish family. It's not clear if the takeover was forced as part of "aryanisation" or obtained with the tactical connivance of the original Dutch owners to get round the anti-semitic Nazi legislation of the 1930s. The Sieglers called this economic digest the *Archiv der Gegenwart*. Archive of the *Times*.

Friedrich, the older brother, who would become a senior Luftwaffe officer, was the author of Luftsieg uber Polen (Air Victory Over Poland) whose lurid cover art depicted a Stuka aircraft raining bombs down on Polish territory during the blitzkrieg that had set the world on fire. Inside there were numerous photographs of German aircraft and Luftwaffe leaders including Göring.

Friedrich spent quite a lot of his time during the war, while ostensibly carrying out his airforce duties, organising the printing of the Wehrmacht soldier's pocketbook issued to serving personnel, including a special version for the SS.

Heinrich, who was also known as Heini, had experience in the German financial sector. He'd worked for a banking trade organisation, and he previously applied for a job as the manager of the spa at the famous German spa town of Baden Baden, describing himself as "sportsman". In 1940 he was working in Berlin at the same time as Gisela was darting back and forth between Vienna and the capital.

Both brothers not only demonstrated a great deal of early

enthusiasm for the Nazis but also had an extensive back catalogue involving spying.

Friedrich was involved in intelligence work during the 1934 Nazi attempt at a takeover in Austria in which the Austrian leader Engelbert Dollfuss was murdered. After the failure of the coup, Friedrich Siegler fled to Germany and joined the renegade Nazi party members organisation set up to accommodate Austrian exiles.

Heinrich revealed during a Nazi Party hearing against him over help he gave to his Jewish ex-wife to flee Germany, that he'd been working undercover in Austria for the SD, the SS intelligence arm, while the Nazi Party was banned there following the attempted coup. He was now a lieutenant in German Military Intelligence, the Abwehr, in the local Berlin unit.

The Nazi file on him notes sourly that he was not given the promotion he deserved within military intelligence because of his Nazi Party membership. An indication of the largely anti-Nazi stance of the Abwehr and its leader Admiral Canaris.

Gisela would later be closely associated with an espionage operation to use the Sieglers' Archiv de Gegenwart publication as a front for gathering economic and other intelligence and probably to move illicit money around europe.

But it was a modelling trip to Switzerland in 1942 that brought her back into the sights of British intelligence. She used the cover of this neutral country to write to Jack Profumo.

She posted a letter addressed to him at the Profumo family home, Avon Carrow, in March 1942. It was sent from the oldest and grandest hotel in the Swiss capital Zurich, the Savoy Baur en Ville on Poststrasse. The letter was intercepted by the British censors and the original was sent to MI5. Gisela's security file at the British archive in Kew has the note covering the intercept dated to the 15th of May.

Writer – a Viennese mannequin on a visit to Switzerland appears to be trying to seek information about the addressee [Jack Profumo]

The report goes on to give several extracts from the letter:

> *...surely you are in service but I hope not as a pilot [...] Now let me tell you how I got here. I am here with 16 other girls all mannequins showing our new fashions in Zurich, it's the only way to travel in other countries. We have just been in Budapest and Zagreb. I live and work in VIENNA and I love it much the best [...] Though I am not nearly as happy as I used to be at 88 Seymour Street [...] When I arrived here I wrote to Andrea in St Moritz and he rang me up [...] Do write to him and next time I come he can tell me.*
>
> *Food is rationed terribly at home and one simply can't buy anything, so Zurich is a paradise for us, only we get too little money to buy anything [...] Jack darling I found it very difficult to write this letter I can't get used to the idea that I am free to write to you without a censor.*

The reference to 88 Seymour Street was clearly a reference to their time together as lovers and the mention of the censor suggests they had been in touch before, but that this route via "Andrea" and Switzerland could be an unmonitored method of communicating.

When this letter was sent, Jack was working as a Captain in Air Intelligence Liaison, helping to coordinate air and ground attacks, so he wasn't exactly a pilot, although he would sport wings on his army uniform, which his son suggests he probably wasn't entitled to. Whether he did finally receive this letter or contact "Andrea" in St Moritz isn't known, but Gisela kept a photograph Jack sent her showing him in the uniform of an army captain complete with wings on the chest. This means he sent it to her after 1941 when he was given that rank.

The original of Gisela's letter was investigated by MI5 on the 2nd of May 1942. The conclusion of an officer who signs himself J. Cotton says:

"I have assessed this file from the point of view of counterintelligence. The only "loose end" is Jack Profumo [...] apart from the fact that his father now dead, who had both British and Italian nationality, was a member of Fascio di Londra (Italian Fascists of London) we have nothing recorded against Jack Profumo, who is now serving as Captain in Northants Yeomanry."

However, only the year before Jack had been talking about Gisela and suspicions she was a spy. In her file at Kew there's a minute sent to the MI5 B1B section which was involved in trying to intercept Abwehr communications for counterintelligence against German agents. In this note a D.C. Orr, possibly a police Special Branch officer, says that Jack Profumo MP called "here", in 1941 and spoke about her.

> *In 1936 in Oxford he had met a German girl called Gisela Klein who was ostensibly studying English and got to know her well. She was always hard up. Later she became a mannequin and made a large number of useful contacts. Lady Astor is alleged to have expressed the opinion that she was a spy.*
>
> *"Apparently, there was some trouble about a visa with regard to her having overstayed the period allowed by her permit and she returned to Germany. Later she turned up in Cairo and Alexandria as a fashionable dressmaker and is said to have known every officer in both places. At odd times she appeared in Paris, the South of France and the USA. The last time Profumo heard from her was at the beginning of the war when she wrote from Dusseldorf. Apparently, her parents had "disappeared" but her two brothers were serving in the German army.*

More than year after the war started Jack was, on the very best face of it, being "economical with the actualite" over the strength of his relationship with Gisela. This was the woman to whom he'd written on the back of his photograph.

"I did love you, I do love you, I will always love you, Jack."

He knocked three years off the time he'd known her. Misrepresented the position with regard to her no employment visa and prosecution in 1935 and failed to mention that she apparently stayed with him at Avon Carrow in 1937 after visiting Egypt, and that he was probably visiting her while she stayed with Diana Russell-Clarke in 1938 shortly before her narrow escape from arrest. They'd also clearly skied together in St Moritz, from the "Andrea" reference in her intercepted letter to him and also met the last summer before war broke out when he was in Cannes at the same time as Gisela.

It all seems to point to the fact she wasn't quite the cold embers of a flame from his youth that he was suggesting, and their connection remained close. Later facts would confirm this.

****

The year 1942 would also be busy for one of Gisela's highest-level Nazi contacts, the Ruhr industrialist and engineer Werner Teddy Schaurte, who sent her the code/love poem.

Under lock and key since 1939 after being arrested in Canada at the request of the British, he was being held in a reasonable degree of comfort in the large Dunluce House on the Ballure Road, Ramsey on the Isle of Man.

He was incarcerated with a mixed bag of German nationals, including his 1939 Canadian hunting companion. Count Lothar von Hoensbroech, the German consul to Iceland, Professor Doctor Werner Gerlach and his family, and former German ice hockey champion Wolfgang Kittel, who'd worked in commercial aviation.

Werner's industrial and military importance to the Nazi hierarchy, apparently unrecognised by the British, was highlighted when he became part of an unusual and secretive prisoner exchange in 1942 between Britain and Germany. The details are patchy, but it involved both Werner and Count Lothar von Hoensbroech.

The Isle of Man Museum records show that the Count was sent home in March 1942 probably via Portugal. It seems to have been part of a deal for the British Diplomat Lancelot Oliphant, captured by the Germans as they'd overrun Belgium two years earlier.

A local paper on the Isle of Man ignored Werner's release but did publish an article about the prisoner swap involving the Icelandic consul, under the headline OFF TO BERLIN. It read:

> *A small party of special internees left on Wednesday with luggage labelled Berlin. The former Nazi Consul to Iceland and his two flaxen haired daughters, one aged 20 the other 12.*
>
> *For some months this family have been living in secluded luxury in Dunluce…they have spent their time sunbathing and strolling down the private pathway to a glen leading to a small beach.*

Another report suggested the exchange had involved three men, nine women and a child.

At the end of the war an appeal panel looking at Werner's Nazi connections concluded his involvement in the exchange was incriminating in itself. It certainly confirmed his usefulness to the Nazi top brass including his friend Göring.

The Germany that Werner returned to was rather different to the one he'd left. As Gisela mentioned in her letter to Jack, shortages in the German Reich were really beginning to bite and that included supplies to the fashion industry.

The reality was, for most people even basic clothing was hard to come by. There was coupon-based rationing of clothing from the outset of the war and, in some cases, women had to produce an unserviceable garment before being allowed to obtain another.

The only items not under often severe restrictions were hats. That's why the 1941 beach/leisure wear Hause der Mode picture of Gisela, makes her straw hat and long head scarf combination the strongest elements of the whole ensemble.

After more than two years of trying to make the foreign fashion shows by the Haus der Mode, Frankfurt's Fashion Institute and the Berlin designers profitable, the German war economy really couldn't take the strain of everything being asked of it.

By the end 1942 it was pretty clear to any but the most devoted Nazis that Germany was in real trouble. The Allies had broken through in the Middle East and invaded Morocco and Algeria. Despite the call for German women to give up their fur coats, German troops were freezing and dying fighting in the Russian winter and under the onslaught of Soviet troops in Stalingrad. The German surrender there at the beginning of February 1943 and Goebbels broadcast speech in which he called for "Total War" saw the fashion industry largely turned over to the war effort. Models and those who organised them weren't really in demand anymore, but fortunately for Gisela she had her second string, as spying was still in vogue.

She kept a reference from Alfred Kunz the head of the Haus der Mode dated the 14th of April 1943:

We hereby confirm that Miss Gisela Klein has been working for us for a long time to our satisfaction.

Miss Klein has proved to be a very reliable and exceptionally hard working employee, who is also very useful for travelling and as a representative due to her image and manners.

Miss Klein is leaving her previous place of work at her own request and we can warmly recommend her to others.

A file on Gisela in the United States Archives which was only declassified in April 2025 at the authors request, reveals odd details about what she was doing in Vienna apparently just after leaving the Haus der Mode. The American Counter Intelligence Corps carried out a background check on her in 1950. It says between January 1943 and December 1944 she was registered (although from the evidence, not living) at an address in Vienna solely used by German military officers. American intelligence couldn't find evidence she'd worked for the Haus der Mode at all but records showed she was employed for three months in 1943 by a "raw materials" trading company with offices on the Tirpitzufer in Berlin, a location which also housed the headquarters of the Abwehr alongside those of the German Military High Command. This company was called ROGES and didn't have an office in Vienna and the Americans were unable to find out what her job was.

Gisela's activities however came back clearly into focus in her association with the Sieglers. Friedrich and Heinrich Siegler had plans to expand the activities of the *Archiv der Gegenwart* into a cover for economic and other espionage with intelligence gathering operations in both France and Spain. On their behalf Fraulein Klein would be off and travelling once again.

14

LES BOSCHES

"WE'LL ALWAYS HAVE Paris," Humphrey Bogart told Ingrid Bergman as he sent her away from the Nazis to safety in the 1942 film Casablanca. Gisela had Paris as well and she was heading back there, although it wouldn't prove to be safe for her this time in the morally grey boulevards.

Before that though, there's a clue she travelled across the Atlantic again. In June 1943 the Royal Canadian Mounted Police made an inquiry to MI5 about a visit by her to Victoria in British Columbia on Canada's west coast. The American Counter Intelligence Report from the 1950s has her still working for the raw materials company based on Berlin's Tirpitzufer. In Canada, Victoria was a focus of pilot training and shipbuilding for the Allied war effort. British intelligence later learned that Abwehr air intelligence in Paris was under constant pressure at this time from Berlin to provide information about the air war capacity in North America.

The request for information about Gisela has been redacted in her British file and Canadian files from this time mainly reveal an obsessive interest in the activities of communists rather than beautiful German spies. All that remains in Gisela's file is the reply from the British to their Canadian counterparts.

Titled 'Secret' it was sent to Commissioner S.T. Wood of the R.C.M.P at the Justice Building in Ottawa in Ontario.

"She is known to have made friends with some well-known young men here," MI5 said. It also mentions her connection to British officers in Egypt and that she was reported to be on "intimate terms" with the German military attaché in Paris.

The letter enclosed a photograph of her "for your records" and was signed on behalf of the Director General of MI5 Sir David Petrie. He was the man brought in to sort out the chaotic state of the security service which was overwhelmed by the demands placed on it during the first year of the war.

There is no such mystery about her presence in Paris, although pinning down the exact time she arrived there is clouded by some of Wolfgang Krause Brandstetter's evasive answers and lies under later questioning. While in a British prisoner of war camp he admitted to his former mentor, the publisher John Holroyd Reece, that he was holding back intelligence information from his interrogators. He was unaware the meeting between them was specially arranged in an "M" room at the "London Cage" in Kensington Palace Gardens and they were both being bugged by the British and his comments recorded and transcribed. He said Gisela arrived in Paris in December of 1943. French Intelligence said she was there from April 1943.

Paris was a city which had learned to live with, accommodate and make a profit from, Les Bosches. More than a few of its inhabitants were actively on the Germans' side, not just in spirit but in action.

On the Rue Copernic in the 16th Arrondissement, where Gisela lived while seeing Joe Kennedy Jr and the "German Military Attache," there was a small Art Deco liberal reform synagogue. The oldest of its kind in France. In the dark of the evening of the 2nd of October 1941 it wasn't the Germans but French collaborators, men of the Mouvement Social Revolutionnaire, a fascist party, who attacked and bombed it. One of a number of synagogues damaged that night.

The city adapted itself remarkably quickly in other respects to the German way of doing things. Everything ran on German time now, an hour forward. Bars, restaurants and entertainments were back up and running even as the last of the occupants who fled the invading Germans trailed slowly back. The French were paying the day to day running costs of the occupation, a revenge for the reparations imposed on Germany after the First World War.

Paris was a sought-after full time posting for the Germans. It was also a preferred destination for soldiers on leave, a luxury break from the vicious fighting in Russia. Men in field grey uniforms packed into risqué performances from the semi-nude female performers of Montmartre's Moulin De La Galette and sought to strike up conversations with women, many of whom still managed, despite the privations they faced, to be as well dressed as possible.

Some later claimed the Parisian adherence to the codes of fashion, and the use of excessive volumes of material in haute couture was a form of resistance to the Germans. At the very least it helped to keep their spirits up in increasingly tough circumstances.

French women nicknamed the uniformed German female auxiliaries, with brevet caps perched on their heads and a "blitz" lightning flash on their uniform sleeves , "Grey Mice" but there was never any real doubt who held the upper hand.

For the city's inhabitant's food and where it could be found was the main interest. The shortages were extreme as the Germans shipped everything they could get their hands on back to the Fatherland. Soup kitchens were operating for the poor, but some, usually women, would have to scavenge in the main market Les Halles looking for edible scraps.

For the occupying forces there were special German soldiers' canteens and officers, German women and the wealthy French could eat well on the black market in the restaurants and cafes.

The writer, philosopher and soldier, Ernst Junger, who was

posted to Paris as a German army staff officer, recorded how he dined at the Ritz and socialised with people like the French actor and director Sacha Guitry, and the film star Arletty. He regularly noted his meals and the people he met in his diaries during the occupation. In the autumn of 1943, he described someone pouring liquid butter onto white bread toast for him. Not a feature of most Parisian lives.

Junger coolly observed what was going on around him but seems, like many Germans, to have been largely divorced from the day-to-day reality. He was far more interested in cultural conversations in the intellectual salons of Paris while seemingly oblivious that a small present given to him by a French man whose Jewish wife had been taken away in one of the regular round ups, might be a desperate attempt to get him to help in some way.

The Parisian couture industry was made of tough material and still survived, even after its German competition had largely imploded. Some famous names had moved their operations to Britain and the United States. Elsa Schiaparelli left for America but kept her salon open. Edward Molyneux and Charles Creed returned to their roots across the channel in Britain. Even so there may have been as many as 100 French couture salons still operating in 1944.

There was a plan to move the whole industry, lock stock and barrel, to Berlin and Vienna. The French couturier Lucien Lelong, a designer Gisela recorded herself as having modelled for, later claimed that after protracted discussions he persuaded the Germans to abandon the idea, because of the difficulties of moving the multitude of small suppliers of items like buttons that supported the main fashion ateliers.

There was money to be made for those who could adapt. Lelong was employing 400 people in 1942 and Elizabeth Arden even produced an iodine dye to mimic the stockings now unobtainable for French women. The German expertise in artificial materials also saw French designers starting to use these new textiles.

Coco Chanel on the other hand, moved into the Ritz hotel after closing her couture business and sacking her staff, although the perfume side, which she didn't fully own, remained open. She tried, unsuccessfully, during the occupation to dispossess her Jewish partners. Her collaboration with the occupying forces took the form of the dashing and handsome German spy Hans Gunther von Dincklage, 10 years her junior.

She was later quoted as saying, "When you are my age and a man wants to sleep with you, you don't ask to see his passport."

Dincklage ran a Nazi propaganda and intelligence operation in Paris in the 1930s as well as an espionage operation involving his wife Maximiliane von Schoenebeck known as Katsy, which targeted French naval officers. They used her Jewish ancestry to portray themselves as refugees from Nazism. Even after they divorced, she retained the Abwehr's protection in Paris by being enrolled as an agent. Dincklage returned under the occupation as an Abwehr officer. German Military Intelligence took over of the Art Nouveau style Hotel Lutetia in the Saint Germain area of the city

Gisela's new accommodation in Paris was noted in the intelligence file in the French archives:

"...in 1943 she stayed at the Hotel Reynolds, 6 Parc du Monceau in the eighth district where she occupied an apartment which had a monthly rental of 3,000 francs. This hotel was uniquely reserved for Germans".

It was a prestigious location near the English style gardens of the Parc Monceau and not far from the Arc de Triomphe which at the beginning of the year provided the backdrop for a very well attended rally by the militia of the fascist Parti Populaire Francais. Some of the French crowds lining the Champs Elysees were giving the Nazi salute as the men marched past.

Gisela was living a life not dissimilar to her previous time in Paris. She obviously had fond memories, as she took her daughter off to a particularly favoured restaurant during a visit in the 1970s. She also pointed out her apartment to her daughter during a taxi ride near the Champs Elysee. If you were young, female and German, life could be very good indeed.

One of Gisela's contemporaries described her own experience of occupied Paris at this time as the "most wonderful and unforgettable time of my youth" with visits to the opera and theatre and lavish dinner parties with the French aristocracy.

Inga Haag, like Gisela, also worked for the Abwehr in Paris. She was a well-connected, glamorous and aquiline brunette from an anti-Nazi Prussian family. She'd met Hitler who she described as:

"Not good looking; he had a chicken skin neck with large pores. He was almost revolting."

Inga was recruited to work for Admiral Canaris, the Head of the Abwehr. She was based at their headquarters in the Hotel Lutetia in Paris. Canaris nicknamed her "the painted doll" and while she was still in Berlin, sent her off to the famous Hotel Adlon, not far from the Brandenburg Gate where everyone important stayed. She sat in the lobby and listened in to the conversations and reported back to him.

She described the Abwehr unit in Paris as the equivalent of MI5 and MI6 rolled into one and said she and her colleagues even had their own personal table at the Ritz on the Place Vendome.

During Inga's time in Paris the anti-Nazi Abwehr was, she claimed, involved in supplying useful documents to help Jews on the run. The Abwehr used her as a courier for this because she was elegant and could therefore pass as a young Parisienne, something else she had in common with Fraulein Klein. What Inga didn't mention was that some of the ID cards and passports were also probably for the Abwehr's Jewish agents of which there were a number. Some of these would refuse to be transferred over to the Nazi SD intelligence service after it gained overall control of the Abwehr in 1944.

Meanwhile Gisela's organising abilities, referenced by Kunz of the Haus Der Mode, and obvious from her capacity for travel were what was required of her in Paris. She was to be the representative of the Siegler von Eberswald's, *Archiv der Gegenwart*, French edition. This enterprise had received the approval of the German military high command to operate as a cover for espionage and intelligence gathering activities. Compiling the *Archiv der Gegenwart* which provided facts and figures about other countries was the perfect excuse for soliciting useful information and a reason for travel. Alongside fashion, Gisela's specialist subjects.

French intelligence described the *Archiv der Gegenwart* as a weekly political and economic magazine and Gisela's British file mentions her travelling to Italy, Greece and "other countries" on business for the archive.

The Siegler von Eberswald brothers were both in Paris at the same time as Gisela. Friedrich, a Lieutenant Colonel in the Luftwaffe, was running air intelligence from the building of the luxury soap maker Roger and Gallet in Rue du Faubourg St Honore. Heini was also in the city on *Archiv der Gegenwart* and other shady business, often relating to the transfer of money. Both the French and the British intelligence services later assumed he was merely the civilian younger brother of the Luftwaffe Siegler and didn't realise he was an Abwehr officer.

The French noted he was staying in the Hotel Bristol on the Rue du Faubourg St Honore, reserved for diplomatic personnel, although they didn't draw any further conclusions from that fact or that later they weren't able to trace him at all.

There was also someone else Gisela undoubtedly knew. The former Air Military Attache at the German embassy in Paris from

1938 was back in town. The balding, pipe smoking Friedrich Carl Hanesse, who was often seen with a slight smile on his inquisitive face. He was also based in the Roger and Gallet Building. He was now a Luftwaffe General in charge of intelligence amongst other things and in November 1943, according to French intelligence, was arranging the dispatch of sabotage agents to Great Britain and the United States. Significant if it was Gisela in Canada that year.

General Hanesse also had another sideline. He was organising the looting of art and other treasures on behalf of his kleptomaniac superior Hermann Göring, who, as the war had begun to go badly for Germany and he'd fallen out of favour with Hitler, retreated into obsessive art collecting, much of it stolen from Jewish owners at knock down prices. The Germans were bureaucratically documenting these transactions to give them a spurious air of legality.

Later yet another familiar face for Gisela arrived. The tall, dark hair and piercing blue eyes of Wolfgang Krause Brandstetter, who told Allied interrogators he'd been anxious to get back to Paris because of a girlfriend, although he didn't specify which one. In the official records he was back in the city from the beginning of 1944.

He'd been forced to leave a cushy posting in Paris nearly two years earlier. The German Foreign Office Propaganda and Intelligence unit targeting Britain was axed because some senior staff were accused of involvement in a plot to oust the German Foreign Minister Joachim von Ribbentrop.

The plot partly centred on Ribbentrop being seen as an obstacle by various elements within Germany, including officials of the Foreign Office and the SS General Walter Schellenberg, who wanted to start peace negotiations with the Allies. A file was prepared which described Ribbentrop as "mentally incapable" of carrying out his duties. The plot backfired on its conspirators and in the ensuing Nazi investigation into that and various sub plots, the propaganda and intelligence department in which Wolfgang was working was labelled as a "most highly objectionable conglomerate of graft, careerism and terror."

One of Wolfgang's superiors ended up in a concentration camp and Wolfgang was sent back to an anti-aircraft battery in Germany, which by then was being pounded regularly by Allied bombers. He used this time to write the travel book and autobiography *Welt im Wurfelbecher,* World in a Dice Cup, and later managed to pull some strings and get himself seconded back to the Abwehr in Paris on the air intelligence side with Friedrich Siegler von Eberswald above him under General Hanesse. Wolfgang like the others also worked out of the Roger and Gallet building.

He was, he later suggested, only really a glorified office bureaucrat, decoding intelligence reports from agents, organizing wireless sets for them and liaising with an Abwehr radio listening post based at St Cloud in the western suburbs of Paris which was receiving coded messages. He was particularly interested in reports about Allied convoys which could be targeted by the Luftwaffe in the English Channel.

As with Gisela, this was not the whole story by any means. His espionage activities were much more extensive than he initially admitted and he had a lucrative side enterprise.

Wolfgang was running an English language bookselling operation, bizarrely as part of an officially sanctioned Nazi economic initiative. The business which involved both the Albatross paperback brand and the German Tauchnitz imprint was set up pre-war with the help of John Holroyd Rees and the Brandstetter Printing business of his stepfather Justus. There were thousands of copies of books in storage in Paris ranging from Steinbeck's *Of Mice and Men* to Katherine Mansfield's *The Garden Party and Other Stories.*

Wolfgang was also very friendly with an aristocratic French family, the De Brions with whom he was also involved in publishing deals. His extra mural business life at one stage landed him in serious trouble with the Nazi authorities and he had to promise that the publishing operation under the Albatross brand was not a foreign Jewish-owned business but was under full German control.

He was allowed to continue on the basis that the business was German, although it wasn't. What the Nazi investigators also didn't realise was that Wolfgang was only sending back to Germany the costs of the operation and was squirreling away the profits. He bought gold and silver bullion which was stashed with a Parisian lawyer. With a certain lack of imagination, he called his illicit gains his "black fund".

For Gisela, Paris was certainly fizzing with old friends in old haunts and a full social life, her natural metier. But try as she might, she and the other Germans intent on enjoying "Gay Paris" still found it impossible to ignore the outside world. Paris was being bombed by Allied aircraft and acts of resistance, including attacks on German soldiers, were becoming more common.

While the jewellers Van Cleef and Arpels on the Place Vendome continued to supply German officers with sparkling items for their girlfriends or wives, the news of the destruction being wreaked on German cities was filtering back and highlighting the relative safety and comfort of the occupiers of Paris in contrast to their families at home.

People in Germany were living in an increasingly dangerous and mad world. The danger came from the skies, the madness from their own side.

The worse things became in Germany, the more the Nazis doubled down on their perceived internal enemies. In December 1943, Elfriede the youngest sister of Erich Maria Remarque the author of *All Quiet on the Western Front* and Marlene Dietrich's old flame in Cannes, was executed by guillotine on the orders of the vicious hectoring Nazi judge Roland Freisler. She'd been denounced for making anti-Nazi and Hitler remarks in the fashion salon she ran in Dresden.

Christmas day in Paris, where the Army Command and the Abwehr were largely united in their hatred of Hitler, brought the news the planned invasion of Europe was to be commanded by the Supreme Allied Commander Dwight D. Eisenhower. The announcement was made in a radio broadcast in the United States by President Roosevelt the day before. The German response to the inevitability of this invasion would have a direct effect on Gisela and the planned *Archiv der Gegenwart* espionage operation.

The Siegler brothers had decided that the Editor at the archive's office at 10 Rue de la Pepiniere, was to be Prince Joseph Schwarzenberg, a Viennese aristocrat in his 40s whose family, like the Siegler von Eberswalds, was a product of the Austro-Hungarian empire with origins in Bohemia. Gisela's cover was to be in charge of organising the paper supplies and printing for the operation and using her contacts to liaise with the relevant German authorities, particularly the Nazi Propaganda Ministry.

At the beginning of 1944 as the Germans organised their defences, the prince was called up to join a German Army Sicherung regiment. These security divisions were used to fight partisans and run intelligence operations targeting resistance. Most of the Sicherung regiments operated on the Eastern front where they were associated with numerous war crimes, but it seems likely Joseph Schwarzenberg III was destined for the 325th Security Division which operated in France and was responsible for the defence of Paris and its surrounding area.

In an attempt to get this order reversed, Heinrich Siegler appealed to the intelligence unit where his brother worked and they in turn contacted the Abwehr Luftwaffe command unit, recently created in Wiesbaden in western Germany. The reply was not what the brothers wanted. The prince's army call up was confirmed and the final straw was that German Military High Command West said it no longer had any interest in the *Archiv der Gegenwart* as a cover for spying.

The later French files on Gisela were completely unaware of any of this. They assumed that because of her looks and social life there could only really be one role for her with Heinrich Siegler. The same role the Paris man of the *Times* newspaper had assigned to her with the German Military Attache.

The French file notes that Heini Siegler stayed at the Hotel Bristol on three occasions in 1944. Between February and March, again in April and May and finally in July.

"Gisela Klein was never his secretary," an entry pronounced firmly with the absolute certainty of the absolutely wrong: "It seems more likely that she was his mistress. She knew him very little and said that he came to Paris to try to set up a weekly magazine. His project did not come to fruition because of the German debacle."

Accepting that she knew Heini Siegler very little and that he was only interested in a magazine was the first mistake. She knew both Siegler brothers well, and the German defeat did nothing to the *Archiv der Gegenwart* operation which was already defunct before that time. This version of what had been going on coloured the later investigations into Gisela. Only a few ever got a partial glimpse of the truth about her, but for the moment her attractively camouflaged armour was intact. She was going to need its full protection and all her skill and cunning because 1944 was going to be the toughest year of her life.

15

VALKYRIE

THIS BLOW TO the *Archiv der Gegenwart* operation saw Gisela looking for some other work. What she was actually doing around this time and precisely when she was doing it is open to question. There was, as so often, a discrepancy in the official records and interpretations of her movements.

Wolfgang Krause Brandstetter said she worked for the German occupation authorities in the Rustung Kommando, part of the German forces supply chain, as 1943 turned into 1944. French intelligence identified her as working later in 1944 for a German specialist unit trying to suppress the black market as a "secretary/ interpreter".

Wolfgang was being economical with the truth once again and the French didn't fully understand exactly who she was working for and its importance. A connection also missed in 1950 by the American Counter Intelligence Corps check on her activities in Vienna. The company the Americans said she was working for, ROGES actually put her at the heart of intelligence gathering and war looting activities organised from Berlin.

ROGES full company title was Rostoffhandelgesellschaft and although ostensibly a commercial operation, it was run directly at the behest of the Wehrmacht High Command and other parts of the Nazi state, organising the payment for and the shipment of war booty back to Germany from the occupied countries. In 1942, 40 train wagons a day were leaving Paris stuffed to the gills with black market materials for the German war economy.

ROGES also directly funded sections of the Abwehr in Paris who had a major role in purchasing on the black market, aided by the enforced exchange rate between Germany and France which made everything cheap for the Germans. Apart from the attractive prospect of making money, black market connections also allowed the Abwehr to create intelligence networks and strings of informers. However, the obvious opportunities for fraud and graft had gotten so out of hand that in 1943 Göring personally authorised attempts to regulate what was happening.

In Paris one of the most prolific and successful black marketeers, Henri Lafont, was under the protection of an Abwehr officer, Herman Otto Brandl, whose Otto network was a major player in the ROGES purchasing system. Later Lafont and his gang transferred their allegiance to the Nazi Sicherheitdienst (SD) who took over the Abwehr from 1944. Lafont's gang which had several names including the "French Gestapo" branched out into anti-Jewish and anti-resistance activities.

French intelligence were completely unaware of Gisela's connection to ROGES when they later interrogated her about her knowledge of a black marketeer called Madam Moutafolo.

A question which apparently caused her to hesitate before answering which was noted by her questioner. There was a good reason for her to be careful about what she said.

Madame Moutafolo was also known as Melita Stullenberg. She was running an illicit and large-scale black market trade in textiles and was said to have made more than 60 million francs from her under the counter activities.

Moutafolo/Stullenberg also informed on a Belgian resistance network to the SD and its members were arrested with the usual terrible consequences. Anything other than a passing connection with this woman put Gisela in the orbit of the Abwehr, SD Intelligence and black marketeers and she clearly knew it.

After the pause Gisela blandly said about Madame Moutafolo: "I only went there at the weekend and haven't seen her since. I don't know what has become of them."

During this time in Paris she also worked for another German-run enterprise. A more glamorous operation than the *Archiv der Gegenwart* or the nasty world of the black market and its informers, but one where there were still, the Abwehr believed, intelligence opportunities..

Her employer was Continental Films in Paris, whose head office was at the prestigious address, 105 Champs Elysees. Continental was the Nazi controlled French film industry. It was part of and paid for by the Goebbels propaganda empire. Its remit was to provide entertainment which could be shown in Germany as well. Gisela's contacts with the Nazi propaganda department in Paris were so good that she was always used by the *Archiv de Gegenwart* operation to obtain the necessary permits.

The Abwehr in the form of senior officer Emil Klieman butted heads with the Head of Continental, the producer Alfred Greven, who apparently refused at least two official requests to use Continental's film activities as a cover for intelligence work.

During the German occupation Continental produced around 30 feature films, ranging from light comedies and adaptations of Georges Simenon's Inspector Maigret detective stories to the 1943 noir thriller *The Raven*, (Le Corbeau) about denunciations in a small community. *The Raven* was later accused of being Nazi propaganda, although the Nazis also hated it and stopped it from being screened in Germany.

Gisela's officially recorded role at Continental seems to have been to use her language skills to transcribe French film soundtracks into subtitles for German cinema release. While working at the Champs Elysees HQ or on the social circuit in the city she met a young woman, six years her junior, called Anne Buydens. Anne was born Hannelore Marx. Hannelore, who like Gisela came from a wealthy family, left Germany in the 1930s, and had an arranged marriage of convenience with a Belgian friend, changing her name and passport in the process. She was, according to her later autobiography, working for a Paris film company called Sonor, which she described as British in origin, but which also seems to have been German registered in occupied Prague. Gisela and Anne were doing identical jobs subtitling films. After the war Anne was working as a publicist in the film industry in Paris when she met and later married a visiting American film star. She would become Hollywood royalty as the well-known philanthropist, Anne Douglas, wife of Kirk Douglas. She and Gisela reunited on America's west coast many years later when Gisela took her daughter to stay at the Douglas family home in Beverly Hills.

Back in 1944 there was another clue to Gisela's intelligence involvement. This was revealed unwittingly by the British traitor and double agent Ronald Sydney Seth who'd turned up in Paris. Seth agreed to work for German Intelligence on an espionage mission to Britain. It seems to have been an operation involving both the Nazi SD and the Abwehr. His later debrief/interrogation by the British also provided a unique insight into some of Wolfgang's spy running activities and his desire to disguise his relationship with Gisela.

Seth was a bespectacled former Ely Cathedral school chorister. He was tall with fair hair and when photographed had a slightly studious air which gave no real hint of his clearly vivid internal life or capacity for deception and double dealing. He was at Peterhouse College at Cambridge University at the same time as Wolfgang was at Gaius and Gonville. He went into teaching and was appointed Professor of Literature at the University of Tallinn in Estonia.

At the beginning of the war, he joined the BBC and was then commissioned as an officer in the Royal Air Force. He never seemed to sit still for any length of time and subsequently joined the SOE, which was tasked by Winston Churchill to "set Europe ablaze". Seth's knowledge of Estonia saw him parachuted into the country to help to organise the resistance to the Germans. In the appropriately named Operation Blunderhead one of Seth's tasks was to disable the Estonian shale oil industry, a vital source of fuel for the Germans.

Accounts varied as to what really happened after Seth hit the ground in occupied Estonia. Knowledgeable German sources suggested he hurt his ankle and surrendered to them, either straight away or shortly after being unable to find the supplies parachuted in with him.

Seth maintained alternatively he went on a sabotage spree with improvised weapons before his capture after which he was tortured and an attempt made to execute him by hanging which was frustrated when the "apparatus" failed. He also maintained he'd been sentenced to death by a Nazi People's Court. Claims described as "fantastic" by his British interrogators.

"Seth is rabidly anti-Soviet to such an extent that all his actions and loyalties are subordinate to this ruling passion" his security file noted.

What is clear is the SOE agent agreed to work for the Germans, whether because of his anti-communism or because, as he later claimed, he was waiting for the first opportunity to escape and get back to Britain. In November 1943 he was sent to Paris for instructions for the spying mission in Britain. He was the protégé of the Abwehr's Emil Klieman in Paris. Seth was handed over for training to another man who was introduced to him as air force

Oberleutnant Dr Braun. His description of his time with 'Braun' was revealing. As always Seth was the hero of this encounter.

> *Braun after our first meeting dined me at Claridge's. (Hotel Claridge on the Champs Elysees) He obviously intended to make me drunk, so that I would talk. In spite of my various vicissitudes, I was glad to find that the hard head that membership of the Peterhouse rowing club had given me had not weakened.*
>
> *As a result after a bottle of wine, two bottles of champagne and two cognacs it was my host who talked. He told me his real name was Brandstetter of Tauchnitz books and he was hoping to get to England himself as an agent.*

Whether Wolfgang's claim he wanted to go on a spying mission in Britain was the truth or merely an attempt to enthuse Seth for the job the Abwehr had for him isn't clear. Seth would also reveal that Wolfgang's role wasn't, as he later pretended, largely bureaucratic intelligence work.

He acted as Seth's Abwehr instructor in secret writing and personally provided him with training in British Army, Naval and Airforce intelligence with lectures at his Avenue Niel apartment on the meaning of military insignia and flashes, tank, aircraft and ship recognition, and the composition of secret messages.

These lectures finished suddenly in February 1944 when Oberleutnant Dr Braun disappeared. He was busy with other operations.

Seth later gave the British what he must have believed was a damning assessment of Wolfgang's abilities as an intelligence officer:

> *He was a most unsuitable man for this work. Officially he had a room at the Hotel Scribe but privately he had a flat at 83*

Avenue Niel where he kept his mistress, a young French actress called Madeleine. I visited this flat twice and he discussed my operation in the presence of this girl, who spoke English.

Apart from this apparent breach of security, Seth also complained that Wolfgang Brandstetter talked about codes to him on an open telephone line, but it was the reference to Madeleine who spoke English which was significant.

Brandstetter later revealed under interrogation several other things about "Madeleine Fontaine" that strike a familiar chord.

She was, he said, about 25 years old, tall and slim with fair hair and blue eyes. Her face was long and she used a slight but skilfully applied amount of make-up. He added ungallantly but not untypically for the self-regarding Wolfgang, that she was not a lady and smoked and drank a lot.

Apart from being slightly younger and the eye colour, Madeleine's description was basically a less classy version of Gisela.

Madeleine also, Brandstetter said, had a connection to Continental films. She was said to be Flemish – Gisela was half Dutch, and she apparently spoke and or understood French, English and German. The Flemish origin story certainly helped to explain Madeleine's underlying accent, although Ronald Seth seems to have swallowed the idea that she was French.

It was not in any way surprising that Wolfgang talked about Seth's British mission in front of his "mistress" because she was clearly the enterprising Gisela from Dusseldorf. No trace of Madeleine Fontaine, or the sister Wolfgang seems to have invented for her were ever found. He must have come up with elements of this story on the hoof when suddenly confronted by the British with Seth's evidence that there was a blonde woman in his life.

Wolfgang also continued to disguise the length of the time he and Gisela had known each other to Allied interrogators by saying they only met when she accompanied a senior Abwehr officer to a party in Paris in early 1944. This officer also, amazingly, according to Wolfgang, only met her for the first time that night as well. They'd not, he insisted, become an item until sometime afterwards because she initially rebuffed his advances. It was thin stuff and clearly wasn't enough for British questioners who returned to the subject.

Under further interrogation, he amended this story to give more, if still deliberately vague, details about her past. He said that before the war she was in England and Palestine, and that she'd been interrogated by the Gestapo on her return to Germany on the outbreak of the war. He also told his British questioners Gisela "indignantly" denied being a member of the Abwehr to him on several occasions.

She was on the face of it, and proved so later, a far better keeper of secrets than Wolfgang while getting drunk on black market champagne, wine and cognac at the Hotel Claridge with the unreliable Ronny Seth.

****

The couple were not the only ones with something to hide in Paris that summer. Senior German army officers were removing the telephone handsets from their cradles in offices and their suites in the requisitioned hotels. They were attempting to block eavesdropping during certain discussions. They weren't worried about the increasing activities of the French resistance or enemy agents listening in, it was their own side that presented the most acute danger.

The man Gisela later claimed had recruited her to the Abwehr, Colonel General Carl-Heinrich von Stulpnagel, was now the Governor of military forces in the greater Paris area. He was known as "the blond Stulpnagel" to differentiate him from his cousin who was also a General and who'd also served in Paris. Despite allegations of involvement in war crimes on the Russian front, Stulpnagel was reportedly an opponent of Hitler from the beginning. He was, along with most of the senior officers of the Abwehr at the Hotel Lutetia, part of a plot to kill the Fuhrer.

There were more than 40 attempts to murder Hitler over the years and his survival helped fuel his messianic vision of himself as a man of destiny. The only destiny General Stulpnagel and his fellow conspirators were confidently predicting was the utter defeat of Germany and its overrun from the east by the communist Soviets, for them the worst possible outcome. They also felt they would be blamed eternally for having done nothing to prevent Hitler's worst excesses. This feeling became particularly pressing in Paris as the conveniently accepted propaganda that Jewish men, women and children were being "resettled", gave way to direct and eyewitness evidence of what was really happening. Everyone in Paris had seen the round ups and knew the Jews were being forced onto trains from the Bobigny station in the city's suburbs.

Ernst Junger, who was on Stulpnagel's staff, recorded in his diary in the autumn of 1943 how he learned about some of the killing methods being used in the eastern Jewish ghettoes, including lorry exhaust gas and victims being forced to stand on a large electrified metal plate. These types of executions were introduced because men forced to shoot Jewish families en masse had started showing psychological problems.

"This is the landscape that reveals Kniebolo's (Junger's codename for Hitler) nature most clearly" ...he wrote in his journal.

Although it seems inconceivable now most people didn't know what was really happening, it was vital to the hideous process of the "final solution" that the millions of victims were kept ignorant of their fate until the last possible moment.

German nationalists ignored their feelings about the Nazis and sat on their hands because of Hitler's successes. With defeat likely it was now clear, if somehow it hadn't been before, how big a mistake that was. Army officers and diplomats were plotting to remove Hitler as a precursor to making peace with the western Allies. They modified a military plan, designed to deal with general insurrection, to allow a complete takeover after Hitler's death. It was called Operation Valkyrie. Stulpnagel even got his friend the leading General Erwin Rommel, famous as the "Desert Fox" to pledge his support.

This secret activity was set against an increasingly tense feeling on the streets of Paris. Air raid sirens were constantly going off and bombers droning overhead. There were raids targeting factories in the suburbs which caused extensive civilian casualties. While Gisela could pass safely as a Parisian woman, or as a privileged German, depending on the time and place, the day-to-day relations between the occupied and the uniformed occupiers were deteriorating. Resistance, including assassinations of German soldiers, increased. Graffiti appeared on walls and fliers urging resistance were left at Metro stations. Some Parisians turned their watches back an hour to the original French time, a small act of rebellion.

Networks of French people sought to keep downed Allied airmen safe from capture and get them back to Britain. Some hid Jews, especially children.

But collaboration was still the name of the game for many, not just in the right wing aristocratic and political classes. The Milice, the fascist style militia created by the Vichy French government in cooperation with the Germans, led the round ups of Jews. The Paris police force continued to be used by the Nazis against its own people and the Germans mounted a show trial of one resistance group in the Hotel Continental in the Place Vendome to highlight that several of its members were Jewish. They plastered the Metro with propaganda posters about the case with pictures of 10 of the men with the headlines "The Liberators?" and "The Liberation by the Crime Army". It wasn't subtle and didn't necessarily work in the way they'd intended, instead serving as a reminder that brave people were fighting back.

Some like Ernst Junger, and many of the French collaborators, continued to fool themselves there was, and could still be, some sort of a unity between the French and the Germans. Certainly, Gisela now felt more at home in Paris than anywhere else.

The real and enormous gulf between victors and vanquished was neatly encapsulated by Junger's description of watching Allied bombs hitting the Saint Germain area of the city during an air raid, with "enormous detonation clouds billowing". He was standing on the roof of the requisitioned Hotel Raphael where he stayed in the chic 16th Arrondissement, and watching the firework display complete with a glass of burgundy with strawberries floating in it.

Elsewhere in the city people who couldn't afford the black market were breeding rabbits and guinea pigs in their baths for food. The Tuileries Gardens in the centre of Paris were now planted with root vegetables as supplies from elsewhere had dried up. On the other side of the coin many French women were keeping up appearances, whizzing around on their bicycles, stylishly dressed. They were so successful at this that later it caused a backlash in Britain when photographs didn't appear to show a population that looked like it had suffered much under the heel of the German jack boot. They had, but fashion was always a form of concealment as Gisela could testify.

On the 6th of June 1944 the long awaited news swept through Paris that Allied forces were invading Normandy. It provided a focus for plans already in the making by both Gisela and Wolfgang. The next day Panzer tanks with young soldiers sitting on them were seen on the Boulevard L'Amiral Bruix. They paused briefly so men could eat in the waning sunlight before setting off on their clanking route to the front line with the Allied invaders.

Gisela later said she'd known General Carl Stulpnagel's niece in Paris, and that she moved in anti-Nazi circles, which included senior Abwehr officers implicated in the plot to kill Hitler. She was seen at a party in the company of General Joachim von Tresckow, who commanded one of the divisions composed of Luftwaffe personnel created by Göring to stop the army stealing his men to plug gaps on the Russian Front. He was involved in Valkyrie. It seems likely given her extensive contacts, that she was aware of the general nature of a conspiracy against Hitler if not perhaps the precise details.

Inga Haag, from the Abwehr in the Hotel Lutetia, had married and moved to Romania with her husband and was also privy to the Valkyrie plan. She knew some of the others who tried to blow up Hitler on the 20th of July 1944. One of them was her cousin, the diplomat Adam von Trott zu Solz, who would have led peace negotiations after Hitler's death and she'd met Claus von Stauffenberg the man who planted the bomb at Hitler's eastern headquarters.

Later she was rather dismissive of Stauffenberg's competence to carry out the assassination. His failure to put a second explosive charge that he possessed in the briefcase bomb combined with sheer bad luck. The briefcase was moved under the table Hitler was leaning over which protected him.

From the moment the briefcase bomb exploded, Operation Valkyrie had all the momentum and tragic potential of a runaway locomotive. General Stulpnagel's call to action came directly from the German war ministry in the Bendlerstrasse in Berlin. "The Fuhrer Adolf Hitler is dead" the message wrongly reported.

Under this belief Stulpnagel gave the orders and all the SS and Gestapo men in Paris were rounded up by Wehrmacht soldiers and imprisoned in the one part of Valkyrie that actually went really well. The German army even bagged "The butcher of Paris" SS Obergruppenfuhrer Carl Albrecht Oberg who'd ordered the round ups of Jews for deportation to their deaths and the execution of hostages taken in reprisal for acts of resistance involving the killing of Germans.

Elsewhere though the conspirators failed to cut communications with Hitler's headquarters and arrest and or kill other Nazi leaders like Goebbels and Himmler. The plot began to unravel. Stulpnagel realised the game was up when General Gunther von Kluge, the overall commander of France, refused to back him because Hitler was still alive.

In Paris it was all over in less than a day. The captured SS and Gestapo men were released and the whole episode was dressed up as a military "exercise". The blond Stulpnagel was ordered back to Berlin. Even with the knowledge he was travelling towards a death sentence, ever the thoughtful gentleman, he still found time to cancel a lunch engagement with Ernst Junger.

On the way he told his driver and the soldier with him he wanted to stop in Verdun. It was the location of the First World War battlefield where he fought and so many of his comrades died. He got out of the car and shot himself in the head with his pistol. In a bitter irony it wasn't a fatal act. He only managed to blind himself. Stulpnagel's life was temporarily saved in a military hospital and he was tried lying on a stretcher in front of the Nazi judge Roland Freisler and hanged on the same day in Berlin's Plotzensee prison.

Even before Operation Valkyrie, General Stulpnagel's staff identified a fallback command location to the east of Paris. The Allies' air superiority over Göring's Luftwaffe and the sheer weight of men and materials coming ashore in Normandy meant they weren't hurled back into the sea as the Germans had hoped.

In the parts of France already overrun by the Allies, Bastille Day, a week before the attempt to kill Hitler, was a focus of extra celebration. In Paris it became an excuse for a mass demonstration with more than 100,000 people singing the Marseillaise and displaying the red, white and blue of the French flag. The Parisians were buoyed by the invasion and it brought them hope. The Paris police decided not to act against the demonstrators, but the people taking part were unaware the Allies didn't plan to capture Paris at all, but divert around it in pursuit of the Germans.

But even with the Germans falling back Gisela was, according to the French files on her, working as a secretary and interpreter, either as they believed for the unit suppressing the black market or perhaps still for ROGES. Whatever the case it's likely her role was to liaise directly with the French Police and the pro-Nazi militia, the Milice as the Germans delegated this sort of work to collaborating French organisations.

The air intelligence war was also giving her lover Wolfgang plenty to do. He was playing a leading part in a very successful German deception operation.

16

WESTERWALD

IT WAS VERY hot and humid in Paris that summer of 1944. In better times Gisela would have joined the annual exodus when those who could afford it headed for the country or the coast, but she was facing forces well beyond her immediate control, as she had most of her life. The daily temperature was so high the Germans feared it might help to trigger a more general insurrection by a near starving population. There was not even milk for babies which led to a public protest by women which was suppressed by German gunfire.

Ernst Junger, taking his leave of the city, talked about the stones of the Basilica of the Sacre Coeur quivering in the sun. While visiting the Cathedral he took a last look out over the heat hazed views of Paris from the Montmartre scarp before descending through the narrow streets lined with the cafes and the restaurants that welcomed the Germans or at least their money.

He said Paris was feminine and only smiled at a victor. A vision contradicted by the role of women in the resistance and the SOE who were there but unseen in Junger's lofty view. As he descended from the hill of the martyr, women, often only young girls, were involved in assassinating German soldiers; hiding weapons; running messages and sheltering and leading Allied air crew through the streets to the next safe house.

In the Hotel Piccadilly on the Rue Pigalle, a small group of young men were living on their nerves in the stifling airless rooms. They kept well out of view of the street by day and avoided the busy nightlife of Paris' traditional red-light area. Next door to the hotel, was a nightclub, Le Prelude, which the young men didn't realise was a notorious hangout for the Germans. A short walk down the road from the hotel, the waif with a big voice, Edith Piaf was singing at the Moulin Rouge cabaret club for the occupation troops who were mostly there for the can-can dancers.

The Allied aircrew hiding at the Hotel Piccadilly and the other locations in Paris only met members of the escape network who were helping them. There was a dark-haired burly man who spoke good English. There was Louis, who was the balding owner of the Hotel Piccadilly. He wore tortoiseshell framed glasses and had really bad teeth.

Some of the evaders encountered the good-looking red-haired woman, Collette, with her fair-haired gaunt boyfriend, known as Captain Jacques, and others, the smiling Jean, a former French air force pilot who'd been born in America. He was friendly and chatty, talking about aircraft and the scrapes he'd been in. He and the others explained that to maintain security the young evaders had to fill out printed forms so the escape network could check their identities via the radio links with Britain. It was vital to the safety of all those putting their lives at risk to help them to make absolutely sure that none of them was a German plant.

The questionnaires were very thorough and started off with name, rank and number. To help identify them accurately, the men were also asked about the type of aircraft they'd been flying, its serial number, their unit identification and how they'd been shot down. Other information included the name of a wife or girlfriend, the name of a pet dog if they had one, and their car registration.

The aircrew filled them out, happy that it would let their friends and family know they were alive and that they'd be on their way home after the checks confirmed they were who they said they were. A day or so later after their details were radioed back someone came to collect them from their hiding place. It was good to be moving again for the next stage of their journey to freedom via Spain.

Elsewhere in the city Gisela was also making her plans and they didn't include a return to Dusseldorf which had suffered extensive damage from fleets of bombers. Her family home on Goltsteinstrasse had already been destroyed. One of her brothers and his wife were living at the apartment in Kapellerstrasse where her late father had been an air raid warden and her mother was now living in Beuel, a suburb of Bonn, with her aunt. There was nowhere she could really call home but Paris. She was worried about the future but she had a new role in prospect and there was always the continuing social life she'd always enjoyed as she charmed and collected people and information.

The tales of hardship in Germany and the course of the war were a regular part of the gatherings she attended with Wolfgang Brandstetter at the quarters of Luftwaffe General Hanesse in the opulent Rothschild mansion, former home of the exiled Jewish family. Despite being in charge of Göring's looting activities, Hanesse ordered the mansion and its contents remained untouched. The General had clearly decided it was unwise to upset such a powerful family at this late stage. For the guests at his table, it was eat, drink and be merry for tomorrow who knows.

Gisela also lunched with Austrian-born, Aristide "Teddy" Doret, an intelligence source, who worked as the Secretary to the Belgian industrialist. Jean, "Johnny" 2nd Baron Empain, also an Abwehr agent. British intelligence later discovered he worked for Emile Klieman of the Abwehr at the Hotel Lutetia and Empain had been recruited via Gisela's friend Teddy Doret.

Johnny Empain had been in the Belgian army when the Germans invaded, was wounded and spent some time as a Prisoner of War. He was a craggy looking man with slicked-back hair and a prominent nose, its visibility not noticeably helped by the small moustache beneath it.

In London in 1934, as a rich playboy, he'd seen the very much younger blonde American burlesque dancer Rozelle Rowland performing at the Dorchester Hotel in London's Park Lane. She was a sensation because her act consisted of wearing nothing but gold paint. Johnny was very keen on Rozelle. He'd already divorced one woman for not giving him a son and when Rozelle, actually Rosie, produced the required male heir he married her and she became Baroness Empain.

He inherited immense wealth because his father's company built the Paris Metro and the family also had their own bank. The family firm which he ran with his brother continued to operate the Paris underground transport system throughout the occupation.

Johnny had a home in Paris and another across the Spanish border. He reportedly spent most of his time in Spain where the Siegler brothers had planned an outpost of the *Archiv der Gegenwart* espionage operation. He and Teddy Doret used the Abwehr to provide their travel documents when needed. Wolfgang dismissed them as low-grade providers of information, but German money was already on the move to Spain and Johnny did have a bank. Wolfgang told British intelligence that Gisela was associated with a Belgian banker called Abrossard, which in reality was probably Johnny. Later the French spent some time trying to find out about other bank accounts Gisela and Heini Siegler had access to and the Belgians and the Dutch also made inquiries about the pair.

Gisela attended at least one party on the arm of the pear-shaped and enthusiastic smoker, Werner Ohletz, a high ranking Abwehr Officer visiting Paris, suggesting her Berlin intelligence connections remained impeccable. He was marked out as a social companion by a sense of humour and proportion. He later declined to become involved in the last ditch stand by the Germans, pointing out he was far too old to run around the mountains wearing a false beard.

Gisela was also acquainted, according to the later interrogation of Wolfgang, with the young oval-faced Oberleutnant Stoll, who had brown hair and grey eyes and who was known for his grating metallic voice. He trained Abwehr agents in wireless operation using British mark II radio sets obtained during operations against the SOE, and he could also helpfully provide false identification papers on demand.

Virtually every day they could all see the high vapour trails of the aircraft above Paris on their way to pound the Ruhr and elsewhere. On one raid early in 1944, American Flying Fortresses hampered by poor visibility over Germany took the opportunity of a break in the clouds to inflict heavy damage on Werner Schaurte's nut and bolt factory in Neuss. The US *Stars and Stripes* newspaper hailed the raid as a success and described the factory as producing "half the high-grade nuts and bolts which hold the Wehrmacht together."

By August the Bauer and Schaurte business had already diversified its production sites to other safer areas including the Harz mountains in the north, where part of the German V2 ballistic missile production programme was also located. The company was using forced labour. As an incentive to the slave workforce, the food they needed to stay alive was allocated on the basis of productivity.

The Luftwaffe was being overwhelmed and desperately needed good intelligence about the Allied air force deployments. At the Abwehr Luftwaffe intelligence headquarters in Wiesbaden, codenamed Wilja, there was much coded radio traffic to Paris, codename Westerwald, about operations and personnel.

There was no going back now for Gisela, only forward into an uncertain world where her options and her high-level contacts were diminishing.

****

On the 15th of August the *New York Times* reported the death of her lover and the Kennedy heir apparent, Joe Kennedy Jr. The news wire services carried the story around the world but it's not clear whether Gisela learned of his death in Paris at this time or later. There wasn't much detail in the front-page story:

> *Lieut. Joseph Patrick Kennedy Jr, 29-year-old son of the former United States Ambassador to England was lost last Saturday, the Navy said today, while piloting a Navy plane on a special mission in the European theatre.*

It was a bald statement for an act of brave but typically competitive sibling rivalry by Joe Jr.

His younger brother Jack had been awarded the Navy and Marine Corps medal and a Purple Heart wound medal for saving the lives of the crew of his patrol torpedo boat PT 109 in the Pacific Ocean. The vessel was hit by a Japanese destroyer, sliced in half, and sunk. Jack rallied the survivors and undertook several long-distance swims between remote islands to get help and rescue.

Jack dryly described his actions: "It was involuntary. They sank my boat." It showed his capacity for clear thought and action under pressure in a crisis.

Probably spurred by his brother's conspicuous valour, Joe Jr, a pilot in anti-submarine patrol aircraft had stayed on in Britain after completing the required number of missions and then volunteered to fly a B24 Liberator aircraft modified as a drone and packed with explosives. The technology of the time just about allowed the plane to be flown and dived onto its target under radio control from a nearby "mother" aircraft. However, the flying bombs needed a human crew for take-off. They parachuted to safety afterwards. The target for this mission was a Nazi complex in France, southwest of Calais where the V3 vengeance weapons, a series of super cannons designed to hit London, were under construction deep underground.

The Liberator bomber successfully got off the runway at RAF Fersfield, southwest of the city of Norwich, with Joe Jr and his co-pilot Lieutenant Wilford John Willy at the controls. They were followed by the drone's "mothership" and a camera unit in another aircraft to film the action. Joe's bravery was to be recorded for posterity. Shortly after the explosives on the B24 were armed and Joe radioed the confirmation code words "spade flush", prior to bailing out, the aircraft was obliterated by an enormous explosion.

The detonation of 11 tons of high explosive happened at 2,000ft in the air. The following aircraft were hit by debris and the tremendous blast caused damage to houses in a wide area below. No remains of either of the pilots were found.

It was a terrible end to Joe Kennedy Sr's dream for his first born, but before his death Joe Jr wrote to his father suggesting that in the event he didn't return from active duty, Jack was more than capable of taking over as the family's Presidential hopeful. With Joe also died the details of the warning he gave Gisela about the British bombing raid on Dusseldorf. Only she knew the full truth of it and she only told part of that to her daughter more than two decades later.

On the same day the death of Joe Jr was announced, the Paris Police went on strike having sniffed the strong scent of new masters on the wind. Gisela was already aware that planning was underway to evacuate Paris by elements of the intelligence services including Wolfgang. He was told to go to Reims by his immediate superior

Major Buttlar of 1 Luft, to organise alternative headquarters as part of a retreat.

Getting out of Paris was slow as the lack of police officers on the streets meant that traffic on the exit routes was jammed with the vehicles full of non-fighting German personnel heading away. The German female auxiliaries, the Grey Mice, were seen waving goodbyes with some in tears as they left.

The garrison commander in Paris was now the slippery Dietrich von Cholitz. He was picked for the task because he was known to obey orders no matter how unpleasant they were.

The city was to become a German bastion. Mortar crews and soldiers were building defensive positions in the famous Luxembourg Gardens where the leaves on the chestnut trees had turned brown and scabby in the summer heat. German engineer units placed explosives under bridges across the River Seine to ensure their demolition in the face of the enemy and SS soldiers were seen examining the supports of the Eiffel tower.

Wolfgang and Gisela initiated the first stage of a plan to deal with the inevitable. He made arrangements to move out from his room at the Hotel Scribe and the apartment at Avenue Niel, where he'd been seen with "Madeleine Fontaine." Gisela was no longer to be found at the flat where she'd been officially living at 4 Rue Clement Marot. They were hiding together a short stroll from the Luxembourg Gardens and Palace in an apartment belonging to Comte Jacques De Brion, one of the French aristocrats who'd been in a publishing venture with Wolfgang.

The apartment was in a discreet Parisian building which spoke of old money, with a solid stone block wall at street level and a painted and substantial double wooden front door. Their new address was 9 Rue Conde in the 6th Arrondissement.

Even though they were now living together full time with an extra intimacy imposed by their plans, how much Wolfgang shared with Gisela about his other activities up until this moment isn't clear. Given Ronny Seth's evidence, probably all of it. That summer he'd been deeply involved in an intelligence operation to obtain vital information about the fighter aircraft strafing German troops in the Allied drive towards Paris and the bomber squadrons in the skies above France and Germany.

The operation was a complex web of treachery and betrayal and a number of those involved, including some women, were never properly identified or brought to justice. Wolfgang posed as Jean or John, a French airforce officer who'd been born in America to gather information from downed Allied airmen who thought they were in the hands of a French escape network.

After bailing out of their crippled aircraft or crash landing they were taken in by genuine members of the resistance who risked their lives to shelter them, but at one handover between groups they were passed onto a bogus link in the chain. This false flag operation was often created by the convinced Nazi and SD Agent Jacques Desoubrie, Captain Jacques amongst other aliases, who'd inveigled his way into the real resistance networks posing as a supporter.

He then offered them an apparently successful opportunity for moving the men on to safety. Many of the people who helped to hide aircrew were enthusiastic and brave amateurs or concentrating on more direct acts of resistance and were only too happy to have this option on offer. The whole deception was being run by the Nazi SD and the Secret Police, the Gestapo, with the assistance of the Abwehr.

Similar deceptions were being run in Brussels and Antwerp. In Chartres to the southwest of Paris and in apartments and hotels in the capital like The Piccadilly on the Rue Pigalle, where the glasses-wearing proprietor Louis Gianoni with bad teeth was involved; Wolfgang using his alias, visited the sheltering aircrew there and got information by chatting to them and using the specially prepared "identification" forms.

The use of these, requiring far more detail than a prisoner of war was under a duty to give, was spectacularly successful. Most of the men felt that their continued journey to freedom was dependent on their full cooperation with the people who were helping them. Only a few ever refused to fill them in. As a result, the Germans were often getting near real time information about attacking squadrons and what was most effective in bringing aircraft down.

After the radio checks were supposedly made, the aircrew were collected for the next stage of the journey and then find the vehicle they were travelling in stopped by French police or the Gestapo. In either case, they were driven directly to the Gestapo headquarters on the Avenue Foch in Paris. The fake resistance members accompanying them were always armed with pistols in case of trouble.

There's no evidence Gisela was one of the handful of women involved. Although one of the aircrew, Joe Sonshine, mentioned a tall blonde woman, who was apparently married to a short dark man called de Costa at the place he stayed in Paris at 4 Rue Mendelsohn just before he was taken off into captivity.

The evaders certainly gave a clear and unambiguous description of the American French pilot John or Jean, who told them he'd been born in Pasadena in California and worked at the Lockheed aircraft corporation plant.

It was clearly Wolfgang and he eventually admitted so to Allied interrogators. According to American aircrew, his knowledge of Pasadena was really good. It should have been given that he'd spent far longer there than his entry visa allowed on his espionage mission in 1938/39.

Wolfgang later, and with very good reason, tried to limit his role in this operation by claiming he'd only ever been involved in deceiving about 25 Allied airmen. He also claimed never to have seen the airmen on his own, but always in the company of another German called Schnell, who pretended to be a resistance commander, and sometimes in the company of Draga, the alias of Yugoslav journalist Miodrag Jevremovic, who changed his appearance all the time, dyeing and curling his hair and sometimes wearing glasses. Draga had been working as a German agent in Spain and France since the 1930s. But in any event the bogus escape operation in Paris was so successful that between June and August 1944 several hundred Allied evaders and escapers from Prisoner of War camps were captured in this way after giving up useful information.

Wolfgang was also involved in interrogating some of them at the infamous Gestapo headquarters on the Avenue Foch. He maintained he always played the nice cop, but some of the men detailed their inhumane treatment around this time. They were beaten up and had their identification dog tags ripped off them followed by threats of execution as spies because they'd been captured in civilian clothes.

They were categorised by their Nazi captors not as enemy prisoners of war but as "terror fliers" who were reducing German cities to rubble. The airmen were incarcerated in Fresnes prison, crammed into the small cells. Others held in Fresnes included members of the resistance like Suzanne Spaak, whose portrait was painted by Rene Magritte. She joined the Red Orchestra like the Berlin model Ina Lautenschlager and used her extensive upper class social contacts to provide medical aid for Jews and helped to save the lives of more than 160 Jewish children. She was captured in October 1943 and wouldn't survive what was to come.

As Wolfgang set off for his journey to Reims, 168 of the captured aircrew were taken from Fresnes and marched several miles in the sweltering humidity to a railway goods yard near the Gare de l'Est. Amongst them was an American airman, First Lieutenant Levitt C Beck who'd been flying a Thunderbolt fighter supporting a bombing mission on a bridge over the River Seine to the southwest of Paris. He crash landed after a dog fight with German Focke-Wulf aircraft. His evasion followed the now well-worn route to the Hotel Piccadilly on the Rue Pigalle. He was driven there by the red-haired Madam Antoinette Orsini, alias Collette, the girlfriend of the treacherous Captain Jacques Desoubrie, and along with the others hiding inside was told there had been a change of plan and they were driven straight into the hands of the Gestapo.

At the railway goods yard Levitt Beck and the other prisoners were put into cattle trucks with two buckets, one with water, the other for use as a latrine. Their only views of the outside world were small ventilation hatches in the sides of the wagons with barbed wire stapled across them. Their destination was five days away in hellish conditions. They were not heading for German prisoner of war camps but Buchenwald concentration camp.

Gisela was still relatively free to move around Paris from the Rue Conde apartment on a bicycle she'd borrowed from one of her contacts. Cycling made her just like all the other young Parisian women in a city where the divisions were not just between the occupier and the occupied. The resistance was split into several competing factions of which the two main groups were the Communists and the supporters of the Free French under General de Gaulle. They were arguing about whether there should be an open uprising. Distant gunfire from the battle with the Allies could be clearly heard like summer thunder and there were attacks on German troops and random acts of murder by some troops on passers-by. Despite this, on sunny days the Parisians still headed for the banks of the Seine to sunbathe and sit on the beach that had been specially constructed for the 1937 Exposition.

Gisela retained her German passport, but as well as the bicycling Parisienne she appeared to be, she also had the paperwork to back up this new version of herself. She had a French identity card in her name from the Prefecture of Police. It had been issued a few months before when Les Flics were rather more compliant. It probably came via Oberleutnant Stoll of the Abwehr, the wireless set trainer and procurer of such things. The identity card said she was a secretary and was valid until November 1944. Wolfgang later said that the reason he'd obtained his false identity document from another source was that everyone knew identities provided by the Abwehr came from the French authorities in Paris making them easier to spot. He claimed he'd been told off for getting his on the black market by Oberleutnant Stoll, who offered to get him an officially sanctioned ID.

Having a genuine but potentially suspicious French carte identite was the least of Gisela's concerns. Focussing on the need to lie low and prepare for her new role allowed her to put to the back of her mind an overriding worry. The Abwehr believed that she was going to act as a stay behind agent for them, but there was another more fundamental reason she was planning to avoid the chaos of Germany and find somewhere safe. Even as Wolfgang had set off for Reims on his scouting mission for a new headquarters for Paris Luftwaffe intelligence, there were clear signs that she was in the early stages of pregnancy.

17

LES MISERABLES

FOR GISELA THE stress of having to hide in a city she'd loved can only have been intensified by the new feelings as her body prepared her to carry a baby. Like that decisive moment before she'd jumped from the parachute tower at the 1937 Paris Exposition there may have been an element of excitement alongside the anxiety. A tiny bit of that old delight in the risk of stepping off into the unknown with a new place or new people. Leaping towards an uncertain future with Wolfgang by her side.

Many years and a continent away when she thought she might be near her end she wrote from the heart to her daughter and son:

"I am not afraid of dying nor do I mind it. I am just very tired of all the struggle, the hard work and the insecurity in my life."

Gisela's life up until 1944 had already contained plenty of hard work and struggle but she was undoubtedly entering the most insecure time she would endure. In the 1930s she'd crisscrossed Europe, the Middle East and the United States in a blur of travel. Always moving, working without permission, ready to move again as Germany called on her skills as an expert collector of people and information.

Now she was a stationery target, no longer able to leave malign interest far behind her and the timing couldn't have been worse for a child.

Wolfgang was still a parachute of potentially uncertain material who might well fail to deploy. The pair of them holed up on the Rue Conde were playing a dangerous double game. If it worked, they might still land safely, whatever the outcome of the battle that was heading to the streets around them

There were probably tensions between the pair of them living in the flat in isolated and claustrophobic conditions. The hunger and uncertainty wouldn't have helped. Wolfgang later said he fell out with "Madeleine Fontaine" at his Avenue Niel apartment because she'd become pregnant. After giving her money for an abortion she'd left and he'd never seen her again.

This was probably a later lying riff on the true situation with Gisela at 9 Rue Conde. Some evidence suggests his confidence, to the point of arrogance, in his own abilities, made him think he was going to get the girl, his baby and the "black fund" and ride off into the sunset.

Oberleutnant Krause Brandstetter returned to the city from his scouting expedition for a new Luftwaffe intelligence headquarters on the 17th of August. He'd found a small castle, the Chateau de Thugny-Trugny, which suited the Luftwaffe unit's purposes, sited on the line of retreat to the north east of Reims. Once back in Paris he could see the whole place was rapidly descending into chaos. There was a palpable sensation that something was going to happen and it wouldn't be good if you were German.

The Paris police were still on strike and had, like the general resistance, divided themselves into competing factions of Gaullists, Socialists and Communists. The Metro workers were also on strike and the acts of opposition were growing bolder. Mainline railway workers were hindering train movements as the Germans attempted to ship themselves and looted art treasures back to the Fatherland.

General Dietrich von Cholitz didn't have the men or equipment to mount an effective defence of Paris and he knew it. In the meantime, he was talking to people he thought could help to influence the population and keep things calm while non-fighting elements of the occupying forces left and the wider German retreat from the advancing Allies could route through the city safely.

The Abwehr at the Hotel Lutetia and the Luftwaffe intelligence unit at the Roger and Gallet building were burning their records before making their escape. The smoke and charred scraps from the pyres of papers and files floating over the city were a scorched echo of the scenes as the Germans had arrived in 1940 and the French had burned their secrets.

Reporting back to his unit on the Faubourg St Honore, Wolfgang was ordered to be ready to leave for Reims in a few hours. This didn't fit in with his and Gisela's plans at all. He later maintained he'd written a letter to his Commanding Officer saying he still had his packing to do and he would leave the city the following morning using his own transport.

Wolfgang also claimed he'd composed a second secret letter to his superior telling him that he was in fact going to stay behind as part of the plan they'd already discussed. In what capacity or why never became clear in his British file and some British intelligence officers doubted he revealed his intentions in this way at all.

Assuming he was telling the truth about the second letter it seems likely that he was covering himself in a specific way. Perhaps not as a stay behind agent like Gisela but something rather more daring in line with his suggestion to Ronny Seth that he wanted to go to Britain on a mission. He may have been suggesting he was planning to become a double agent.

The available evidence shows what had the makings of a very neat plan which covered both him and Gisela whatever happened. One would stay put and the other hedge their bets.

As the Germans made their escape from Paris, staff cars could be seen jammed to the gills with everything from carpets to wine. Lorries with troops clutching loot in the back rumbled through and a soldier in one opened fire on a group of Parisians who were standing watching the conquerors leave with their tails between their legs.

Life in the city continued in spite of the surrounding drama. It had to, people needed to eat and sleep, and it being Paris, love and hate. Gisela joined the other women on foot or on their bicycles hunting for any meagre supplies. The rumour mills and the concierge of their building ever alert for opportunities that sent everyone rushing for the pitifully small amounts that were available, often now only turnips. Wolfgang and Gisela had access to French ration cards, either some of the many fakes available or official ones, but even having secured some food the ability to cook it was severely limited by the lack of gas and electricity. On the banks of the Seine old men fished, hoping for a plump Perch to provide a meal.

The fuse for the bomb that would engulf them all was lit two days after Wolfgang's return. Police officers seized a massive prefecture building near the Cathedral of Notre Dame on the Ile de la Cite and began singing the Marseillaise. The French Tricolor was hauled up on the roof. The move had been triggered by elements within the divided force who supported General De Gaulle.

The resistance also began to act. Posters were stuck up on walls urging a general mobilisation against the Germans in the name of the French republic. Citroen Traction Avant cars with the Cross of\ Lorraine or FFI (French Forces of the Interior) painted roughly in white on the sides began to speed about the streets. The insurrection spread out as groups of resistance men and women without uniforms operated more openly. They were identified only by makeshift armbands, and some didn't even have those.

Local government buildings were seized and the resistance

began, despite very limited weapons and resources, to prepare Paris for liberation by the advancing Allied armies.

The uprising had begun way too early. General De Gaulle was still urging the Supreme Allied Commander General Eisenhower to take the city in direct contradiction of the existing strategic plans which intended to bypass it altogether. The rationale was simple. Paris would swallow soldiers and resources and thousands of tons of food a week for the hungry population which it would be the responsibility of the Allies to provide.

Gisela and Wolfgang's life together in the flat on the Rue Conde was frozen in a moment when it could go either way. In one direction the Germans attacked in force and wiped out the poorly organised and badly armed resistance and in the other the Allies arrived and Dietrich von Cholitz chose to obey Hitler's command that Paris should be turned into a field of ruins around them.

Even as the city's fate hung in the balance there was a touch of performance about the activities on the streets. Some Parisians were recording snatched scenes of the unfolding drama on both still and film cameras. Young men and women posed looking heroic with their rifles, pistols or British mass-produced Sten sub machine guns.

German soldiers made several abortive attempts to storm the Prefecture containing the rebel police officers, taking casualties and leaving a blazing lorry behind in the process. It was only a kilometre away from the apartment at Rue Conde and the intense bursts of rifle fire and machine guns around the Prefecture would have been an alarm call to Gisela and Wolfgang that the most dangerous phase was beginning.

Later as barricades began to spring up on the streets, at the corner of the Boulevard St Michel and the Boulevard Saint German a group of appreciative onlookers watched resistance fighters behind a defence made of ripped up street cobbles and sandbags. They shot up any Germans and their vehicles that strayed into range. Lobbing petrol bombs at troops and less effectively at tanks. As the bullets began to fly the audience took shelter before re-emerging. Seeing and being seen were still an essential part of the city's culture.

But not all the French in Paris were looking forward to liberation from the Germans. While the ranks of the fighters on the streets would soon be joined by those desperate to be on the winning side, derisively called the "August resistance", the Milice, the French fascist militia were still fighting alongside the Germans. French right wingers who'd either directly or tacitly collaborated hid in their homes or fled, fearful of the reprisals threatened by the posters that had issued the call to arms.

It was just a question of whether the Allies would get to Paris before the rebellion was destroyed for lack of ammunition, if not courage.

The Swedish Consul in the city, Raoul Nordling was playing a role as an intermediary between some parts of the resistance leadership and General Cholitz who alternated between describing those rebelling as terrorists and taking a more placatory position. A ceasefire was actually agreed although it was honoured more in the breach. Some parts of the resistance refused to comply and army and SS units retreating through Paris unaware of and certainly unsympathetic to any ceasefire, shot civilians whether they were resisting or not.

Through the cooling open windows of their apartment Gisela and Wolfgang could have heard the constant dissonance of war. It was too dangerous to peer out. There were snipers operating in the city and nervy members of the FFI were capable of firing indiscriminately at people in windows they thought might be armed members of the Milice. In more than one instance the resistance stormed apartment buildings where snipers were thought to be and killed the completely innocent.

In the far distance the couple could hear the low grumble of heavy artillery. Much nearer the crack of rifles and chatter of sub machine guns, then the squeals and clatter of tank tracks and thrumming of lorry tyres on the cobbles from the German garrison at the nearby Luxembourg Palace and Gardens.

The days of waiting for limited but always disturbing information, and the mental strain of endless private or shared worries must have made the time they spent at 9 Rue Conde seem endless. They'd gone from the victors to the hunted, knowing that the city they'd enjoyed and loved could go the same way as Warsaw. There the Germans destroyed museums, art galleries, theatres, churches and historic buildings as a vicious and pointless reprisal following an uprising by the Polish resistance.

It was the prospect of another Warsaw and entreaties from De Gaulle that led to the change of heart by the Allies. Hitler had ordered General Cholitz to defend Paris and maintain it as a strategic part of his plans to bring the fight back to the Allies. The corpulent and monocle-wearing Cholitz was cannier than the cartoon German general he appeared to be. Even as he blustered, he knew he would be on trial for what happened to the City of Light and it was more likely that those judging him would be speaking French and English than German.

Although he made the preparations to blow bridges over the Seine, he didn't give the go-ahead while still maintaining that he was "only a little General. I receive orders. I execute them." Although his reports back to the German High Command, in common with many other commanders, gave the appearance of adhering strictly to the strategy demanded by the Fuhrer. He was playing a difficult double game and he wasn't the only German doing so.

Gisela and Wolfgang were way ahead of him. Wolfgang had his black fund nest egg of gold and silver coins sitting in the safe of a Parisian lawyer and Gisela was armed with something just as effective as hard cash, which must have given her a degree of confidence despite the precarious situation and the worries about the coming baby. She had brains which she could hide at will behind her charm and looks that caused most men to massively underestimate her.

The signal for the start of their operation came 10 wearying and hungry days after Wolfgang returned to Paris and they'd gone into hiding. The bourdon Emmanuel, the largest and most historic of the bells of Notre Dame Cathedral rang out to announce the Allies were in the city. Notre Dame was joined by the bells of Sacre Coeur on the Montmartre hill along with a chorus from other churches.

The French were allowed by Eisenhower to provide the spearhead of the assault on Paris alongside American troops. General Philippe Leclerc de Hautecloque who'd previously described his American allies as "bastards" for not giving him the go-ahead, led the Deuxieme Division Blindee into the city on the night of the 24th of August. He ignored orders on his direction of attack and ran into some stiff pockets of German resistance and lost tanks and 300 men.

The news of the arrival of the Allied troops spread quickly although the church bells were premature. There was hard fighting at various German strongpoints including the Luxembourg Gardens. It wasn't until the afternoon of the 25th that General Cholitz formally surrendered and began his later and largely successful PR campaign to portray himself as the saviour of Paris.

It still wasn't safe for the couple at Rue Conde. On the streets the celebrations were intense. To such a degree that the Catholic Church felt the need to make it clear via pamphlets that women and girls should save themselves and their bodies for marriage. But the joy was mixed with equal if not greater levels of savagery and revenge.

The author and broadcaster Malcolm Muggeridge was on

hand to witness the scenes. He was due to liaise with French Intelligence as one the very few British Military Intelligence officers in the city at this stage. At Wolfgang's former accommodation the Hotel Scribe, Muggeridge saw the writer and personification of macho, Ernest Hemingway, hung about with hand grenades, "like monstrous pearls", holding an alcohol fuelled court of his admirers. The Liberation of Paris and its vicious aftermath was just the sort of wild west show Hemingway adored.

Muggeridge then encountered another intelligence officer, Victor Rothschild, and they set themselves up in some comfort in the Rothschild Parisian mansion on the Avenue Marigny where only a short time before, Luftwaffe General Hanesse had been living and entertaining Gisela and Wolfgang.

After enjoying a Paris that was anxious to show the Allies its friendship and wipe the slate clean, Muggeridge and Rothschild finally formally reported for duty just a five minute walk away at Hanesse's former HQ at the Roger and Gallet building on Faubourg St Honore.

During the day Gisela, if not Wolfgang, would have been able to venture out onto the streets but the Paris police understandably, were still keeping a low profile until it was absolutely clear who was in charge.

"It was when darkness began to fall that one became aware of the breakdown; with no street lighting and the tall houses all silent and locked and boarded up, like sightless eyes." Muggeridge recorded. "Inside them I imagined cowering figures, hopeful of surviving if they remained perfectly still and hidden".

Muggeridge met and accompanied one of the many bands of the French Forces of the Interior who were roaming the city. He watched them take valuable objects from people and could never work out if they were just a criminal gang or whether some patriotic intentions lay behind their actions which included forced searches of property and, they liked to boast, summary executions. He heard later that the leader of the group had a history of collaboration.

Two days after the German collapse in Paris with more than 10,000 German prisoners taken and in excess of 4,000 dead, Wolfgang, wearing civilian clothes, ventured out onto the streets. He left Gisela and the apartment at 9 Rue Conde and made his way across the River Seine. He was heading to a flat on the Faubourg St Honore. The well-connected de Brion publishing family had arranged a meeting with Allied officers from T Force, a specialist unit created to hoover up information and people likely to be useful in the continuing war with Germany.

In what became an almost obligatory statement from most Germans, Wolfgang explained to the four Allied officers who arrived to interrogate him that he'd never been in sympathy with the Nazis but more than that had actually maintained contacts with the resistance through the de Brions and a Dominican Priest, Father Raymond Bruckberger who had been imprisoned by the Germans but then released. He certainly had maintained contacts with the resistance in the fraudulent escape line operation but not quite in the way he was suggesting to the people he was now intending to serve.

If Wolfgang was hoping to ingratiate himself with the members of T Force's air intelligence section, he wasn't entirely successful.

> *Probably the real reason for his remaining is a girl with whom he has been living and the fact that his personal comfort would be greater here than in Germany. P/W (Prisoner of War) is a weak character. He is a willing talker especially if he is given good treatment and special considerations. It is highly probable that he knows a great deal more than he has thus far divulged.*

Wolfgang went on to give the Allied intelligence officers details about the organisation of Luftwaffe intelligence, agents codenames although very few if any real identities, and said he'd seen some messages from a female agent based in Britain who went by the German codename Tramp.

One report from her recorded the explosion of a VI "doodlebug" flying bomb near Marble Arch and another described "grey" tanks passing by in a different location.

This linked him and Gisela once again to the head of the Abwehr's Hotel Lutetia operation, Emil Klieman who ran Tramp and also organised stay behind agents in France. What none of them knew at this stage was that Tramp was also a British agent named Treasure, used as part of an operation run by the Twenty Committee – so called because the Roman numerals for 20 are XX standing for double cross – which had deceived the Germans about the intended landing sites on D-Day.

It was perhaps the information about Tramp who had a role in misinforming the Germans about the location of flying bomb hits, to introduce inaccuracies into their ranging, that led one officer to make an observation in a letter in Wolfgang Brandstetter's file:

"Krause Brandstetter is singularly well informed concerning Abwehr activities, and for reasons which I will explain to you when I deliver this letter certain of this information is of a highly delicate character which necessitates very limited distribution."

After two days of questioning Wolfgang was formally arrested at 11.30 on the morning of the 29th of August. It was noted despite being dressed as a civilian he did have a uniform and military identification available which afforded him the protection of the Geneva Convention covering the treatment of prisoners of war. A treaty the Germans had completely ignored with the 168 air crew sent to Buchenwald concentration camp. Two of those airmen died there from the maltreatment they received - the American fighter pilot,

Lieutenant Beck who contracted pneumonia, and the sole survivor of a British bomber crew, Flying Officer Phillip Hemmings. The others were eventually transferred to a Prisoner of War camp after Göring was alerted to what the SD and Gestapo had done.

Wolfgang was searched by the officers who arrested him and the items he had were carefully listed. Some, like the membership card of the German tennis club in Paris, reflected the joys of the occupation for those lucky enough to get a posting.

Like Gisela he had a French identity card. Bearing the serial number 1835 it was apparently issued by the Prefecture de L'yonne, based in Auxerre, 170 kilometres to the southeast of Paris. His false name and details were Bernard Albert Werbecque, born the 2nd of October 1910 in Pasadena, California. The place that John or Jean had talked about to the Allied evaders and Wolfgang had given as his destination during the 1938 espionage trip to America.

This was the ID he said he'd obtained from Father Bruckberger, his claimed resistance contact. Bruckberger was indeed the Chaplain to the FFI, and was seen moving about the city in his smoke and bloodstained white habit as he tended to the wounded and dying of the resistance during the liberation, but he was also reported to have close links to Joseph Darnand, the fascist who'd created the Milice who was credited with saving his life after he'd been captured by the Germans for resistance activities. It's not clear how he came to be supplying fake identities to Abwehr Officer Wolfgang and on what basis.

Wolfgang also had with him a red leather pocketbook and diary which contained some notes of interrogations of Allied aircrew, and a label for a uniform with the name Rolf Brandstetter, Soldat Feldpost No 03188. Another potential disguise allowing him to become a basic soldier in the German forces.

It must have been an agony of waiting for Gisela, not knowing whether the plan was working and constantly fearing that it hadn't.

Every hour that passed without Allied troops or the FFI kicking the doors in and arresting her allowed hope to continue.

In all Wolfgang underwent three field interrogations by officers from T Force before he was shipped back to Britain for further questioning and assessment. He was identified as highly useful to the continuing war effort. During these bouts of questioning, he revealed Gisela's existence in the city and where she was in hiding. He was clearly keen to play down her role. Perhaps he was hoping she would be afforded good treatment or perhaps he was aware that the Allied officers weren't warming to him sufficiently and felt the need to offer them someone else.

A summary of Wolfgang's interrogations and the information he gave, prepared by staff at the Headquarters of T Force of the 12th Army Group on the 29th of August, the day of his arrest, has her as item No 7 on one of its pages.

> *P/W's mistress is KLEIN, Gisella Hendrika.(Sic) She is a German citizen (mother was Dutch) and has French identity papers valid until November.*
>
> *She will be found at the flat of JACQUES de BRION, 9 Rue Conde. The French (Commandant HAYES) have been informed and will deal with the matter tomorrow.*

Gisela's fate had apparently been sealed but, as so often in the past, things would not be quite so straight forward. Gisela would not be sitting meekly in the apartment of Jacques de Brion awaiting her fate. She'd already taken matters into her own hands. She was never one to willingly hide her light under a bushel and she wasn't going to start now.

18

THE KLEIN AFFAIR

IN EARLY SEPTEMBER 1944, Paris was without effective law and order and particularly justice as the "wild purge" continued but money and connections could still get you a good meal.

Gisela was back in her favourite haunts once again. It seemed that, armed with her French identity and with a stack of useful Parisian contacts, life might be about to turn a significant corner. The city had only suffered relatively minor damage and the activity on the streets suggested civilisation was returning to normal even if it was all a thin veneer.

Gisela could count her blessings. She had survived the liberation, the lack of food, and what she must have been hoping, was the temporary loss of Wolfgang. She was out on the most famous street in Paris where the Germans had marched in victory in 1940 and the French and the Americans had done the same only days before.

She was going to mark her 29th Birthday on the following day and she must have been enjoying the food that was brought by the same waiters who'd served her during the occupation in one of the many restaurants on the Champs Elysees. *Le faim est le meilleur condiment*, as the French put it. Hunger is the best sauce.

Her table companion(s) at this meal aren't known. It seems

improbable given her extensive address book that she was eating alone. It may have been Anne Buydens or Petra Kilka, a German actress whom she knew, or it could have been any of the Parisians she knew. These included the actor and film director Jean de Limur, who said he met her at the Ritz, where the Abwehr had their own table, and considered her for a film part, or the French fighter pilot and Vichy Deputy of the French Parliament Count Jean de Beaumont. In his case it was a further coincidence that the Abwehr Officer Emil Klieman told British intelligence that he'd thought about utilising some former French pilots who volunteered themselves to Carl Friedrich Hanesse and had been referred to him by Friedrich Siegler von Eberswald. Gisela linked them all.

During this meal a group of armed *fifis* (FFI) entered the restaurant. There must have been a moment of gnawing fear which killed her appetite completely when she saw them and hoped they'd come for someone else. The dining room went quiet. There were plenty of others eating at the tables who had something to hide. Accusations saw people swept up who'd done nothing or just provided the Germans with basic services. Gisela's fear turned to terror as they checked her papers and decided to arrest her. She wouldn't have been hard to spot from her description. Perhaps one of the aproned waiters or waitresses remembered the "striking" woman from a recent time when her companions were wearing what was now the wrong uniform.

Taken outside by the men as other diners averted their gazes or stared at her in contempt it was likely here that she was tied to a tree. Something she told her daughter about, although when she did so, she said it was because her papers weren't in order.

Gisela was used to being looked at. She relied on it to a degree but this was completely different. The most public humiliation possible on a street where she'd worked and led a busy social life. Eyewitnesses of the abuse of the women paraded in public and accused of collaboration spoke of the hunted animal fear in their eyes as they were subjected to public scorn and abuse.

Passersby would have jeered at the blonde Bosche, calling her a bitch or a whore or making a deliberate point of not looking at her, as they'd done to the occupying German troops. She was being led to the chaotic factories of revenge and retribution which blindly processed everyone fed into them.

Elsewhere in the city Malcolm Muggeridge dined with a senior French officer and Coco Chanel. She'd ensured that American GIs got free bottles of Chanel perfume immediately after the liberation, a PR stunt that was a measure of her guile. After witnessing the tough but physically slight couturier in her element, Muggeridge concluded that no matter how small the millstones of revenge ground, they would never grind her. He was right. She fled the accusations of "collaboration horizontale" for her work for the Nazi SD and took off for Switzerland and her Abwehr lover Gunther von Dincklage.

It was only eight days since Gisela and Wolfgang had said goodbye to each other. At first it seemed to have gone well. The de Brions had kept her informed and she knew he'd been arrested and she thought he was probably helping the Americans. The officer who'd led the initial interrogation team was a Major Walter Hochschild from the United States.

She'd been seen by Police Commandant Hayes from the Petit Palais and clearly used her highly developed social skills on him. He apparently told her to come back in four days. She then, at his suggestion, typed out a detailed chronology of her life and movements. Her French file said that with the help of the de Brion family she'd also been to see the American military authorities and been released by them. It meant she must have thought her bases were now fully covered with both the French and the Americans.

Something changed that. It may have been no more than bad luck. There was no effective coordination between the competing authorities within Paris which meant that she'd joined the thousands incarcerated on the basis of allegations, often anonymous, which coupled with no effective record keeping meant that charges were often completely unknown by both the captors and captives. At the very least she'd been identified as the consort of a German intelligence officer.

Her British file suggests that the FFI took her to Fresnes Prison. If the hellhole where the captured Allied aircrew had been maltreated, and where Suzanne Spaak was murdered in her cell by a Gestapo officer just under a month before, was terrible under the Germans, it was as bad if not worse now.

Malcolm Muggeridge visited the jail as part of his intelligence duties and met a prisoner who'd also been there under the Germans. The man told him bitterly that it had been like life in a Chateau before.

The 67-year-old industrialist and vehicle manufacturer Louis Renault, accused of collaboration, died after allegations he'd been beaten in Fresnes at this time. A nun said she'd seen him hit on the head by a warder wielding a steel helmet. A later post mortem examination showed a fractured vertebrae in his neck.

Gisela's French file in the Paris Archives covering this period paints a different picture of what happened to her. It says that after being taken from the restaurant on the Champs Elysees she was held at what seems to have been a makeshift FFI office on the Rue Paquet in Paris for five days. It doesn't mention Fresnes. What happened to her there isn't known but there is little doubt she was not treated well, no one else was. She never spoke of it afterwards and ignoring and compartmentalising terrible memories was a common reaction to trauma for a whole generation in the Second World War. The only other thing she told her daughter was that she'd been so hungry during this period that she'd re-eaten a piece of bread she'd vomited, presumably from morning sickness.

Either there or elsewhere she was interrogated. Her French files contain two transcripts of her answers to the questioning. There were many more unrecorded interrogations.

In the first questioning session, a Captain Marin asked why she'd created the document she'd titled Curriculum Vitae. She must have been carrying it with her or there'd been searches of the flat at 9 Rue Conde or her official home at 4 Rue Clement Marot.

She replied that Commandant Hayes of the Petit Palais asked her to produce it.

The policeman had done her a favour. It was a very useful crib sheet and allowed her to skate neatly over a couple of potential issues about her activities before the war and the occupation.

This document, which also gives a list of people who could provide references, is retained in her French file. In it she says she was working in fashion in the UK throughout 1934 and makes no mention at all of the lengthy return that year to Germany to look after her "sick mother", which seems most likely to be the time that she was formally recruited and trained by the Abwehr which gave her access to travel documents and the freedom to move around.

She also gave a conflicting account to the French report on her reasons for leaving Paris and her flat on the Rue Copernic in September 1938 to travel to Italy, where she'd had her passport renewed. She claimed this time it was because she'd lost her documents allowing her to stay in France. No mention of marriage or fear about hostilities or concentration camps, or for that matter the further trip to Cairo in 1938 she told Jakey Astor she was making.

Fortunately for Gisela the French interrogators were completely unaware of any of this and in any case had other interests. They were only concerned with her activities and connections in Paris and the possibility of other Germans hiding in the city.

Her file titled 'Affaire Klein' seems to show an unnatural speech style in the typed records of the questions and answers. They were probably produced from notes afterwards by the secretary who was present for some of the interrogations.

She was asked about the Germans she'd known in Paris and named the niece of General von Stulpnagel and a couple of others who were connected to the July plot to kill Hitler. She clearly felt she needed to burnish her anti-Nazi credentials. She was backed up on this by one of her French referees who said she "detested" the Nazis, although he'd been involved in the *Archiv der Gegenwart* operation and so had an interest in saying this.

In the first interview dated to the day of her arrest, the 4th of September 1944 she was also briefly questioned about two women. One was a Spanish national called Madame Villa Ceballos, who later admitted to the same interrogators that she was a mistress of Joachim von Tresckow, Luftwaffe officer and a Director of the Heinkel Aircraft Company. Gisela said she'd met her at one of two possible social occasions. Ceballos was questioned as to whether Tresckow had ever used her to deposit large sums of money, which she denied.

The question that seemed to be most significant to the interrogator – because the record showed Gisela hesitated before answering – was, as mentioned, about Madame Moutafolo or Melita Stullenberg the textile black marketeer and SD agent who informed on resistors in Belgium.

Gisela said she'd been to stay with her for the weekend but was very vague about the details..

In the second interrogation two days later, she is once again asked about her weekend chez Moutafolo. The interrogator is aware of her pregnancy because he asks:

"How were you during your stay…?"

"I was fine although a little tired," Gisela replied. "I rested for about an hour in the afternoon."

It wasn't exactly a serious cross examination and didn't discover Gisela's employment by ROGES or that her connection to Melita Stullenberg undoubtedly involved intelligence gathering, although Gisela's connection to the world of fashion also chimed with Stullenberg's black market textile operation.

She was pressed about her access to bank accounts and various people but the second interview didn't produce any real information. However, there was an unexpected turn to the events unfolding in the interrogation room. This is revealed in a separate note on the end of the page from Captain Marin and records a different conversation altogether:

Marin says:

"At one point in the questioning I got the secretary to leave and had the following conversation with Klein".

Making the secretary leave must have made the situation much more threatening and possibly the precursor to violence. Gisela was alone with this man and perhaps others. The record claims the conversation went like this.

"As you are aware many Germans are still at large in Paris," Marin said. They both knew what he was talking about. German stay-behind agents and saboteurs.

"Are you now prepared to help us find them?" Her reply came after a few "simulated tears".

"Yes, I promise to do everything I can, but is it dangerous?"

Marin answered, "We will take you under your protection."

Her reply, "I am entirely at your disposal."

This exchange has the stilted air of the sort of the "verbal" confessions British police officers used to claim had occurred when villains "confessed" in the back of the police car on the way to the station. Even so, Gisela had no real choice and whether her tears were simulated as suggested by the cynical Captain Marin is debatable. She was pregnant, and in the hands of the French who had every reason to despise her. Her lover was gone and she was alone and fending for herself. She was a quick thinker and knew her presumed knowledge of Germans hiding in Paris gave her a chance.

The film director, screenwriter and actor Jean De Limur provided this assessment of her to French intelligence:

"I think she's extremely resourceful whatever the situation. I think she's an intelligent girl but she's more into the worldly and easygoing side of things. She's a very international girl, the kind of girl you find all over the world. She's perfectly capable of espionage but I've never noticed evidence of it."

Around this time and on the basis she was now working for the other side, her files indicate she was transferred into the hands of the Service Speciaux, which was the Free French intelligence unit, formed under General De Gaulle. Malcolm Muggeridge was attached to them as a liaison officer.

The unfortunately abbreviated SS, which appeared on the number plates of the unit's cars, was soon the subject of ridicule and the name was changed to the Directorat General des Etudes et Recherches.

The DGER took over a series of Art Deco buildings on the salubrious Boulevard Suchet, previously the headquarters of the German Navy, the Kriegsmarine. As Gisela began the task of trying to help the French catch other Germans lying low in Paris, as far as the French were concerned there was still no really solid link between her and the Abwehr operation in Paris. The only thing the French had was that her lover was an Abwehr officer who was helping the Allies with their inquiries. She clearly knew a lot of the German occupation forces and therefore could be helpful but overall she was just a pretty, pregnant blonde socialite, who might be of some use while they chased the important people.

That view should have changed. The information that could have done it wasn't obtained in Paris but from the village of Arkley 10 miles north of London. Arkley View was a large house which in 1939 became the location of the Radio Security Service with the enigmatic postal address Post Box 25.

It was the centre of the British interception of the Abwehr's coded wireless traffic by a chain of listening units called Y stations and also by volunteers who monitored enemy Morse code transmissions.

The encoded messages collected from the frequencies the Abwehr were using were sent to Arkley View and then forwarded via teleprinter to Bletchley Park, which had developed from a codebreaking cottage industry at the beginning of the war to a large industrial cypher-breaking complex employing some 9,000 people. Bletchley read the Abwehr's messages from 1941.

Bletchley decrypted a chain of messages beginning on the 6th of September 1944 showing the Abwehr's continued interest in Wolfgang Krause Brandstetter. On that day there's a transmission from Berlin to the Abwehr headquarters in Wiesbaden saying that he is required for an "urgent and special mission" and saying he should be dispatched in person at once to "Belinde." This was the Abwehr codename for Schlosss Baruth, an Abwehr Headquarters 70 miles to the south of Berlin.

Wiesbaden reports back that Wolfgang has been missing since the 19th of August in Paris where he'd been with the permission of his commanding officer to settle personal affairs. The message referred to a separate report that also said he was missing.

Then there's a message from Westerwald which had been the Paris codename but which must have been in use by the elements of the Luftwaffe Abwehr who'd retreated to Reims. It was sent to

Berlin on the 10th of September and said that nothing was known about his whereabouts.

This triggered a return wireless transmission from Berlin to the Luftwaffe Abwehr HQ in Wiesbaden. The Bletchley Park decrypt reads:

"Secret. Are the whereabouts of Oberltn Krause Brandstetter known (has anything been done in the way of investigations?) Is there AFU link with Gisela (Klein?-text doubtful?)."

This was the smoking gun which showed a number of important things. It proved the Abwehr/SD in Berlin knew about Gisela's separate and continuing presence in Paris after the liberation and they viewed her as having a stay behind role. The reference to AFU is the Abwehr acronym for Agentenfunk in German, which means Agent Radio.

This Bletchley Park decrypt prompted MI5's Captain J E B Hill from the B1B section to write:

"This is the first positive evidence that Klein is connected, other than by emotional ties, with the GIS (German intelligence services) There has, however, never been any indication that she knows enough about wireless to operate as a stay behind W/T (wireless transmitter) agent herself."

Given that large numbers of the SOE wireless operators in Europe were female this seems rather too dismissive especially as Wolfgang under later interrogation linked Gisela to Oberleutnant Stoll, the Paris Abwehr radio trainer and provider of fake identity documents. Captain Hill goes on to give this assessment of her.

"Her activities for the last ten years are certainly consistent with a high level of espionage although hitherto it has been impossible to say definitely that she is more than a widely travelled and remarkably well befriended adventuress."

This comment is followed by a further note on the British Klein file from the lawyer and intelligence officer Helenus "Buster" Milmo.

"I spoke to the war room, Mr. Roberts, concerning Klein. He has already signalled Paris this further information. There is no further action we can take."

There is no evidence in Gisela Klein's French file that this information in any form at all ever reached the DGER intelligence officers holding her at the Boulevard Suchet where she was detained in an improvised prison. Although the British in Paris were told, there was at this time an absolute embargo on revealing the existence of the Ultra decrypts of the German Enigma code machines to the Free French who were not seen as trustworthy. There were even difficulties disseminating Ultra intelligence to British units who had French liaison officers. The information about her could only have come from reading coded Abwehr radio traffic and British intelligence were not going to blow the most important and closely guarded secret of the war over Gisela, no matter what she'd been up to.

In any case they knew through British liaison she'd already agreed to help the French intelligence officers, and they had Wolfgang helping them. So all the bases seem to have been covered.

There's only one reference to the assistance that Gisela provided to French intelligence. This comes in the form of a handwritten report which assesses her usefulness. It seems to be dated to sometime in November or December 1944. The assessment of her says firmly:

"Gisela Klein is not a known German informer at the spy agency. (presumably Abwehr)."

This seems to miss the point about Gisela activities altogether and naturally it doesn't mention information contained in the Bletchley Park decrypt at all. After giving a brief summary of her life including the visits to Britain and her modelling, the author remarks that she's an anti-Nazi and despite her fiancé being a prisoner of war the inquiries discovered no suspicious activities.

The author's sympathies are very clear.

"She is a pretty and elegant woman" And he, and it is undoubtedly a man, reaches two conclusions after suggesting she is something of a social butterfly with a taste for the high life:

"It appears certain, after long inquiries and interviews that she's not been involved in any form of espionage….and: She is four months pregnant and she accepts that in the matter of our 'Heinis' she doesn't actually know anything about Germans living in Paris."

Basic security dictated German stay behind agents wouldn't know about each other and there is of course no mention of her intelligence or the clear assessment of the film producer Jean de Limur that she was "extremely resourceful" or indeed her prewar activities and high level connections in Britain and France that had been referenced by Captain Hill of MI5.

She'd been both skilful and very lucky. She'd fallen neatly into the information gap between the French and the British. This coupled with her charm and beauty and the natural compassion on the part of the officers interviewing her over her pregnancy, all worked in her favour, but it wasn't to be the end of her problems.

19

FRENCH WITH TEARS

THE LIBERATION OF Paris meant the population wasn't actually starving anymore but if the people hoped there would be a quick return to much better times those hopes were dashed.

In October 1944 the *Manchester Guardian* listed the food available for a family of three in the city. No milk at all except for children under three years of age; 3 ounces of butter a month; one egg a week; 3 ounces of meat a week per person; 10 ounces of bread a day.

Pregnant women need extra calories especially in the later stages and whatever the Parisians were getting, Gisela was getting far less. For her the misery of hunger and incarceration only intensified as she faced imprisonment in the severe cold of a winter of freezing temperatures that blanketed the city in snow as a bleak Christmas turned into a frostbitten January. The accompanying freezing fogs kept aircraft grounded and helped Hitler's desperate and doomed gamble with an armoured German assault though the hills and forests of the Ardennes to try to reach the port of Antwerp and split the Allied forces heading for Germany.

In Paris there was virtually no fuel for heating, barges that should have delivered it were frozen in, and coal supplies were limited to three sacks for a family for the whole winter. Gas for cooking or hot water was only available for a few hours a day. Some of the "auxiliary" guards at Fresnes prison ran a lucrative sideline in extra clothing for inmates who were freezing in their cells.

Gisela kept a special memento of the eight long months she spent in captivity in Paris. It obviously meant a great deal to her. It was an unusual letter and an act of kindness from someone who claimed not to know her at all and who signed himself Wladimir Zoliwski. He gives his address as Room 31, of wherever she was being held. It could have been Fresnes or Fort de Charenton, where she was imprisoned alongside other political prisoners, or the makeshift jail at Boulevard Suchet or finally and most likely a mental asylum on the Rue Tolbiac in Paris which seems to have been pressed into service as a prison for her.

"This letter is going to surprise you. It is not J.J. who writes it but a friend. You have never seen me and I have never seen you [...] he told me to open all letters that came for him and this is the answer."

It's not clear who JJ was and the writer reports he has been moved to another location. Gisela's mystery correspondent offers to get letters sent to people outside and goes on to suggest who she should contact to try to arrange for her transfer to a place he calls Hausman where she could be seen and looked after by the American Red Cross, "before you go to the maternitee." He sent her a little money or food and tries to cheer her up:

"Do not worry too much and keep smiling yourself, the things are never as bad as they seem and it's in the long run the end of things that matters."

He said he would try to arrange for her to get a food parcel every now and then and concludes:

"This correspondence in prison between two people who have never seen each other is quite a strange thing but with great charm."

She was now heavily pregnant and this act of kindness obviously touched her very deeply.

Her French contacts also tried to help her. These included the fighter pilot and French Parliamentary Deputy Jean De Beaumont who'd been swept up for collaboration along with tens of thousands of others around the same time she'd been arrested at the restaurant on the Champs Elysees.

He was later freed and alongside the De Brion family finally came up trumps for her.

This is recorded in a document for the Military Government of Paris, 5th Bureaux dated around March 1945 which said these people presented "the beautiful Klein" as someone at odds with the politics of her own country and as an anti-Nazi. It says the de Brions had been pressing for her to be transferred to a maternity clinic and they dismissed her multiple connections to other German intelligence officers as "friends of her fiancé".

The report says it was difficult to really ascertain Gisela's true feelings towards France but…

"It seems we can trust the families in question who have signed their respective declarations and confirmed them in writing."

It was the bureaucratic equivalent of a Gallic shrug of the shoulders and suggests she should be sent to a clinic under surveillance until a final conclusion to her case could be reached.

Gisela gave birth to her baby son at a maternity clinic at 36 Cours Vincennes in the 12th arrondissement of Paris on the 16th of May 1945.

The files don't reveal if Wolfgang knew about the safe delivery of his child at the time, although he did later. His attempts to go over to the Allies were not quite as successful as he'd hoped. Despite providing them with a large amount of information about the Abwehr's activities in Paris including both accurate and misleading details about Gisela, he remained vague enough about some information to make them suspect he was holding out. This was confirmed during the bugged meeting with his former mentor John Holroyd Reece where he admitted as much.

Wolfgang was busy during his captivity. He made attempts to become involved with the Political Information Department of the Foreign Office, which was based at the British Broadcasting Corporation's Bush House at the Aldwych in London. The PID was a cover name for the Political Warfare Executive which was running various propaganda radio stations and broadcasts aimed at the German army and public. It was the British equivalent of the German Foreign Office unit he'd been working for in Paris as the "English Expert" before it was disbanded over the plot against Ribbentrop.

He was also interviewed by the American Office of Strategic Services, the intelligence service which was the forerunner of the CIA and by the United States Office of War Information, another propaganda unit. The OSS seem to have approved of him and although there were concerns he might be a double agent, at least on the British side, he was used for at least one propaganda broadcast to Germany by the Americans which was recorded at the Levy Studios on New Bond Street in London.

The British distrust of Wolfgang was growing. A member of the Political Information Department writing from Bush House refers to a negative report on him and goes on to say:

"I have not mentioned anything to the Americans who used this turn."

That report was summarised in his file by Lieutenant Colonel Vivian Home Seymer of MI5. It refers to Wolfgang and another German Prisoner of War called Kulitz.

> *Our records show that both these subjects are unsuitable for any employment in the Allied war interest; nor is it clear that there are any grounds that these prisoners of war could expect treatment different from that accorded to ordinary Nazi prisoners of war. Whatever efforts they may have made to*

convince us of anti-Nazi sympathies probably springs from one loyalty only, and that is to themselves.

His final fall from grace was recorded in February 1945 in a note written and signed by Dawn Rockingham-Gill, the personal assistant to the Head of MI19 which processed the intelligence from eavesdropping on prisoners of war.

"...you may be glad to hear that Brandstetter was removed from No7 P/W camp a week or more ago. This was done at the special request of Lt Colonel Holt, BBC Security, and you may rest assured that his broadcasting activities are now at an end. PID are also 'wise' to him."

MI19 had apparently picked up on Wolfgang's attempts to bribe a British officer, with promises of post-war publishing work. He wanted the unnamed man to retrieve his black fund of gold and silver in Paris. He was worried that the French lawyer he'd used might be forced to hand it over to the French authorities.

The British had discovered that he'd been prepared to lie to his Abwehr/SD superiors about the profits from the Tauchnitz Albatross publishing enterprise and there was a further full examination of his role in deceiving the aircrews who were sent to Buchenwald.

Colonel Alexander Scotland, the head of the London District Cage – the secret interrogation centre – based in Kensington Palace Gardens, expressed the view that his role in the escape line operation made it possible to treat him as a war criminal.

He'd been transferred to the London Cage in November 1945 where Colonel Scotland had a notorious reputation and where war crimes were investigated. There were numerous allegations of brutality and torture including the use of prolonged marching and exercise as interrogation stress techniques, alongside sleep deprivation and starvation, all strenuously denied by the Colonel.

It's perhaps telling that a photograph of Wolfgang after his release shows him looking particularly gaunt and thin.

The French also requested Wolfgang's return to them in Paris as part of a war crimes case. That request was apparently granted but for reasons that are unclear in the records held in the British National Archive, the transfer doesn't seem to have happened.

Gisela was doing rather better in her captivity. A photograph taken in Paris on the 8th of May 1945 shows her holding her baby son in a cast iron bed in the maternity clinic. He looks healthy and his little cot is beside her bed. She's smiling in the photograph but unsurprisingly after her captivity and the birth she looks tired although still managing to look beautiful. On the back she'd written in German, "Horst, two days old". Her honey blonde hair, which had grown long during her captivity, had been curled up at the front in a "pompadour," a fashionable and practical look on the streets of Paris at the time, and she had every reason to be hopeful about the future for herself and her son.

At the Hotel Majestic in Paris where the German Headquarters had once been, a United States Serviceman Edward Winegard was part of the US forces now based there. He enlisted in New York in 1943. He was born in Florida and described himself as a salesman to consumers, probably for the Queensboro Stove Company in New York. He was married to a woman called Olympia Marie and had a home in the Queens district. The French files on Gisela describe him as a specialist engineer and the British said he was of German origin. He was 5ft 8ins tall with blue eyes and fairish hair. He was a good looking man and wore a moustache which made him resemble the film star Ronald Colman. He was six years older than Gisela and was in charge of the temporary prison at Boulevard Suchet where she was being held.

She told her daughter that Edward had "wooed her properly", something that clearly appealed to the formal part of Gisela's nature and probably helped her to reconcile herself to the very unequal nature of their original encounter and the way their relationship began, as prisoner and the jailer who brought her chocolates. Perhaps for appearances, they later maintained they'd originally met in New York in 1938/39, but for the soldier away from home the plight of a beautiful German woman held captive in the jail he was running was guaranteed to bring out his protective feelings. Her beauty and his desire to rescue a damsel in distress was a heady combination undoubtedly intensified by life away from home in post occupation Paris.

Ed arranged her formal release from the maternity unit. Now in her early 30s Gisela's ability to attract men in uniform was in no way diminished. Her French file claimed that before Ed appeared on the scene she'd already formed a substantial fanbase amongst the Americans serving in Paris. She chose him.

She still had Parisian friends who stood by her. On her release she went to stay in an apartment provided by Jean Charles Reynaud and his wife. Monsieur Reynaud had told French intelligence officers investigating Gisela that he had Austrian connections and a role at the *Archiv de Gegenwart* operation under its French title Archives Contemporaire. He said Gisela was referred to him by someone called Zukowski. There was no mention at all of the Siegler brothers or of course of the use of the operation as a cover for espionage. Reynaud said Gisela's role was to deal with the German authorities and in particular to obtain the necessary permits from the German propaganda department in Paris.

He also contradicted Gisela's previous assertion to her French questioners that she'd never dealt with banking matters at the Archive. They were all skating on very thin ice but as Gisela settled down to freedom in Paris, as well as convenient individual amnesia about what had happened, there was a more general desire to forget and create a myth about the occupation of the city and the role of its inhabitants that concentrated on the relatively few who'd actively resisted the Germans. In the retelling it was always many.

As specialist tribunals in Paris investigated cases described as "national indignitee" an offence falling short of treason and punishable by being stripped of rank or employment, Gisela's travels were about to start again. She, her son Horst and Ed Winegard were on the move as Ed followed his work. They went to the French town of Verdun to the north east of Paris which was liberated by the US army 7th Armoured Corp on the 31st of August 1944.

It was a logistics centre for American operations and Ed in his role as a specialist engineer was reporting on damage to infrastructure. A surviving report from him gives his assessment of a series of tracked crawler cranes at a port facility at Granville on the French coast and whether they could be repaired and he travelled to various ports and docks as part of this work.

While Gisela and Ed were living in Verdun, Gisela used the alias Mrs. Edward Adam. She kept an envelope addressed to her with that name on it. It's not clear why. The French did receive a request from the Dutch for information about her and Heinrich Siegler von Eberswald, although they dismissed this connection as of no importance with the line about her not really knowing him and probably being his mistress. The Belgians also put her and Heinrich on a list of persons of interest. She may have still been worried about her deal to help the French and the possibility of reprisal.

It was probably living in Verdun that triggered Gisela to tell Ed about her connection to Carl Heinrich von Stulpnagel, who tried to kill himself there on his way back to Berlin after the failure of Valkyrie. As with Jack Profumo, the suggestion she was a beautiful espionage agent clearly didn't dampen his enthusiasm for her and he was good to Horst.

The couple moved again as Ed's working life took them from

place to place. The next stop must have induced a wistful joy in Gisela. She was back in an old hunting ground; they went to live in Saint Rafael on the French coast 30 miles to the south west of Cannes. Their home in the Villa Antonin in San Rafael attracted, according Gisela's British file, the interest of the American intelligence services.

It seems Gisela's connection to German Military Intelligence wasn't over. Her British file said that in 1947 or 1948 the couple were in trouble with American intelligence because they'd "harboured" a German chief of a spy ring.

The German was unidentified in the British report and a search of other sources hasn't produced a name. But it could have been Wolfgang who'd by then been released by the British.

There's a story Wolfgang demanded a sports car to allow Ed to adopt his son. It may have been at this time. The deal was struck and Horst always regarded Ed as his father.

Gisela and Ed finally married in 1948 in Hamburg which was in the American controlled sector of Germany. That year the Russians blockaded Berlin, cutting off the British and American areas in the city from the rest of West Germany. It required a massive airlift of supplies to stop a complete Soviet take over. Europe was settling down to the Cold War conflict between east and west. The Abwehr's Russian operation went over lock stock and barrel to the Americans.

Alongside the country she'd loved being split and ruined, Gisela had to accept a particular effect of her marriage. German law at the time meant that for a woman, marriage to a foreign national led to the automatic loss of her German nationality. Ed arranged for Gisela to be given American travel documents which her British file describes as showing her as "stateless".

She was not alone. There were millions of displaced and now stateless people all over Europe, from the survivors of the Holocaust to ethnic Germans who'd been expelled from the countries that had been part of the Greater Reich or the Eastern Europeans who'd fled the arrival of the communists.

There are no apparent surviving wedding pictures of the couple although one kept by Gisela shows them in a nightclub or restaurant in Montmartre at a table with friends, a well-dressed, dark haired, florid looking man and a good looking dark haired woman in a floral dress and high-waisted belt. A violinist is playing for them and they're all looking at the camera. There's champagne in an ice bucket on the table. There's a reason for thinking that it might be a formal celebration of some sort. Ed is wearing a double breasted pin striped suit and white shirt and tie and Gisela a silk blouse, pearl three strand choker, pearl earrings and a dark plaited heart shaped hat perched on the back of her head.

Apart from unifying them as a couple, the wedding and Gisela's travel document obtained on the back of it had a practical purpose. They were going to leave France and head for somewhere exotic where Ed had lined up a job.

It was an irony that Gisela would be the one to get a full time job working for a propaganda radio station. On the 9th of August 1949 the Winegards arrived in Tangier by air. The Voice of America radio station, first started in 1942 to counter Nazi propaganda, had set up a relay station in Morocco as part of its expansion to deal with the perceived new threat from the Soviet Union. Both Gisela and Edward now had jobs there.

Her life in Tangier mirrored the city's bohemian and complex history and it saw the turbulent return of the man who told her on the back of the photograph she still treasured that he would always love her.

20

TANGIER SUMMER

IN THE LATE 1940s and early 1950s, the city of Tangier had them all: diplomats, spies, gun runners, gold smugglers, dodgy aristocrats, writers and artists, well known and unknown, and these all came complete with a thriving social and gay scene. The raw ingredients of the spicy and complex tagine were seasoned by Tangier's unusual governance which saw the Sultan of Morocco, the United States and various European countries all possess legal powers over the people who lived in what was called the International Zone.

A taste of some of the more extreme excitements Tangier had to offer came some months before Ed and Gisela's arrival, when the adventuress, alleged killer of two husbands, and suspected spy, the Comtesse Marga d'Andurain was murdered on her yacht in Tangier by a young man who was said to have been a Gestapo agent during the war. It's likely that Gisela at the very least knew of her. Marga Andurain was connected to the Abwehr and SD black market activities in Paris and was so notorious that she was known as one of the "Countesses of the Gestapo". Her body was never found.

The city's bohemian allure had a gravitational pull for life's outsiders. The 25-year-old writer Truman Capote arrived in Tangier in the summer of 1949. His visit was deliberately spoiled by his rival and arch enemy for life Gore Vidal turning up on the dockside to greet the ship from Marseille.

Capote described the city in a travel feature for *Vogue.*

"If you are someone escaping from the police, or merely someone escaping, then by all means come here."

Gisela, her son and Ed flew into Tangier's hot and dusty airport in August from Casablanca. They were coming to a place that the Americans regarded as important in a Cold War which was warming up. The North Atlantic Treaty Organisation, NATO, was created early in 1949 ensuring mutual defence for the Western allies and Morocco was seen as an important base for American strike aircraft. This was part of the US policy of trying to contain the Soviet Union with an ability to launch nuclear bombers from Morocco towards the Ukraine, the oilfields of the Caucasus and even Moscow.

Ed was involved with electrical engineering for the Voice of America and also worked for Atlas Constructors, a joint venture by five civil construction firms in the United States who'd been awarded the contracts to build military airbases. Gisela obtained a job working as a clerk in the Naval section of the VOA. In her own later scribbled CV summary, she describes the job as "Secretary to the Naval Commander". This unit was involved with the development of offshore radio ships in the Mediterranean which could be moved to wherever they were needed. These were to be fed their daily programming, originating in the US, from the powerful shortwave transmitters of the Tangier relay station.

Gisela took to Tangier and the city and its inhabitants clearly took to her. She was back in a cosmopolitan scene, her best life. Truman Capote described the social activity as "dark till dawn". It was a busy kif smoking portal to the unknown and Gisela would sample the hazy pleasures of the local marijuana although alcohol was really Ed's preferred stimulant and that played its own part in what happened later.

The pair were out on the town regularly. Ed even attended

a fancy dress party as the bespectacled Capote, whose high-pitched voice and openness about his sexuality made him easy to caricature. Gisela featured in a social round-up newspaper article, which she kept, detailing the comings and goings in Tangier. It showed once again she was well connected.

"Mrs. Edward Winegard, whose husband is employed by Atlas Constructors and who is one of the most beautiful of American hostesses in Tangier, has just moved into a new apartment on the Rue Dante with a wonderful view of the bay".

The brief but gushing report also noted that she was being visited by Clemence Bonnet "one of the kindest Tangier residents". The dark haired, dark eyed and elegant Clemence Bonnet Matthews was from a long established Tangier family. Her grandfather, Felix A. Matthews was the United States Consul in Tangier in the 19th century. In her own home in the city Clemence had her portrait on the wall by the Tangier artist James McBey. He was most famous for his oil painting of Lawrence of Arabia in full flowing robes and headdress. Clemence was accompanied on this visit to Gisela's new flat by Jane Bodden "with whom she shares her home" and who the reporter breathlessly informed Tangiers was "one of the most popular American residents."

But things for one of the most beautiful "American" hostesses were about to go terribly wrong. In the spring of 1950 Gisela was sacked from her job in the Voice of America's naval section. The reason officially given was that it had been discovered that she'd worked as a spy for the Germans and that she was still 100 percent pro-German. It was probably this that triggered the American Counter Intelligence Corps investigation that year which discovered her connection to the black market company and intelligence operation ROGES.

There were obvious tensions between her and Ed as well. There's reference in her British security file to Ed having talked about her under the "stimulation of alcohol" which is what probably led to her sacking.

It couldn't have been easy for either of them. Gisela's wanderlust was still apparent. There seems to have been an attempt to obtain a United States visa in 1949 although the American calendar system, putting the month first on dates of birth had prevented the British from identifying her and they also hadn't realised she'd married, changing her name. The first time she'd done that for a legal purpose.

Tangier, cosmopolitan as it was, still wasn't London, Paris or New York, or Berlin or Vienna come to that. Truman Capote also described the evening social scene in *Vogue* as "neither especially inspired nor varied," while no doubt availing himself of all the pleasures on offer. Gisela was always busy working officially or unofficially and socialising but without a job, on her own for a lot of the time and with a small boy to look after, the long hot days must have dragged and she had time to think about her past.

For Ed, a combination of a beautiful wife who drew all the attention and jealousy when that attention came from other men proved too much. There were bitter rows between them which went public.

On the 22nd of September 1950 a notice was published in a Tangier newspaper saying that Gisela had left her husband and he no longer accepted responsibility for her debts.

Two days later Gisela showed a lawyer based in Tangier a torn half of a typed note which she said she'd picked up in their flat just before she left him.

The note was an indication of the depth of the rift between them. It seemed to show Ed was preparing grounds to divorce and disgrace her. The ripped document said she'd spent eight months in jail in France for espionage and her son was the offspring of a German officer with whom she'd lived.

The actual trigger for their split was revealed the next day.

Ed stated that his wife had left him because he'd discovered that she had recently been receiving "endearing" letters from John Dennis Profumo. The letters were written on House of Commons headed notepaper. Jack was back in Gisela's life. Very probably he'd never really gone away.

Jack was still an unmarried man about town when his continuing connection to Gisela was revealed.

He'd lost his parliamentary seat in Kettering in the Labour party landslide of 1945 that swept Winston Churchill and the Conservative Party from office but got himself back into the House of Commons in February 1950 for the safe Tory seat of Stratford on Avon. This allowed him once again the illicit perk of using House of Commons stationery for love letters.

Gisela was not the only recipient. He was still generous as ever with his affections, dating a number of high profile women. While Gisela was living at the Villa Antonin in the South of France he met a married actress called Valerie Hobson and they started an affair. According to their son David, she identified Jack straight away as a commitment-phobe, but that didn't prevent the liaison continuing and a Paris trip together in 1949. In an echo of Gisela, Valerie already had a young son.

What Gisela's feelings about Jack were at this time aren't really clear. Like Valerie she knew what he was and how he was with women. She'd been quite mobile in her affections herself, but she was lonely with Ed away and travelling for work on the various American projects Atlas Constructors were running in French Morocco. She would have enjoyed the letters from her first close British boyfriend who could so easily have been much more. Jack could on the evidence, write a good love letter and he was the man whose pictures she still had tucked away. The man who'd said, in what must have felt like another world altogether, that he had loved her, did love her and would always love her. She needed to be wanted and it seems that Ed only fully realised that when Gisela left him. Like many men of the Second World War generation, Ed's lifestyle was often fuelled by alcohol which when it gets its addictive grip, is not the support it seems to be, especially in personal relationships.

MI5 compiled a report to add to Gisela's dossier in October 1950 based on what Ed said about her after she'd left him and while he was drowning his sorrows. It seems that Tangier was a very small indiscreet world and some of that world was reporting private conversations to the British intelligence services. In this case the MI6 officer based at the British consular office.

Ed revealed Gisela was recruited as a spy to the *Archiv de Gegenwart* operation by General Stulpnagel, something she must have told him, conveniently ignoring the reality of the situation and her other close connections to Werner Schaurte, Wolfgang Brandstetter and multiple Abwehr officers including the Siegler brothers. Ed also said they'd fallen foul of American intelligence in the South of France over the unidentified former German spy who stayed with them at the Villa Antonin in San Raphael.

Despite this very public and fiery split Gisela did return to Ed and they reconciled, continuing to live in Tangier where the gossip undoubtedly soon moved on to fresh events.

In November 1951, she applied for a visa to visit Britain. Ed didn't need one as a US citizen. She described herself as a "housewife" and gave Jack Profumo as her reference, referring to him with a question mark as the MP for South "Cattering" instead of Kettering but giving an accurate address for him at an elegant stucco Georgian villa in Chester Terrace in London's Regents Park.

The British passport control office in Tangier sought further clarification on this application from London who in turn demanded more information. The reply was that Gisela was now unwilling to provide specific references but had spoken of having a "great many friends" in Britain, which was certainly accurate socially, if not amongst the officers of MI5 and the staff of the Home Office immigration section. Gisela's statement about her connections was coupled with a claim from the British officials in Tangier, which if it was true, cast the whole plan by the couple to travel to Britain in a much more sinister light:

"We have good reason to believe that Mr. and Mrs. Winegard have recently engaged in blackmailing activities and now think it is possible that their intended visit to the UK is connected with this affair."

Having dropped this bombshell, the Passport Control Office in Tangier said that it would be grateful for an early reply to this application from the Home Office, which unsurprisingly was a firm no, given what they'd just been told and Gisela's extensive MI5 file. She had the initials RD retained on the Home Office Suspects list according to her British file. This was the letter code for Refuse Visa. Refuse Leave to Land.

The subject of these claimed "blackmailing activities" is not revealed anywhere else in her British file. The obvious conclusion is that it related to Jack Profumo although given Gisela's "great many friends" in the UK the cast list isn't just limited to him. However, the use of Jack as her reference on the original application and her later refusal to specify anyone to the Tangier officials points to a change in the circumstances between her and Jack. Gisela's daughter believes her mother really did love Jack and certainly she kept more photographs of him than anyone else along with a 1960s German newspaper report about the Profumo Affair. Perhaps Ed's jealousy had been ignited when he discovered that she'd used Jack as her referee and he threatened to expose him for the pursuit of another man's wife or intriguingly for something else Gisela had told him about the well-connected Member of Parliament.

Jack had only himself to blame. It was his continuing appetite for risk and subterfuge in his love life, from German spies to married actresses to Christine Keeler, that would lead to his complete downfall.

Before issuing the visa refusal the British also contacted the American Legation in Tangier to see whether Gisela would be granted a visa for travel to the United States.

"The US legation is reluctant to give a definite answer as to whether Mrs. Winegard would be permitted to reside in the United States, but unofficially we have been given to understand that she would not be granted a visa for that country."

However, Ed was not going to let the refusal to allow them visit the UK pass without further explanation. He wrote a letter addressed to the British Home Secretary on the 22nd of March of 1952 from their flat on Rue Dante in Tangier.

He pointed out that Gisela had become stateless on their marriage because of German law and gave a brief resume of his work activities. He said they had not yet applied for American citizenship for Gisela because that had to be done after their return to the US. He wrote:

"I should be very interested in learning upon what grounds this application has been refused."

If Ed suspected that he hadn't got his wife's whole backstory and the British authorities were going to provide any further information on their reasons for the refusal, he was to be disappointed. A note from Home Office Passport Control Department in April deployed the bland and infuriatingly blank stance of the British need to know principle.

"Would you please arrange for the passport control officer to inform the writer that the Secretary of State, in accordance with his general policy, is not prepared to assign a reason for his decision in individual cases."

Before this dismissive reply Gisela was already travelling. She'd left Tangier and taken Horst to the fashionable Austrian ski resort of Kitzbuhel to the east of Innsbruck in the Tyrol. Kitzbuhel attracted an international set before the war and there was a saying at the time:

"People go to St Moritz to show off, to St Anton to ski and to Kitzbuhel to flirt."

The resort was always a favourite with the German elite because it was easily accessible. Leni Riefenstahl the former dancer, actress and director of the 1934 Nuremberg rally propaganda documentary, Triumph of the Will and the Venice festival winning film about the 1936 Olympics, had a home and editing studio at a house on the Black lake.

The place also attracted senior Nazis. Joachim von Ribbentrop leased the Horlahof villa for his family and Carl Oberg, the SS commander in Paris, who Gisela undoubtedly met during her time in the city, was captured in May 1945 hiding disguised as a private in the Austrian army in the mountains near the town, complete with a two-year supply of food. He was spotted by a Major in the United States army who remembered his bald egg-shaped head. Oberg tried to blame his actions in Paris, including the round ups of Jews and the reprisal shooting of hostages, on General Carl Heinrich Stulpnagel who was in no position to deny the claims.

There's a photographic record of Gisela's visit to Kitzbuhel in 1952. She is standing on a snow slope on skis with spring bindings and heavy boots and holding ski sticks. Her blonde hair has a slight natural wave. She's wearing a crew-neck sweater, the standard ski apparel of those days, with the collar of a blouse showing and dark ski pants. She's smiling directly at the camera. In front is her young son, who clearly takes after her. He is just getting his adult teeth given the gaps in his smile. He has a plaster cast on one leg from a skiing accident and is wearing shorts, a jumper, a knitted balaclava and zip up boots. He is clutching a snowball in his mittened hand.

He doesn't remember much about the trip all these years later except that Gisela belonged to a group of ladies who skied at Kitzbuhel and that two of them had a given him a little gift in the bar area of the hotel in which they'd stayed.

"She was very ladylike," he remembered of his mother. "She kind of had an air about her."

There was something else about Gisela as she rode the ski lift to the top of the piste for a run or twisted and turned on the edges of her skis down the slalom course as part of an amateur competition where everyone got a prize. She was pregnant again.

The baby was born in Tangier on the 24th of October 1952. Ed and Gisela announced the arrival of their daughter Lisl with a specially printed card sent from their address at the flat on the Rue Dante. Their son's main memory of this time, when children were expected to eat what was on their plates, was that he could dispose of food he didn't particularly like over the balcony with the lovely views of the bay.

Ed's work on the American airbases in Morocco was drawing to a close and when Lisl was a year old they were on the move again. This time back to Verdun where Ed was once again connected to the US military base. The family settled into an apartment of the Rue de la Magdelaine in the historic centre of the city not far from the Cathedral. Gisela and Ed carrying their daughter up the stairs of the Victory Monument in the centre of the town commemorating the battle of 1916 and walking through Liberation square to their new home.

Gisela seems to have settled in her marriage if not necessarily in her location. Ed was working with the 313th Army Engineer Construction Group whose headquarters were in Verdun. The group was running heavy equipment and dump trucks for reconstruction and civil engineering works and for the first part of the year in which the family arrived, some men from an engineer battalion were involved in salvaging the remains of a US B24 bomber that had crashed during the war.

Despite heavy winds and rain, the salvage operation drew spectators from France and Germany to inspect a tragic reminder of the fleets of aircraft that had brought savage destruction to both countries only a decade before and whose operations were the subject of the dark intelligence war in Paris by the Luftwaffe Abwehr and SD.

Living in Verdun meant Gisela was also able to take her children to visit her mother and aunt in Germany, but all their lives were changed irrevocably by the end of another war involving the United States. The *Stars and Stripes* army newspaper reported on the 9th of April 1955 that the 313th Army Engineer Construction Group was being folded into a different unit and its colours returned to its homebase in St Louis, Missouri.

It was part of a reorganisation of the US army in Europe driven by the end of the Korean war and partly by French politics. The French tolerance for American bases on their soil was rapidly diminishing.

At the end of March 1955 Gisela realised the ambition she'd apparently harboured since the outbreak of the Second World War caught her in Cannes and which had apparently been thwarted by Dusseldorf's Gestapo.

She, Ed and the children boarded the SS Ryndam run by the Holland America line which was sailing from the Normandy port of Le Havre. The ship was rather different to Gisela's previous trip on the stylish Aquitania. The Ryndam was built as a far less graceful cargo freighter carrying a few passengers, then fully converted for the 1950s transatlantic immigration market.

Gisela seems to have procured a new German passport for

this trip as she is described as being from Germany with the relevant documents, as is her son who travelled using Wolfgang Brandstetter's surname.

Life on the Ryndam was similar though in other ways to Gisela's 1938 transatlantic crossing. There was a mixed bag of French, German and officially stateless people alongside Gisela, Ed, and their young family in the 850 tourist class berths. Most of them hoping for the new life that the Statue of Liberty proclaimed, as it had done for previous generations arriving at the old Ellis Island immigration processing centre.

Everything they had in the world came with them, recorded on the ship's manifest. Gisela was listed as having four suitcases and three trunks while Horst's name had six suitcases and two boxes in the ship's hold attached to it.

There's a family photograph of them all on the Ryndam during the days they were on board. They look like a typical white mom and pop American family from the mid 1950s.

Against the backdrop of a ship's lifeboat, Horst is wearing a checked shirt under a sweatshirt with a drawing of the Western film star Gene Autrey on his horse Champion on the front. Lisl, carried by her father, has a soft toy tucked into her cardigan and is clutching a small chocolate easter egg which she's already sampled. Ed is in a sports jacket, dark V-neck pullover, white shirt and tie while Gisela has her hand on Horst's shoulder as she smiles at the camera. Once again she looks stylish in a light crew-neck sweater, flecked woollen overcoat and a chiffon scarf tied at her throat.

It was a new beginning and Gisela did her best to be the all-American suburban mom with two kids and a husband. In 1958 a court in Cleveland, Ohio, where the family had settled in the suburb of Rocky River on the shore of Lake Erie, gave Gisela American citizenship and although she and Ed later divorced, they remained close. She would fly out to the Middle East where he was working to be with him after a heart attack. She saw him in hospital and was planning to bring him the BLT sandwich he'd requested for breakfast the next morning, but he died overnight.

Gisela continued to be a hard worker. She became a girl scout leader, worked for the US postal service and after the family's move to Californian had herself rejuvenated by a plastic surgeon and then trained for and passed her realtor exam to set up her own business selling properties.

She rarely talked about the past, even her childhood. Gisela could never bear to watch anything about the Second World War on their TV. Even though she was reunited with Anne Douglas, her old friend from Paris, she never saw the 1966 black and white war film *Is Paris Burning?*, starring Anne's husband Kirk Douglas as General Patton. It was about the final days of the city and the liberation. Gisela and Anne knew far more about the dark reality of the German occupation of the City of Light and what followed than Kirk probably ever realised.

It had been a long and perilous journey for the striking woman from Dusseldorf, who entranced a generation of young and not so young men. She and they had galloped, talking, laughing and dancing towards the Second World war and paid a heavy price – millions like Joe Jr the ultimate price, for their open and secret allegiances, right or wrong.

Gisela was proof of Maxwell Knight of MI5's belief that women make better agents than men, a view apparently shared by Stella Rimington, the first woman to run Britain's domestic security service.

For her children the process of finding out about the past of Gisela Klein, model and spy, hasn't been easy. Lisl was shocked to discover her parents had met in a jail. Everyone has a view of their mother formed from their earliest days. Facts that don't fit into our beliefs or show her to be fully independent of us with a very different life before our existence are perhaps a direct challenge to our own story. Spies and mothers do share something in common though. They usually know more about you than you know about them.

Gisela's son who amongst other things inherited her discretion, put it simply: "Every family has secrets, she kept it buried."

Her daughter, who also inherited her looks and blonde hair and love of travel, believes her father Ed reinforced Gisela's desire not to talk about her life in the 1930s and the Second World War. The past is a foreign country and our parents who live there are strangers.

In the hills behind the Californian coast where the Birds of Paradise flowers nod their spiky heads in the wind that blows up from the Pacific, the daughter of the intelligent, witty and companionable model and spy summed her up.

"I don't blame her because we weren't there at that time. She was far tougher than I ever knew."

Some of the last words come directly from Gisela herself. She was writing immediately after one of the small strokes she thought might bring her life to its end and which would gradually take her memories and then take her from her family. She puts all the men who admired her, the couture, the espionage, and her capture in Paris in their place.

"To my beloved children I have this to say. You were the biggest love in my life. You have given me the most happiness and I thank you both for your love and devotion and the help you were to me in a somehow hard and turbulent life."

Gisela Klein died aged 77 on the first of May 1991 in Orange County, California. She kept her secrets till the end. Some of them will never be known.

Epilogue

A GREAT MANY FRIENDS

Germany

Wolfgang Krause Brandstetter. In July 1948 the last group of German Prisoners of War in Britain left by ship for home from the Harwich Parkeston Quay where the young Gisela had arrived 15 years before. Wolfgang was released in that year or just before as his British security file has him located in West Germany in 1948.

The Brandstetter printing business in Soviet occupied Leipzig was seized by the Russians as war booty because the firm had produced maps for the German army. Wolfgang married a woman whose family ran a cement business, a profitable enterprise during the massive reconstruction that Germany required. According to family history he used her money to rebuild the Brandstetter publishing operation in Wiesbaden in West Germany where the Luftwaffe Abwehr had their old headquarters. It's not clear what happened to Wolfgang's black fund in Paris. He'd desperately offered it to the British to help the war effort after they'd discovered its existence.

Wolfgang had two daughters and there was clearly some continuing connection between Gisela and Wolfgang, because in 1963 Gisela told her son his father had died. Horst was confused by this information because he'd always regarded Ed and not Wolfgang as his father.

Wolfgang is buried in the same cemetery in Wiesbaden as the *Luftwaffe* General and former Paris Military Attache Friedrich Carl Hanesse.

General der Luftwaffe *Friedrich Carl Hanesse.* The former first world war pilot and Military Attache in Paris and the man who ran the Luftwaffe and Hermann Göring's office in occupied Paris, joined the German retreat in August 1944 as Gisela and Wolfgang went into hiding. He continued as the commanding General of the Luftwaffe supplemental corps between September 1944 and February 1945 before officially retiring. He was captured by the French and was released in December 1946. He moved to Wiesbaden in common with a surprising number of former senior Third Reich military commanders and died aged 82 in May 1975.

Werner Teddy Schaurte. Gisela's poem sender, friend and business associate of Göring and member of the SA who was pictured with Hitler and who had such a keen interest in the aircraft technology of the Third Reich, rebuilt the war ravaged Bauer and Schaurte business back up again after the conflict. He fought a long battle to ensure that his deNazification status meant his business would not be taken away from him. In later years, like many former hunters, he developed an interest in preserving wildlife, particularly the rhinoceros, and became involved in the Worldwide Fund for Nature, helping to set up a major game reserve in Africa.

Annemarie Heise. Even as the bitter fighting for Berlin was underway in the spring of 1945 the fashion salon run by Annemarie Heise executed the wedding dress order for Eva Braun. Annemarie Heise survived the war and continued in the clothes business.

In 1949 she was listed as the costumier to the film Eine Grosse Liebe which was entered in the 1949 Cannes film festival. The film was directed by Hans Bertram who in 1941 had made Kampfgeschwader Lutzow a propaganda film about a bomber crew over Poland. Her work is preserved in some museums usually because of its association with Eva Braun and also in numerous pictures in photographic archives including the dress modelled by Gisela held by the Vassiliev Foundation in Paris which notes that Heise took a dim view of the Nazis because of their anti semitism. This it's claimed was after a film star friend of hers was forced to divorce his Jewish wife by Joseph Goebbels.

Heinrich Karl Julius *Siegler von Eberswald.* Abwehr officer and former SD agent in Austria, Heini Siegler, who the French thought was just a magazine publisher, was captured by the Russians in Vienna. He was a Prisoner of War and was released in the late 1940s. He went to live with his much younger second wife Johanna in Baden Baden where he'd applied to be the manager of the Spa before the Second World War.

United States

John F. Kennedy. Gisela Klein kept a letter from the brother of the man she "dated". It was a reply to her and Ed Winegard's congratulations on his winning the Presidency. The letter was sent on the 6th of December 1960 and he thanks them for their thoughts.

"I hope that my record during the next four years will sustain your confidence. With every good wish I am sincerely, John F Kennedy" he wrote.

Jack Kennedy's Presidency wouldn't last four years. Like his older brother Joe, who should have been President, Jack's life was cut short. He was assassinated in Dallas,Texas in November 1963.

Anne Douglas, Anne Buydens, Hannelore Marx. Gisela's friend Anne Douglas met the film star Kirk Douglas as a publicist on the set of the 1953 film Act of Love which was being filmed in France and they married She is credited with sorting out the star's chaotic finances and for the longevity of their marriage which lasted for 66 years. They had two sons together and she always said she took a "European" view of Kirk's infidelities. There is a photograph of Gisela, Lisl, Anne Douglas and her son Eric at the Douglas family home in Beverly Hills.

France

*Jean de Beaumont.*The French aristocrat, Deputy for Indochina, and pilot, Count Jean Bonin de la Bonniniere de Beaumont, who Gisela used as a referee after her capture by the French. He supported Petain's government after the German invasion which is what probably led to his arrest for collaboration. In September 1949 he was noted in the *Queen* newspaper as staying at Drumlanrig Castle in Scotland with the Duke and Duchess of Buccleuch, where other guests had included Princess Elizabeth and the Duke of Edinburgh. Before the war he was an Olympic clay pigeon shooter and was later heavily involved with both the French and International Olympics from the 1950s to the 1970s. He had two daughters and a son.

Great Britain

Geordie 5th Duke of Sutherland. Geordie George Granville Sutherland Leveson Gower, the 5th Duke of Sutherland's wife, Lady Eileen died in 1943. He remarried and continued his life much as before. Photographs of him in later life make him look weak and unhappy in some way the camera doesn't fully define, rather like his friend David, the Prince of Wales, the man who gave up the British throne for Wallis Simpson. Geordie never had any children, except for perhaps Princess Diana's stepmother, Raine Spencer, and he died in 1963 at Nassau in the Bahamas. He is buried in the grounds of Dunrobin castle in Scotland. On his death his titles were shared between his niece and a distant male relative.

Hanmer Cecil "Pat" Hanbury. Three years after taking Gisela to Paris, Pat Hanbury married Prunella "Bimby" Higgins, the daughter of an Air Commodore. He fought with the Grenadier Guards in both Tunisia and Italy and was wounded during fierce fighting for Monte Camino in Italy where he was awarded the Military Cross for his bravery. He stayed in the army until 1958. His wife's family had an estate in Bedfordshire and he ran that afterwards. He had two children, a daughter and a son. He held the ceremonial office of Lord Lieutenant of Bedfordshire and died in 1994 aged 78.

Michael Isaacs. "Lord Erleigh" 3rd Marquess of Reading. The young man whose connection to Gisela triggered the letter from the *Times* Correspondent in Paris to British intelligence, was a tank commander in the Queens Bays, the 2nd Dragoon Guards, and was awarded the Military Cross as the British were pushed back by the rapid German advances in 1940. After the war he was a banker and member of the London Stock Exchange. In 1940 he married the car racing, aircraft flying, society beauty Margot Duke, who in at least one photograph held by the National Portrait Gallery looks rather like Gisela. They had four children.

Diana Russell Clarke. The reason Diana Russell Clarke went to work at the Bletchley Park decoding centre, according to a family story, was because she didn't want to join the Women's Auxiliary Territorial Service because she didn't like the uniform. Her first marriage was to someone she met at Bletchley which didn't last. She also met her second husband at Bletchley and that did. She recalled seeing his blue eyes through the hatch in one of the huts at Bletchley used to pass messages for decoding on the Enigma code machine simulators by her and the other Bletchley "Debs". In the 1990s she gave her first and only public talk about her time at Bletchley to the Burford Society in which she detailed the British attempt to arrest Gisela. Her son found a very poor recording of this talk and managed to clean the audio so that the story was preserved.

Jack Profumo. According to his son David's account, John Dennis Profumo fathered a child during the Second World War. Janine, the baby's mother was the wife of a right wing Vichy politician who conveniently went over to the Allies and was later central to a bizarre plot to steal Marshall Petain's coffin.

Jack's political career flourished through the 1950s and in 1960 he was made Secretary of State for War and tipped for even higher office.

On the 8th of July 1961 Jack and his wife, the actress Valerie Hobson drove up to Cliveden past the Fountain of Love to stay with Bill Astor, the man he'd helped in the Fulham constituency in 1935.

At the open air Cliveden swimming pool Jack met the young and attractive Christine Keeler. She was described by one elderly peer of the realm to the author as "catnip to men." In that she clearly shared something with Gisela. Jack started an affair with her but was apparently warned off by MI5 because she was associated with a Russian military attaché. After the details of the brief affair began to leak out Jack lied to his political colleagues and to Parliament about his relationship with her. The scandal that engulfed them all was satirised in a limerick.

Oh, what have you done said Christine
You have ruined the party machine
To lie in the nude may be terribly rude
but to lie in the house is obscene

Many of Jack's friends and colleagues including Bill Astor abandoned him. Astor was disgraced as well. He was accused of having an affair with Christine Keeler's friend, Mandy Rice-Davies. On being told during a subsequent court case that Astor denied an affair with her, Rice-Davies famously replied, "Well he would, wouldn't he?". He died in 1966 from a heart attack in Nassau in the Bahamas. Jack went to work for a charity for the homeless in the East end of London and never spoke publicly about the matter.

Gisela's file and place in Jack's life were part of some bureaucratic paper shuffling between MI6 and MI5 at the time of the Profumo Affair.

"Although it is not particularly relevant to the current notorious case, [...] thought you might like to have a copy of a report from our representative in (place redacted but clearly Tangier) dated 2nd October 1950, which makes mention of an association between Gisela Klein and Profumo which began c1933 and had not ceased at the time of this report."

"Not particularly relevant" is a masterful understatement. Had the press at the time known of Jack's relationship with Gisela, who like Christine Keeler, MI5 had linked to a Military Attache, there is little doubt the row would have been even more intense than it was. Given the continuing repercussions of the defection of the Soviet spies Burgess, Philby and Maclean just over decade before, it's not impossible that serious questions would have been raised about his true loyalties in the 1930s and later. As it was Jack has been credited, probably unfairly, with the end of general public deference to the ruling classes and the eventual fall of the Macmillan government.

He was far luckier with the woman he finally chose than perhaps he deserved. Valerie stuck by her husband throughout and in 1975 Jack was made a Commander of the British Empire at Buckingham Palace, signalling a public return to favour.

Some of the papers relating to the official inquiry by Lord Denning into the Profumo Affair will not be declassified until the 2040s.

ACKNOWLEDGEMENTS

MY PROFOUND THANKS go to Lisl and Horst and Wolfgang Brandstetter, named after his uncle, for his help and loan of Welt im Wurfelbecher. Aly and Josie Maclean; Margaret Enefer; Kate Robinson and Gillian Slovo for their help and suggestions during this book's long gestation.

The author Janetta Maclean for her research in Canada. Archive staff at Dusseldorf and Neuss and North Rhine Westphalia and the UK National Archives at Kew; Philipp Steinhoff of Geneaologia Badenia for his determined research in Germany and France.

The staff at the British Library for newspaper searches and a copy of Geordie Sutherland's autobiography. The staff at the Wiener Library in London and the Museum of Rural Life in Reading which holds Nancy Astor's Papers and also personnel at the Broadland Archives at the University of Southampton where Gisela's connection to "Rabbits" Mount Temple was revealed.

Thanks to Dr Thomas Cheetham at Bletchley Park for his help on Ultra and the Free French. Also, to various staff at the United States National Archives and the Kennedy Archive in Boston. Their speedy replies to emailed inquiries mark them out as exceptional.

My gratitude to Nigel and Penny Barraclough for their help and lunch and to the "super recognisers" who both confirmed and knocked down several possible identifications.

I am deeply indebted to my agent Andrew Lownie for his support. My thanks to Christine Costello and Nick Webster for spotting inconsistencies and egregious spelling mistakes etc. Any errors of fact are mine alone and I will endeavour to correct them in any future editions. Finally, apologies to everyone who has had to listen to me droning on about this story for the last five years.

A GREAT MANY PHOTOGRAPHS

Gisela modelling in Berlin 1942

(Top left) Jack Profumo and Gisela at Avon Carrow. *(Top right)* 1930s glamour London. Gisela photographed by Shaw Wildman. *(Above)* Gisela's bit of fluff. The 5th Duke of Sutherland

(Above left) Wolfgang Krause Brandsetter, publisher and spy. *(Above right)* "I did love you, I do love you, I will always love you Jack x" from Gisela's box of photographs.

(Above left) Jack Profumo in wartime captain's uniform kept by Gisela. *(Above right)* Kennedy wearing regalia during his graduation from Harvard in June 1940. Credit John F. Kennedy Presidential Library and museum, Boston

(Top left) Gisela in Oxford, 1933. *(Top right)* John F Kennedy pictured with his father Joe Kennedy, 1940

(Top left) Hyannisport, Massachusetts, USA, 1940; The Kennedy boys: *(right to left)* John F. Kennedy, Robert F. Kennedy & Ted Kennedy

MISS KLEIN *is tying* MR. J. D. PROFUMO'S *cap, while* MISS McMINNIS *and the* HON. MICHAEL ASTOR *watch. Mr. Profumo was second, on his Decent Fellow, in the University Grind at Somerton.*

Photo taken in Somerton, 1935, features Gisela Klein, Jack Profumo and Michael Astor.

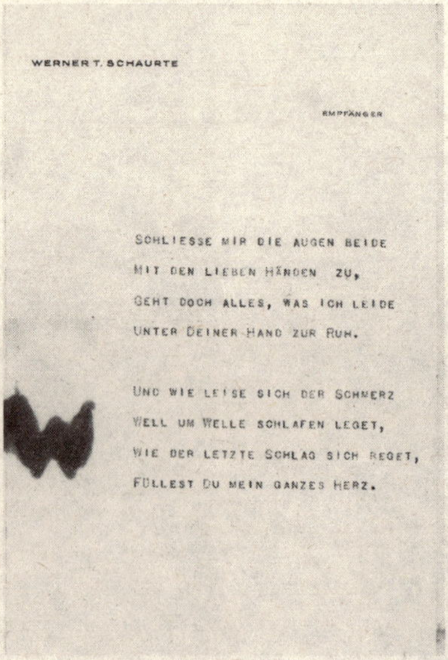

WERNER T. SCHAURTE

EMPFÄNGER

SCHLIESSE MIR DIE AUGEN BEIDE
MIT DEN LIEBEN HÄNDEN ZU,
GEHT DOCH ALLES, WAS ICH LEIDE
UNTER DEINER HAND ZUR RUH.

UND WIE LEISE SICH DER SCHMERZ
WELL UM WELLE SCHLAFEN LEGET,
WIE DER LETZTE SCHLAG SICH REGET,
FÜLLEST DU MEIN GANZES HERZ.

(Top left) Love or code poem by Werner T Schaurte sent to Gisela. *(Top right)* Gisela pictured in Egypt, 1936

Ruhr Industrialist Werner Theodor Schaurte pictured with Goring. Credit: Nuess Archives

NOTES ON TEXT

Chapter One

1. *They seemed to know how she'd come to possess it and they took her outside....* Gisela Klein told her daughter about being tied to a tree and that it was because her papers weren't in order. They certainly weren't, she had a French identity card despite being a German national. The possession of the ID was amongst details about her revealed by Abwehr officer Wolfgang Krause Brandstetter during interrogation by officers of T Force in August 1944. Personal files of the Security Service. British National Archive at Kew. KV2/160
2. *Hundreds if not thousands in the city would die at the hands of their neighbours.* Estimates vary for extra judicial killings across the whole of France but are put at between 10 and 15 thousand.
3. According to the file kept on her by British Military Intelligence. Gisela Klein's file KV4/146 at the British National Archive at Kew is supplemented by further information about her in the file of Wolfgang Krause Brandstetter KV2/160.
4. *...to be beaten and abused and have their heads shaved.* There were as many as 20,000 women known as Les Tondue, the shorn women. Source: Imperial War Museum. IWM London.

Chapter Two

1. *A young woman of striking appearance* KV6/146. Personal files of the Security Service held by the UK National Archives at Kew. A report from Valentine Vivian head of counterintelligence at M16 in 1938 to MI5. He would later become MI6's Deputy Chief. The public release of this file in 2017 triggered brief newspaper reports about Gisela Klein's relationship with Profumo. The interest still fuelled by his later downfall because of the sex and spy scandal of the 1960s.

2. *The squeeze was now at its worst.* January 1933 unemployment rate was 23%. "Concentrations of high unemployment in the North of England and throughout Wales." Abstract: Industrial, Regional and Gender divides in British Unemployment between the wars. October 2020. Meredith M Paker. University of Oxford.
3. *...one of thousands* Controls on foreign domestic servants were relaxed as early as 1930 and around 20,000 women from Germany, Austria and Czechoslovakia arrived in Britain on domestic visas before the outbreak of war in 1939. Refugees from National Socialism in Wales. University of Aberystwyth. Second World War Holocaust Programme led by the Imperial war Museum. (https://wp-research.ac.uk)
4. *...many of these were told to listen.* My Eriksson, a domestic servant, arrived in 1936. She described herself as a Swedish widow but was in fact German. She was connected to German agent Walter Simon, and she maintained an extensive contact list of other domestic staff including Olive Scott who worked at 10 Downing Street. KV2/535/536/537/538. Also, Margaret Newitt who ran a domestic agency for German and Austrian servants who was interned in 1940. KV2/3327. Also see The Rise of the Abwehr, Hitlers Nest of Vipers. Nigel West. Frontline Books 2022.
5. *...records show she never joined the Nazi party.* Bundesarchiv Lichterfelde. Nazi Party Membership Gisela Klein: "No references to Gisela Klein could be found in relevant holdings and personal collections kept by the local office of the Federal Archives in Berlin Lichterfelde. Clues can be identified. In particular, the research on membership in the NSDAP was negative. Only a short note from the repatriation office of the foreign organization of the NSDAP regarding the "return immigrant from France" and the deregistration from Bad Kohlgrub to Berlin from 16.7.1941 could be proven (NS 9/6418)."
6. *...told people she was anti-Nazi.* Reported by MI5 about her, and she also told French intelligence officers the same thing and that she'd moved in anti-Nazi circles. KV6/146 UK National Archive at Kew.
7. The ticket that Gisela Klein purchased bringing her to Harwich came with a hidden surcharge. See Total Espionage, Germany's Information and Disinformation Apparatus 1932-1940 by Curt

Riess. First published 1941, the book details the German development of the Soviet Total Espionage doctrine.

8. Hitler Youth had burned what were described as "unwanted" books and paintings in front of the city's Rhine Hall. Dusseldorfer Kunstszene 1933-1945. Werner Alberg, Dusseldorf Stadtmuseum. Copy at IWM London.

9. *...marked the Fuhrer's accession to power by using members of his own workforce to create a storm troop of brown shirts*, the Nazi Sturmabteilung, the SA. Neus-Grevenbroicher Zeitung News May 2, 1933. From Association of victims of the Nazi Regime/ State Association of Anti Fascists of North Rhine Westphalia. NRW.WVN. BDA.de

10. *...faithful to an ideal of the German nation* Gisela Klein, described by a sponsor in Egypt as "100 percent German girl", (KV6/146). She would be dismissed from a job working for the Voice of America radio station after the war because of her pro-German views and her detention in France for espionage. She would regularly return to Germany for visits after moving to the United States in the 1950s and would even compare the weather in California unfavourably with that of Germany. She could never bear to watch anything on TV about the Second World War. Author interview with her daughter.

11. The German National Archive notes drily. "Supplementary cards (from the 1939 census) for Thuringia and the majority of those for the Rhine province were stored at the reserve post of the Reich Office of Genealogy in Schloss Rathsfeld in Robla/Hartz where they were probably eliminated in 1945." www.bundesarchiv.de/EN/Content/Publikationen/essay-zimmermann-supplementary-cards.html finden.

12. *...an air raid warden in the block of apartments*. In Hausbuch Kapellerstr 9b he is registered as "Luftschutzhauswart. Correspondence with Claudia Wehofen. Dusseldorf City Archive.

13. In Great Dunmow Gisela stayed in a large house called Rood End Author visit and viewing of Rood End House courtesy of Mike Perry. mikeperryphotography.co.uk

14. *Dr Geoffrey Barber, his wife Daphne, and their one-year-old son Nicholas*. Details about the Barber family are limited but he later

served in the Royal Navy and wrote a book about Sexual Hygiene for Public Schools. They married in 1931, and Nicholas was born in May 1932. The Chelmsford Chronicle from the 15th of September 1933 and Ancestry.co.uk provided details of Nicholas' birth and Daphne's community involvement.

15. *...continue her studies of English.* KV6/146

16. *...carried their porcine prizes away.* Most of the results of the Dunmow Flitch Trials dating back to 1445 can be found at www.dunmowflitchtrails.co.uk. The first recorded entry in 1445 notes a winner as Richard Wright who was also not an Essex local, he was from Norfolk. It doesn't mention the name of the wife to whom he was publicly devoted.

Chapter Three.

1. Avon Carrow, an impressively odd and faux medieval former hunting Lodge. Author visit and tour of part of Avon Carrow house and garden.

2. David Profumo recounts a story of an on-course book maker's comments about his father. *Bringing the House Down*: A Family Memoir by David Profumo. 2006. John Murray. David Profumo allows himself some latitude over details about the lives of his mother and father. In the foreward he says: "I cannot vouch for the absolute accuracy of these narratives.......and I expect there are mistakes, some of which may be deliberate." Perhaps understandably he politely declined the author's request for access to further information about Jack and Gisela's relationship.

3. They were of *"foreign descent"* as one note in the file on Gisela puts it. KV6/146.

4. *MI5 would report he was a member of the London branch of the Italian Fascist party...*Ibid.

5. *... the security service had thoroughly penetrated.* Defense of the Realm. The authorised history of MI5. Christopher Andrew. 2009 Penguin Books.

6. *...on the 23rd of May 1934 by tuning a valve radio set to 767 kilohertz.* RADIO TIMES WHITSUN ISSUE 20th May 1934. 1900 Regional

Programme Midland. Opera. "A great lady, bored by her court life allows herself to be hired as a servant to a young farmer."

7. *He was sent to the Vocational Guidance Department of the National Institute of Industrial Psychology Bringing the House Down* David Profumo. John Murray 2006.
8. *One contemporary of the pair would tell M15 she was: intelligent, witty and companionable.* MI5 report. Probably Jack Profumo. KV6/146.
9. *...whom she would later, broadly, and vaguely, describe to the British authorities as a "great many friends"* Details of 1950s British Visa Application. KV6/146.
10. *The first steady girlfriend was a lovely German blonde named Gisela Klein, who seemed to share his taste for japes. Bringing the House Down* David Profumo. John Murray 2006.
11. *...a one hundred and sixty horsepower Fairchild, an American make.* Probably bought in late 1936 or 1937 as the Fulham Chronicle article from 1938 about Jack and Maina's near accident describes the aircraft as just over a year old.
12. As the aircraft landed people on the ground heard a scraping noise. Fulham Chronicle 9th September 1938. Warwickshire and Warwickshire Advertiser. 10th September 1938.
13. *With Gisela away in Germany, Jack who had a continuously roving eye would become associated with another beautiful woman with strongly pro-German tendencies.* Photograph of "John" Profumo and Jeanne Stourton at the Opening of the Punch Club in 1934. Source Alamy.
14. *She famously shouted Heil Hitler after kicking her later husband, the gentle and long-suffering Sherman Stonor, Baron Camoys, down the stairs.* From Author Interview with Jeanne's daughter Julia Stonor and her book about her mother: *Sherman's Wife*, Julia Camoys Stonor. Desert Hearts. 2006

Chapter Four

1. *Marianne, perhaps rather brighter than her "Uncle", had, it was later reported, sensed something was wrong with the*

operation and insisted on returning to Germany. KV 2/2642 and KV2/1319 -1323 *UK National Archives* and *The Game of Foxes*. Ladislas Farago. Hodder and Stoughton 1971.

2. *While there she witnessed the referendum that sealed her country's fate.* 90 percent of those who voted were in favour of merging the posts of Fuhrer and Reichs Chancellor. The *New York Times* wrote: "The endorsement gives Chancellor Hitler, who four years ago was not even a German citizen, dictatorial powers unequalled in any other country."
3. *She was not telling the authorities the truth.* KV6/146 UK National Archives at Kew.
4. *An Espionage Training Manual produced in 1934 and preserved in the German National Archives.* RW 5/207 Lecture notes 1934 – 1937 Old reference OKW 1107. Freiberg Bundesarchiv.
5. *Bremen also had a role.* The Abwehr Unit at Bremen according to the KV series at the National Archives at Kew also had an interest in the Middle East
6. *In December 1935 Hitler wrote to Lord Rothermere in a letter.* A translated copy of which is preserved in the Broadlands Archive of Lord Mount Temple at the University of Southampton. Mount Temple, the Chairman of the Anglo-German Fellowship, was also in receipt of a signed copy of Hitler's photograph which is mentioned in a letter from H.G. Von Hussow from the German Embassy dated 21st November 1936.
7. *...the 1935 Paramount production, the Lives of a Bengal Lancer.* Knowledge of Hitler's liking for the film has been attributed to Sir Ivone Augustine Kirkpatrick. First Secretary at the British Embassy in Berlin from 1933 to 1938. He became convinced the only way to deal with the Fuhrer was to "hit Hitler on the head." Also referenced in

Images Behind The Curtain: Hitlers Private Film Viewings. A Master's Thesis by Dodie Cook. 2020, held by the Harvard library. She cites Adolf Hitler: The Definitive Biography. John Toland. Doubleday 1976 and The Lost Life of Eva Braun. Angela Lambert. St Martin's Press. 2007.

8. *A week before Easter, in April 1935, Gisela and Jack travelled to the house to stay as guests together.* The guest book for Cliveden containing Gisela and Jack's signatures during this period are held at the Museum of English Rural Life which is part of the University of Reading.
9. *There was a display of art, weapons and suits of armour and three tapestries given to a previous owner.* Author tour of Cliveden, which is now a private hotel via National Trust volunteer guides.
10. *...including a large red velvet settee in front of the enormous, canopied stone fireplace.* Mentioned by Debo Mitford in her book *Wait For Me.* 2010. John Murray. Other descriptions of Nancy Astor's spiky personality, and dinner with Mr Lee presiding can be found in *Rose, My Life in Service To Lady Astor*, by Nancy Astor's personal maid Rosina Harrison. Cassell & Company 1975.
11. *Mrs. Ethel B Mallorie who wrote to her frequently calling her "my dear friend."* From correspondence and papers of Nancy Astor at the Museum of English Rural Life. Reading.
12. *That night she was complaining about having to attend the 12th Conference of the International Woman Suffrage Alliance which was being held on the 18th of April in Istanbul.* Referenced in Jack Profumo's thank you letter. Ibid.
13. *In December of that year Gisela sent a postcard addressed to Viscountess Nancy Astor at Cliveden., Taplow, England. It was posted from abroad.* Ibid.
14. *The file on Gisela at the British National Archive at Kew shows*

that it must have been the Metropolitan Police in London who carried out an investigation. KV6/146. Nancy Astor had good police connections. At least one senior officer was in correspondence with her seeking her support in his application for a post as a Chief Constable. Correspondence and papers of Nancy Astor at the Museum of English Rural Life. Reading.

Chapter Five

1. *She was flying on a new route between Cairo and Luxor on El Misr Airworks, a British firm with Egyptian funding.* The new service started just as Gisela arrived in Egypt and provided the fastest link between Assyut and Cairo. It was the Middle East's and Africa's first airline. History of Egyptair. Forward in Brochure of Egypt International Airshow.
2. *Gisela's new role in Egypt was as a "fashionable dressmaker" operating in both Cairo and Alexandria.* Contained in letter to MI5 from J Astor about Gisela and "low grade" agent Rudolf Goldschmidt KV6/146.
3. *...some non-Soviet air.* Jack Profumo's diary entry quoted in: *Bringing the House Down*. David Profumo. John Murray. 2006
4. *Schaurte was a regular guest on Herman Göring's 90ft personal Motor yacht Carin 11.* This information comes from an interview with Frau Heller Panzer by a group of school students for an entry in a Federal German History competition. The Life of a Screw Icon. 2011.
5. *One of his Great-Grandfathers was Jewish.* This limited family inheritance was still enough to cause him problems. The Life of a Screw Icon reproduces part of Schaurte's questioning during the post war de-Nazification process where this detail was discussed. Despite using forced labour and his close connections to Hitler and Göring, Werner Schaurte successfully appealed against the original de-Nazification panel findings which allowed him to retain control of his company after the war. Appeal summary North Rhine Westphalia Archive.

6. *Where does propaganda end and espionage begin.* Goebbels quoted by Curt Riess in his 1941 book Total Espionage. G.P Putnam's Sons 1941.

7. *Mr and Mrs J D Astley.* Gisela would describe them to French Intelligence as English friends who invited her to stay. This was in a typewritten list of her movements and the relevant dates she'd carefully prepared in advance of her interrogation by French intelligence officers in 1944. Although she refers to Assiut as Asunt, a helpfully misleading typo. French Archives. Fiche De Renseignments P422741

8. *The German Military Attache at the London Embassy, Baron Geyr Von Schweppenburg was accused.* Schweppenburg describes the incident in his autobiography The Critical Years. Wingate. 1952.

9. *...and the official files betray none of the intense interest that would be shown in enterprising young women.* The KV files at the National Archives about German espionage have remarkably little about most of the 1930s. . "British knowledge of the organization (Abwehr) remained almost non existent until 1938" The Rise of the Abwehr, Hitlers Nest of Vipers. Nigel West. Frontline. 2022

10. *Celine Morriset also known as Lena or Line Mori. German espionage in Egypt.* Miscellaneous reports of suspected spying. KV3/70

11. *It led one intelligence officer to produce a detailed analysis of the origins of the dancers and entertainers.* Ibid.

12. *Sophie Clapham Kukralova,* KV2/3122

13. Photographs of Goebbels from this visit in KV3/69.

14. *This was most likely to have been Lieutenant Richard Derek Cardiff.* Cardiff was the contact Gisela Klein named as the person she was staying with on her application to the British for a visa. KV6/146

15. *...vigorous motoring.* Leicester Chronicle 30th October 1937.

16. *...passed off to the Fuhrer as a misguided freelance operation. Game of the Foxes.* Ladislas Farago. Hodder and Stoughton 1971.

17. *Hitler vehemently re-issued the spy ban in the UK in person to Admiral Canaris in the autumn of 1935. Defence of the Realm.* Christopher Andrew. Penguin Books. 2010. Andrew cites; Germany Military Intelligence, Leverkuehn and Hitler's Spies. Kahn.

18. *...she must also have suggested to him she'd been a Rhodes scholar*

at Oxford in the early 30s. Letter from Ed Winegard contained in KV6/146. Cecil Rhodes will which created the scholarships unambiguously used the words male; him; manly; manhood etc. It wasn't until 1977 that the first female Rhodes Scholars appeared. The Rhodes Project. (https://therhodesproject.com)

19. *Carl Heinrich Stulpnagel was actually in charge of German military intelligence for the "Foreign Armies" branch between 1933 and 1936.* UK National Archives Official Blog Dr Richard Dunley 2017.

20. *Maxwell Knight maintained that when women wanted to command attention.* See also One Girl's War. 1945. By Joan Miller (reprint Brandon Books 1987) who was his personal assistant. Knight was eccentric and collected animals including Baboons as pets. Miller also claimed Knight was gay and deliberately used his unconsummated affair with her to disguise the fact from his staff at MI5.

21. *...the Foreign Secretary Sir Samuel Hoare, who actually recruited Mussolini as a paid agent for MI5.* Hoare was paying Mussolini the then extraordinary sum of £100 a week as part of a counter subversion operation to keep Italy onside during the First World War. Defence of the Realm Christopher Andrew. Penguin 2010.

22. *The 2nd Battalion of the Scots Guards was promptly dispatched to Egypt to reinforce the 1st battalion and bolster the local forces.* Gaumont British Newsreel. Scots Guards Leave on Voyage to Egypt. Film ID VLVAACFKIX030RXHPFGXM7VNX83RO Captioned: From Southampton. www.britishpathe.com

23. *...National Socialists who regarded all semitic peoples as inferior and wouldn't become involved or authorise an Arab Nazi party.* The Nazis tied themselves in semantic knots about who was Aryan to try to keep the Turks and Egyptians happy about the Nuremberg Race Laws of 1935 and developed close links to a number of Arab Nationalists and aimed Arabic speaking propaganda broadcasts at the region. Hitler later personally authorised individual Muslims to become Nazi party members. Presentation to Historical Society Conference 2008. Professor Jeffrey Herf University of Maryland.

Chapter Six

1. *He chose to cycle to work like his 900 plus employees rather than use the expensive motor vehicle he owned.* Author interview with Wolfgang Brandstetter. Justus Brandstetter's step-grandson, who was named by his father Rudi after his uncle Wolfgang.
2. *...a passion for fast cars which saw Horst killed in a racing accident and Wolfgang injured in a car accident.* Wolfgang used the injury to defer compulsory military service. Bundesarchiv Freiberg Pers 6/ 243270
3. *British publisher John Holroyd Reece.* Holroyd Reece's career and some details of Wolfgang Brandstetter are in Strange Bird. The Albatross Press and the Third Reich. Michelle K Troy. Yale University Press. 2017. Reece also appears in Wolfgang Brandstetter's British File KV2/160.
4. *...an article in a Leipzig newspaper.* May 1935 Leipziger Neuse Nachricten quoted in Strange Bird. The Albatross Press and the Third Reich. Michelle K. Troy. Yale University Press. 2017
5. *...funded by British Jewish finance.* According to KV2/160 Wolfgang was retaining the profits from selling Albatross books and not sending them back to Nazi Germany.
6. They variously described him in his official soldier's record held by the German Military Archive at Freiberg as: Bundesarchiv Freiberg Pers 6/ 243270
7. *He recorded his adventures in a travelogue. Welt im Wurfelbecher.* Wolfgang Ernst. Tauchnitz. 1943. I am much indebted to Wolfgang's nephew for lending me this book and for his help.
8. *Edward always displayed a marked and some would show a treacherous affinity for Nazi Germany.* See *Traitor King*. Andrew Lownie. 2021 Bonnier Books.
9. *...two couple of the fox hunting mad Mitford pack:* Hounds in a fox pack are counted in pairs. Two couple equals 4.
10. *It has been suggested Philby was infiltrating this organization to disguise his own real affiliations.* Malcolm Muggeridge is fascinating on the enigma of Philby in his autobiography Chronicles of Wasted Time. Regent College Publishing. 1972.

11. Wilfred William Ashley. Lord Mount Temple. A former government minister was elevated to the Peerage in 1932. His papers and correspondence are held at the Broadlands Archive at the University of Southampton.

Chapter Seven

1. *Hanmer Hanbury was always known as Pat, or Patsy by his doting mother, and in the Grenadier Guards.* His mother Dorothy wrote to Lord Mount Temple she was bringing him home in a letter preserved in the Broadlands Archive of Southampton University. BR 88/15
2. *Whatever the cause, he carried a scar on his forehead ever after.* A set of three photographs in 1938 by Bassano LTD held by the National Portrait Gallery show a pronounced scar running up from his left eye across his forehead.
3. *...who had the distinction of being the first English woman to be enrolled in the fascist party of Benito Mussolini.* Reference to this in Northampton Mercury of 7th July 1939 in a report on Cecil's (Pat's) wedding to Prunella Higgins the daughter of an Air Commodore.
4. *Gisela had a good job as a designer and was also in receipt of a "private" income of £2 10 shillings a week.* An index, to KV6/146 has some date typos apparently putting some of its contents out of sequence. Exactly when Lady Hanbury wrote to the authorities is based on an informed guess of the order of events. It might have been after the trip to Paris with Pat Hanbury.
5. *Gisela's continuous travel was summed up by Malcolm Muggeridge. Chronicles of Wasted Time.* Malcolm Muggeridge. Regent College Publishing 2006.
6. *She tells me that she met Gisela Klein in Germany and was suspicious of her.* KV6/146. At this time, as with the Abwehr, women were not allowed to be officers of MI5/ MI6 only agents or "secretarial"
7. *...a more than stupid treaty.* Translated copy in Broadlands Archive. Southampton University. BR78/24.
8. *No more Paris Models.* June 1933 Hitler to the fashion writer Hela

Strehl. Nazi Chic? Fashioning Women in The Third Reich. Irene Guenther. Berg. 2004. She sources the quote to Bella Fromm a journalist who knew Strehl and who wrote Blood and Banquets based on her secret diaries written in Berlin in the 1930s.

9. *Eva Braun loved Heise so much.* Eva Braun died without paying her bill to Heise and she ordered her bills from the couturier should be destroyed to hide them from posterity. Nazi Chic? Fashioning Women in The Third Reich. Irene Guenther. Berg. 2004.

10. *...one suspected female Abwehr agent who came to Britain in virtually identical circumstances Ingeburg Berta aka Fiedler and Bicker.* She arrived in 1933 to study English. In France she studied French. Arrested by the French in 1939 but not tried. She had a child at the end of the war and went to America in the 1950s. Described by British interrogating officer in 1944 as an inveterate liar and sly, cunning, and resourceful. KV2/3656. US intelligence: an "intelligent and resourceful woman"

11. *Frau Klimt would later be berated by the Mayor of Frankfurt for not producing enough commercial designs.* The exchange is detailed in Nazi Chic? Fashioning Women in The Third Reich. Irene Guenther. Berg. 2004.

12. *The French secret files on her, which officially identify her as located in the French capital in the New Year.* Letter sent from the Prefecture of Police in Paris to the Deuxieme Bureaux 25th November 1938 with attached details of the surveillance. French Archives. Gisela Klein file: 53176

Chapter Eight

1. *Hilmar Dierks, from the Abwehr unit in Hamburg.* Dierks died in 1940 and didn't warrant a complete British KV series file of his own, (he pops up in others) in the UK National archive. However, there is an interesting account of his life at https://www.nisa.intelligence

2. *Dierks was one of three Abwehr officers running a handful of female agents.* It's possible that the details Farrago reports are contained in the 81 linear feet of his papers held by the University of Boston.

3. *...described by her later handler Nikolaus Ritter as "the most beautiful*

spy". She was called Vera Eriksen… Ritter codenamed Dr Rantzau KV2/88. Vera Eriksen aka Starizky aka Shalberg KV2/14,15,16.

4. Thomas Cadett was appointed the Paris Correspondent for the *Times* in 1937 Cranleigh School's website has a section on his life. It quotes a friend in Cadett's obituary in the *Times*: "He possessed courage and gaiety of spirit, an elegant wit and a Rabelaisian sense of humour." https://1865.cranleigh.org

5. *Gisela took what looks like a counter measure to throw them off the scent...* I am indebted to Diana Russell Clarke's son Nigel Barraclough for helping me and for providing a recording of a talk Diana gave in the 1980s to the Burford Society in which she speaks about Gisela Klein escaping arrest before going on to describe her time at Bletchley Park. In what seems to have been a genuine coincidence this time, Diana's late father Edward was instrumental in detecting and helping to break the German High Seas Fleet codes in the First World War. This connection would see Diana go to work at the code breaking Bletchley Park during the Second World War.

6. *In early 1937 he was apparently learning the ropes of the publishing business on behalf of his stepfather's firm.* A timeline compiled with the help of Brandstetter after his capture in 1944, so probably not that accurate, suggests he was working in the Brandstetter Paris Office between April and July 1937. He was back in Berlin in July. KV2/160

7. *...but he isn't listed as a military attaché at the German's Paris embassy during this period. Die Wiedereinrichtung des deutschen miltarischen Attachedienstes nach dem Ersten Weltkrieg* by Manfred Kehrig. Harold Boldt Verlag 1966 Appendix 15 lists all the Paris Military Attaches for the relevant time

8. *...our country has been the object of a secret international propaganda. Looking Back*, the autobiography of the 5th Duke of Sutherland. Odhams Press 1957.

9. *His marriage to his first wife Lady Eileen, who was the senior Lady in the Royal Household, was reported to be unhappy.* Geordie's mother Millicent Sutherland was a friend and confidant of Maxine Elliot the owner of an elegant villa on the French Riviera where Winston Churchill was a frequent visitor. Maxine is quoted on the subject of Geordie in *the Riviera Set* by Mary S Lovell. Little Brown 2016.

Chapter Nine

1. *The Eiffel tower was scheduled for replacement with an even bigger structure christened The Lighthouse of the World but there wasn't enough money.* Lyn Maurice Ferguson Arnold. From Ideals to Ideology. Two contrasting views of Architectural Discourse. 2021 Pages 15.34 Polish Journal of Aesthetics.)
2. *The brutalist German design was by Hitler's pet architect Albert Speer who described it as a "nouveau riche architecture of prestige.* quoting Gaston Gordillo. Nazi Architecture as Affective Weapon. Funabulist Papers Volume 2. 2015
3. *The Exposition actually had a 243 foot tall parachute jump tower.* A clash of Ideology at the Paris Expo. Paul Garson Warfare History Network.com
4. *In Paris the secret watchers, undoubtedly aided by the all-seeing Concierge lurking on the ground floor of her building in the 16th arrondissement.* The art nouveaux building is now the Hotel Victor Hugo.
5. *On the 28th of November 1938 a letter from the Paris Prefect of Police.* French Archives. Gisela Klein file: 53176
6. *She said she had "dated" the eldest son of a very prominent American family.* Author interview with Gisela Klein's daughter.
7. *They both stayed on various occasions with Bullitt's right-hand man and fixer Carmel Offie at his Paris appartment.* Offie who later ran into trouble with the Communist witch hunter Senator McCarthy because of his homosexuality, headed a CIA operation, Bloodstone, recruiting Nazis for anti -Soviet work.

Chapter Ten

1. *One contemporary later described him as:* Richard Flood. Interviewed by Edwin Martin 1964 John F Kennedy Library.
2. *Jack, who struggled with regular bouts of ill health, was in his older brother's good looking and physically robust shadow.* Jack Kennedy had Addisons disease which affects the adrenal glands and Coeliac disease, an auto immune condition triggered by eating Gluten.

3. *He has often sat in my study and submitted with that smile that was pure magic to relentless teasing about his determination to be nothing less than President of the United States.* The Kennedy Men, 1901-1963. Laurence Leamer. William Morrow. 2001.

4. *Joe Jr spent a year studying and socialising in the UK.* He was living in a flat in a block in Earls Court in London which he shared with a friend Aubrey Whitelaw. Whitelaw interview for The Lost Prince. Hank Searls New American Library 1969.

5. *His father had sent him 200 pounds for the trip warning him it was coming out of his million-dollar trust fund.* Telegram from Joe Kennedy Sr in the JFK Library. Boston. Mass. JFKlibrary.org.

6. *Both Joe and his younger brother Jack were in Paris.* The Ambassador. Susan Ronald. St Martin's Press 2021. Ronald puts both Kennedy sons in Paris between June 1938 and the Munich crisis of September 1938. Laurence Leamer in the Kennedy Men also places Joe Jr as working as an attaché for Bullitt. Joe Jr kept various items in scrapbooks from this time including a menu for a diplomatic dinner which included the French Prime Minister Daladier and William C Bullitt. JFKlibrary.org.

7. *Evidence that Gisela was with Joe Kennedy.* Scrapbooks and Albums: Joseph P Kennedy, JR., 1932-1938. JFKlibrary.or

8. *She was clear about the difference in Joe's mind between lovers and the woman he would marry.* Lorelle McCarver Swisher Morre Hearst interview for: The Lost Prince. Hank Searls New American Library 1969. Reprint Silvertail Books 2024.

Chapter Eleven

1. *It is likely that another passenger on board the Aquitania later in December 1938 was also travelling on a similar basis.* Passenger lists via Ancestry, co.uk. These searchable passenger lists provide a wealth of information including revealing details of Wolfgang Brandstetter's use of his genetic father's name on his passport that year.

2. *The Americans were imposing strict immigration quotas on the German Jews desperate to leave their persecution behind.* 110,000 Jewish refugees escaped to the United States between 1933 and

1941. According to the Holocaust Encyclopedia (ushmm.org) hundreds of thousands of others applied but failed.

3. *The ship that brought the two men to Los Angeles became the target of hostile action while still in American waters.* Oakland Tribune. California 11/4/1938 Headline "Nazi Ship Explodes in Estuary"

4. *A fake ID he was carrying on his capture in Paris five years later gave Pasadena as his supposed birthplace.* UK National Archives KV2/160 reports that the ID card carried the name Bernard Werbecque. Born 2,12.1910 Pasadena California.

5. *Germany's espionage was successful and amongst other American innovations it stole details of the accurate Norden bomb sight.* The Norden bomb sight while excellent in tests in good weather conditions in the United States was not as effective in Europe but faith in it helped to keep the US wedded to costly daylight raids over Germany long after the British went over to the far less accurate but greater safety of night attacks.

6. *She appeared in a full-page advertisement in the prestigious magazine. The New Yorker. New Yorker* cutting. Gisela Klein family papers.

7. *That year Bergdorf Goodman created a surrealist fashion window display.* Early in 1938 there was a major Surrealist exhibition in Paris. Artists included Salvador Dali and Duchamps. The surrealist window display in New York was from around the same time. There are several photographs of the Bergdorf Goodman display including at the US Library of Congress. Lee Russell photographer. LC-USF33-011399-M4. Lot 1296.

8. *Three months later the Abwehr sent another photographer's model and spy to New York, Lily Stein.* The FBI website Fbi.gov has a precis of the fate of the 33 members of the spy ring in which Stein was involved. 1n 1942 she was sentenced to a total of 10 years in prison.

9. *...they had left Britain in their light aircraft in mid-August and were planning to stay in Cannes until September.* Market Harborough Advertiser and Midland Mail. Friday 18th August 1939.

10. *...when the British ultimatum was delivered to Hitler by his translator Paul Schmidt. Hitler's Interpreter.* Paul Schmidt. Fonthill Media Ltd. 2016. (First published 1951) Interesting, though partial, firsthand view of Nazi diplomacy and people from an eyewitness.

11. *Privately Hitler called him an "arschloch" (arsehole.)* Professor Christopher Andrew. *Defense of the Realm* quoted by mi5.gov.uk. Vernon Kell "took the personal decision to inform him (Chamberlain) Hitler referred to him in private as an arsehole. The probably shocked Foreign Secretary Lord Halifax underlined the insult three times in red ink."

12. *Her return to her homeland attracted the unwelcome interest of the Nazi secret police, the Gestapo.* KV6/146

Chapter Twelve

1. *That evening at RAF Marham in Norfolk, a 26-year-old pilot, Alec Pringle, hauled on the controls of a bomb laden Wellington aircraft to get it off the runway.* It was the 15th of May 1940. Records of losses for 115 Squadron and details of first strategic raid Archives RAF Hendon and Imperial War Museum.

2. *I can tell you this you utterly contemptible little shit. Troublesome Young Men.* Lynne Olson. Farra, Straus and Giroux. 2008

3. *Anna de Wolkoff, Haute Couture Modes from premises at 37 Conduit Street I London's Westminster 1.* The film of Wolkoff held by Getty Images. Details. UK National Archives KV2/840/2. The spy fiction writer Len Deighton witnessed the arrest of Wolkoff as a young boy and it triggered his interest in espionage.

4. *The founder of that club, the MP Archibald Ramsay. Ramsay was also associated with the antisemitic Nordic league.* The Wiener library has a copy of the Red Book membership list. The members included Anna Wolkoff; Lord Redesdale, William Joyce, (Lord Haw Haw) and Joan Miller who was working for Maxwell Knight of MI5. archivehub.jisc.ac.uk. Also see Miller's memoirs One Girls War (originally published 1945) Brandon/Mount Eagle 1986.

5. *The picture of her modelling for the Berlin couturier Annemarie Heise places her in the German capital in 1940.* Photograph in collection of Andre Vassiliev Foundation Paris. Gisela kept a cropped version of the same photograph without the Heise attribution.

6. *It was via the communist cell to which she was connected and later via the famous Rote Kapelle, (the Red Orchestra).* Obituary of Lautenschlager broadcast in Germany by WDR 5 March 27, 2008.

7. *Also, in Berlin at the same time as Gisela, according to his Nazi party records.* Heinrich Siegler von Eberswald. NSDAP records Berlin Lichterfelde. R9361-2 Nr 941549.

Chapter Thirteen

1. *She called this the happiest time of her life. Author interview with her daughter and her own words in Letter to Jack Profumo 1941.* British Archives Kew KV6/146.
2. *...fashion was worth more to Germany than iron and coal put together. Nazi Chic?* Irene Guenther. 2004 Berg She quotes BA (Bundesarchiv R55 622. Record of this year's meeting with Dr Ley on fashion Issues. 9 Oct 1941)
3. *It was on the first floor near a "small comfortable restaurant".* Haus Der Mode, Vienna as the Reich Fashion City. Wien Museum Magazin. Ingrid Holzschuh and Sabine Plakolm-Forsthuber.
4. *She could give free reign to the drive and ambition.* Her energetic travelling, modelling career and intelligence work were proof of this when she was younger but even in her 60s she study for and pass her realtor qualification in California in order to create another successful career. Author discussion with her son.
5. *Robert Ley, the man in charge of the German Labor Front.* This Nazi organization took over from all other trades unions in the Reich under the Nazification process in the 1930s. In practice it sided with the employers and kept wages low.
6. *There was also a suspicion by British intelligence she was also in Cairo in 1940.* KV6/146. Gisela Klein's British file has correspondence with the Cairo Security Officer about reports she was in Egypt. If she was it was never proved.
7. *The Haus Der Mode was allowed to attend and exhibit at shows in Berlin. Nazi Chic?* Irene Guenther. 2004. Berg.
8. *The Nazi file on him notes sourly that he was not given the promotion he deserved.* Bundesarchiv. NSDAP Heinrich Siegler von Eberswald R9361-2 Nr 941549.
9. *She sent a letter addressed to him at Avon Carrow in May 1942.* British National Archives Kew KV6/146.

10. *Jack Profumo MP had called here.* Possibly 58 St James Street in London where MI5 was based in 1941 and a short taxicab ride from the House of Commons.
11. ...*"economical with the actualite"* A quote from the Conservative MP and diarist Alan Clark about his ministerial role in the Iraqi supergun affair in the 1990s.
12. *He was locked up with a very mixed bag of German nationals, including his 1939 Canadian hunting companion.* Count Lothar von Hoensbroech. A wooden box carved by Hoensbroech during his imprisonment with the three-leg heraldic symbol of the Isle in bas relief on the lid is housed by the Isle of Man Museum after it was donated by his family. Walter Kittel later worked for Werner Schaurte at his company in Neuss and married the Icelandic consul, Gerlach's daughter.
13. *In December 1940 Hitler gave the go ahead to make Vienna Jew free.* The Vienna Mode of Radicalisation. Austria and the Shoah. Somner, Raggam-Blesch, Uhl. House of Austrian History Vienna 2022. Wiener Library.
14. *A local paper on the Isle of Man ignored Werner Schaurte's release. Involuntary Guests.* Alan Franklin 2017. Wiener Library Barcode 107084
15. *The American Counter Intelligence Corps carried out a background check on her in 1950.* The United States National Archive microfilm report was declassified at the request of the author on the 28th of April 2025. Investigatory Report Repository Gisela Hendrina Winegard MSN66623. It is a result of a check on her in Vienna by the Chief of the Counter Intelligence Corps, presumably at the request of the US Legation in Tangier. It names six sources for its information.

Chapter Fourteen

1. *...there was a clue that she'd travelled across the Atlantic again.* KV6/146 Gisela Klein. UK National Archives.
2. *...it wasn't the Germans but French men of the Mouvement Social Revolutionnaire, a fascist group, who attacked and bombed it.* The art deco building was not only subjected to a bomb attack in 1941

but was also attacked again on the anniversary of the first attack in 1980 with a bomb hidden in a motorcycle. Both extreme right and Middle eastern terrorists were blamed. Source: Association for the Protection of the Heritage of the Synagogue Rue Copernic.

3. *...the semi- nude female performers of Montmartre's Moulin De La Galette.* From contemporary photograph. Source Alamy.

4. *...and they were both being bugged by the British and his comments transcribed.* Brandstetter described being taken to a large house for the meeting with John Holroyd Reece who was apparently cooperating with British Military intelligence although they would have their suspicions about him. There is a note on the French file on Reece which suggests that he did or had worked for British Intelligence. The location of the recorded conversation was the "London Cage", an interrogation centre targeting hard core Nazis. They were numerous allegations of torture and mistreatment at the unit which was later involved in investigating war crimes. KV2/160 Wolfgang Krause Brandstetter. UK National Archives.

5. *Ernst Junger, who was posted to Paris as a German army staff officer, recorded how he dined at the Ritz.* A German Officer in Occupied Paris. Columbia Press. 2018...Junger was a highly decorated soldier and the author of the first world war trench memoir Storm of Steel. His place on the staff of General Carl Heinrich Von Stulpnagel, a leading light in Paris of the 1944 Stauffenberg Plot to kill Hitler saw him sacked from the German army. In his journals he describes reading Katherine Mansfield's stories. Undoubtedly the Albatross version sold by Wolfgang Krause Brandstetter to help create his "black fund".

6. *Even so there may have been as many as 100 French couture salons still operating in 1944. Nazi Chic.* Irene Guenther. 2004. Berg.

7. *...visits to the opera and theatre and lavish dinner parties with the French aristocracy.* Ursula Rudt von Collenberg quoted in Les Parisiennes. Anne Seba. 2016. Weidenfield and Nicholson.

8. *The beautiful Inga Haag who was recruited to work for Admiral Canaris.* Inga Haag was recorded in a long interview about her life for the archives of the Imperial War Museum in London. Online at iwm.org.uk. She was quoted in the Guardian Newspaper in 2004 describing Hitler and the plot in 1944 to kill him.

9. *Some of these refused to be transferred over to the Nazi SD intelligence service after it gained overall control of the Abwehr in 1944.* KV2/106 Oberleutnant Werner Ohletz. Head of Mil.Amt.C (RHSA)

10. *The former Air Military Attache at the German embassy in Paris.* The balding, pipe smoking Friedrich Carl Hannesse… In the 1930s Hannesse visited the UK and had postings in Paris, Berne and Lisbon. His connection to placing of sabotage agents in the UK and the USA identified by French intelligence is referenced in the Summary of Traces in Wolfgang Brandstetters UK file KV2/160.

11. *...Prince Joseph Schwarzenberg, a Viennese based aristocrat in his 40.* KV./160 Wolfgang Krause Brandstetter. UK National Archives. Some personal details on Joseph Maria Adolf Titus est zu Schwarzenberg can be found on Ancestry.Co.UK.

12. *A file was prepared which described Ribbentrop as "mentally incapable" of carrying out his duties. The plot backfired on its conspirators.* Unterstaatssekretaer Martin Luther and the Ribbentrop Foreign Office. JSTOR Christopher R Browning *Journal of Contemporary History* Vol 12 No 2 April 1977.

13. 13. He was allowed to continue on the basis that Albatross was a German business….. Source: Strange Bird. The Albatross Press and the Third Reich. Michelle K. Troy. Yale University Press 2017.

14. *The Abwehr headquarters, recently moved to safer location in Wiesbaden in western Germany.* After the war Wiesbaden became the home of a number of retired German Generals including Hanesse. Wolfgang Brandstetter also rebuilt the Brandstetter printing business there.

15. *Gisela Klein was never his secretary [...] It seems more likely that she was his mistress.* French Archives R.G.7 No 2795 Cabinet du Prefet. Premier Bureau 9 August 1946.

Chapter Fifteen

1. *The company the Americans said she was working for, ROGES.*See Collaboratrices. Pierre Brana and Joelle Dusseau. 2024. Perrin. Also: German Black Market Operations in France and in Belgium 1940-1944 PhD Dissertation Cambridge History Faculty 2004 Paul

Sanders. Academia.edu

2. *...her contacts with the Nazi propaganda department in Paris were so good she was always used by the Archiv de Gegenwart operation to obtain the necessary permits.* Information obtained during French questioning of Jean Maurice Noblet an investor in the Archiv de Gegenwart. French Archives. Fiche de Renseignments P422741.

3. *Seth was a bespectacled former chorister [...]Seth was never prosecuted for his activities including being the German stool pigeon "Captain John de Witt" planted amongst British POWs.* He was a prodigious letter writer and numerous officers in his security file seem to have just grown increasingly weary of his manic claims and demands. UK National Archive KV2/380. Seth later wrote spy books under his real name and became the "sexologist" Robert Chartham. He ran a sex clinic and published books about sex which along with anti-communism and espionage was a major interest noted in his KV file.

4. *...that membership of the Peterhouse rowing club.* KV2/160 actually renders this as Peterhead but this seems to have been an error.

5. *Braun after our first meeting dined me a Claridge's...* This extract comes from Wolfgang Brandstetter's KV file and does not appear in KV2/380 about Seth himself.

6. *One of the most prolific and successful black marketeers was under the early protection of an Abwehr officer.* Rationing and the Black Market in Paris during the war. Chris Lloyd aspectsofhistory.com

7. *...Madame Moutafolo was also known as Melita Stullenberg.* She was running an illicit and large scale trade in textiles and was said to have made more than 60 million francs....... The Collaboratrices. Pierre Brana and Joelle Dusseau. 2024. Perrin.

8. *Le Corbeau* is now seen as a depiction of the effects of the occupation.

9. *...officers removed the telephone handsets from their cradles to block eavesdropping.* Detail from Ernst Junger in his journals. A German Officer in Occupied Paris. European Perspectives. Columbia University Press. 2020.

10. *This is the landscape that reveals Kniebolo's (Jungers codename for Hitler) nature most clearly" ...he wrote.* Ibid.

11. *He shot himself in the head with his pistol but only managed to blind*

himself. Either in a delirium in hospital caused by his wound or because of later torture Stulpnagel revealed Erwin Rommel's name as a supporter of the conspiracy. Rommel was given the choice of suicide or a trial. He chose suicide. Because of Rommel's status the Nazis pretended he died as a result of wounds received in an allied air attack on his car some time before.

12. *Stulpnagel realised the game was up when General Gunther von Kluge the overall commander in France refused to back him because Hitler was still alive.* Kluge didn't even last as long as Stulpnagel. Suspected by Hitler in the wake of Valkyrie he was sacked and killed himself on 19th August 1944.
13. *He was tried on a stretcher in front of the Nazi judge Roland Freisler and hanged.* In one of the few examples of divine retribution involving the Nazi's, the ghastly Freisler was killed by falling masonry or a fragment of shrapnel, there are differing accounts, after a bomb hit his court on February the 3rd 1945.

Chapter Sixteen

1. *Jack drily described his actions: "It was involuntary they sank my boat"* JFK Library.org
2. *...the tremendous blast caused widespread damage to houses in a wide area below.* Contained in newly discovered local government war damage records. *Anglian Daily Times* report on damage to houses in Blythburgh, Hinton Thorington Walberswick and Wenhaston. 4th February 2024.
3. *General Hannesse in the opulent Rothschild mansion where the family's major domo still presided. Chronicles of Wasted Time.* Malcolm Muggeridge.
4. *..."half the high-grade nuts and bolts which hold the Wehrmacht together" Stars and Stripes* 7th Jan 44.
5. *This link was created by the convinced Nazi and SD Agent Jaques Desoubrie.* A Belgian he worked for the Gestapo since 1941. He was also known as Jean Masson, Jacque Leman and Captain Jacques. He helped to destroy the Comet escape line and was responsible for the deaths and capture of many resistors. He even shot his red-haired girlfriend Marie Antoinette Orsini alias Collette,

although she survived. Her exact role and degree of culpability in the deception plan was never fully discovered. He was tried and executed in 1949. Another man Guy Marcheret also seems to have used an alias Captain Jack and was involved in the bogus network operation and the betrayal and killing of resistors. He too was shot after trial in 1949.

6. *Although Joe Sonshine described a tall blonde woman, who was married to a short dark man called de Costa at the place he stayed in Paris at 4 Rue Mendelsohn.* 168 *Jump into Hell.* Stanley Booker. Arthur G Kinnis 1999.
7. *He unofficially moved from his room at the Hotel Scribe.* The Hotel Scribe later in 1944 became the base for a number of foreign war reporters and photographers including the fearless Lee Miller, the former *Vogue* model, who was painted by Picasso and who was the muse of the artist Man Ray.
8. *As Wolfgang Brandstetter set off for his journey to Reims 168 of the aircrew, he helped to capture....*82 were from the United States. 48 from Britain. 9 from Australia. 2 from New Zealand and one from Jamaica. Details from The National WW11 Museum New Orleans. https://www.nationalww2museum.org)
9. *Amongst them was an American airman, First Lieutenant Levitt C Beck.* Details of Leveritt C Becks Jr life from The National WW11 Museum New Orleans. Jason Dawsey PhD. https://www.nationalww2museum.org)
10. *Gisela was still relatively free to move around from the Rue Conde apartment on a bicycle she borrowed from one of her friends.* The friend, industrialist and investor Jean Maurice Noblet was later questioned as to whether he lent her the bicycle by the French as part of the file on her called "The Klein Affair". Fiches des Renseignments. Gisela Klein 53176.

Chapter Seventeen

1. *I am not afraid of dying....* Letter from Gisela Klein to her son and daughter.
2. *Wolfgang was told to be ready to leave for Reims that day.* KV2/160/4. CSDIC Interrogation report.

3. *Wolfgang and Gisela had access to French ration cards, either some of the many fakes available or official ones.* A number of French ration cards were in Wolfgang Brandstetters possession when he was arrested as a voluntary prisoner of war. KV 2/160.

4. *...a small group of resistance fighters behind a barricade made of ripped up street cobbles and sandbags.* A photograph of the barricade by Reynaud Lucien is held in the Paris Museums collection. Parismuseescollections.paris.fr

5. *...he didn't give the go ahead while still maintaining he was "only a little General. I receive orders. I execute them."* Said to Swedish Diplomat Raoul Nordling and quoted in Paris 44. Patrick Bishop. Viking 2024.

6. *Although they ran into some German resistance and lost tanks and 300 men.* Source National World War 11 Museum. www.nationalww2museum.org

7. *Geneva Convention covering the treatment of prisoners of war which the Germans completely ignored with the 168 air crew sent to Buchenwald.* The surviving airmen were later sent to Prisoner of War camps after the Luftwaffe were alerted to their situation and Göring personally ordered their transfer out of the hands of the SS.

8. *This was the ID he said he obtained from Father Bruckberger, Father Raymond Leopold Bruckberger was a Roman Catholic Intellectual and Chaplain to the FFI.* He held profoundly conservative views. He was also a writer and film director. He later served with the Foreign Legion. He tried to save the life of Joseph Darnand, the fascist and Vichy leader who was later executed by the French. Various sources including Chronicles Magazine and IMDb

Chapter Eighteen

1. *French fighter Pilot and Vichy Deputy of the French Parliament Count Jean de Beaumont.* Beaumont was the Deputy for the French colony of Indochine (which became Vietnam) between 1934 and 1944. In 1939 he met the Foreign Secretary Lord Halifax in the UK to discuss the "far-eastern question." Western morning News 22 April 1939. He had an interest in the rubber business and was arrested for collaboration amongst 60,000 according to the Paris

Prefect of Police. Reports in the Bradford Observer. Belfast Newsletter 7th September 1944. In 1949 he was noted as staying at Drumlarig Castle with the Duke and Duchess of Buccleuch where other guests had included Princess Elizabeth and the Duke of Edinburgh. The Queen newspaper 28th September 1949

2. *Gisela' French file covering this period paints a different picture of what happened to her. Fiches de Paris.* Military Government of Paris. 5th Bureaux Dossier No 2F.286

3. *...it was probably here that she was tied to a tree.* Author interview with Gisela Klein's daughter

4. *Although she believed it was the Americans...* Gisela told the French questioners this which meant she knew Wolfgang had been interrogated by US officer Walter Hochschild one of the four T Force officers who initially went to the flat on Fauborg St Honore

5. *The film director, screenwriter and actor Jean De Limur.* His film Le Voyage Imprevu, won a special mention at the Venice film festival in 1935 where it was also nominated for the Mussolini cup. Source IMDb.com. In Gisela's French file he said he rejected her for a film part because her spoken French had a German inflection. The reason Wolfgang gave "Madelaine Fontaine" a Flemish background.

6. *The DGER took over a series of Art Deco buildings on the salubrious Boulevard Suchet.* The Duke and Duchess of Windsor lived at Number 24 Boulevard Suchet before the war where they were photographed by Cecil Beaton in 1939. Victoria and Albert Museum vandaimages.com

7. *The unfortunately abbreviated SS, which appeared on the number plates of the units cars.* Chronicles of Wasted Time. Malcolm Muggeridge. 2006. Regent College Publishing.

8. *...the enigmatic postal address PO Box 25.* Radio Society of Great Britain. Visit to Bletchley Park and discussion with archivist Dr Thomas Cheetham.

9. *This was the Abwehr codename for Schlosss Baruth an Abwehr Headquarters 70 miles to the south of Berlin.* Abwehr officers involved in the July 20th plot were based here and the castle's owner was forced to sign it over to Himmler afterwards. This suggests Wolfgang was actually being summoned back by the SD. Details of Belinde in

Cold War Counterfeit Spies. Nigel West. 2016. Casemate.

10. *Her activities for the last ten years are certainly consistent....* KV2/146 Gisela Klein UK National archives.
11. *...the lawyer Helenus "Buster" Milmo who was also working for counterintelligence.* H.P. Milmo was later one of the prosecutors at the trial of leading Nazi's at Nuremberg. He also interrogated but failed to break Kim Philby. He concluded Philby was a Soviet Agent 12 years before he fled. Source: Article in the Independent online by Milmo's grandson based on FCO 158/28 at Kew.

Chapter Nineteen

1. *He said he would try to arrange for her to get a parcel.* He uses the French word colis but may have been referring to a Red Cross parcel which could be requested by an individual for a particular prisoner of war, although as a suspected spy Gisela did not necessarily qualify.
2. *...one of which was clearly not up to snuff for him as he described it as a "pigsty".* KV2/160
3. *His final fall from grace was recorded in February 1945 in a note written and signed by Dawn Rockingham.* Gill, the Personal Assistant to the Head of MI19. There's a photograph of Gill posted on X by Dr Helen Fry who has written about MI19 The M Room. 2012. CreateSpace Independent Publishing Platform.
4. *...you may be glad to hear that Brandstetter was removed from No7 P/W camp a week or more ago.* Camp No 7 at Ascot in Berkshire was called Winter Quarter Camp and was composed of 20 Huts within the Guards compound separated from other prisoners by a double perimeter fence. Source Datablog. The guardian.com
5. *...including the use of prolonged marching and exercise as a stress technique, sleep deprivation and starvation all strenuously denied by the Colonel.* SS Commander Fritz Knochlein, later executed for murdering British prisoners, alleged all of these.
6. *It's perhaps telling that a photograph of Brandstetter from after this time shows him looking gaunt and thin faced.* Published in Strange Bird. The Albatross Press and the Third Reich. Michelle K Troy

2017 Yale University Press.

7. *It seems we can trust the families in question who have signed their respective declarations and confirmed them in writing.* Fiches de Paris. Military Government of Paris. 5th Bureaux. Dossier No 2F.286

8. *He enlisted in New York in 1943, describing himself as a salesman.* United States National Archives. WW11 Enlistment records 1938 -1946 Record Group 64.

9. *...but he was also put in charge of the temporary prison at Boulevard Suchet where Gisela was being held.* KV6/146

10. *Ed arranged her formal release from the maternity unit.* KV6/146 actually suggests he arranged her release direct from Boulevard Suchet but her French file say she was released after giving birth. There's also a reference to other American admirers before he came on the scene.

11. *...his assessment of a series of tracked crawler cranes at a port facility at Granville on the French coast.* US National Archive. Document 000145 Report Edward E Winegard. CWO.18th March

Chapter Twenty

1. *A taste of the excitements Tangier had to offer came in November 1948 when the adventuress, suspected murderer of two husbands and spy, the Comtesse d' Andurain was apparently murdered on her yacht. Time Magazine* January 13th, 1947. "Murder my Pet?" *Daily Mirror.* 6th April 1949 "Victim of murder denies she is dead." See also Collaboratrices. Pierre Brana and Joelle Dusseau 2024. Perrin for references to the "Countesses of the Gestapo."

2. *The 25 year old Truman Capote's arrival in Tangier in the summer of the following year was deliberately spoiled by his rival and enemy for life Gore Vidal turning up on the dockside.* Obituary of Gore Vidal. Washington Post. August 1, 2012, quotes Paul Bowles on this subject in Tanger et autres Marocs Daniel Rondeau. 1997. Folio

3. *If you are someone escaping from the police, or merely someone escaping, then by all means come here. Vogue.* Tangier. Truman Capote. April 1st, 1950.

4. *...and Morocco was seen as an important base for American strike*

aircraft. Bricks Sand and Marble. US Army Corps of Engineers Construction in the Mediterranean and Middle East 1947-1991. Robert P Grathwol. Donota M. Moorhus. Centre of Military History Corps of Engineers. Wikimedia.org

5. *Gisela would sample the delights of the local marijuana.* Author discussion with her son.
6. *Ed even attended a fancy dress party dressed as the bespectacled Truman Capote.* Author interview with her daughter.
7. *Clemence Bonnet Matthews was from a long established Tangier family.* Obituary for Clemence's daughter Anna Gabriela da Silva Araujo Bonnet. November 2020. Tangier American Legation Museum. Legation.org.
8. *Clemence was painted by the Tangier artist James McBey probably most famous for his portrait of Lawrence of Arabia in full Arab attire.* The portrait of T E Lawrence now held by the IWM London.
9. *The note was an indication of the rift between them.* The details of the public split between the pair are in a case summary KV6/146.
10. *...he met a married actress called Valerie Hobbs with whom he started an affair. Bringing the House Down.* David Profumo. 2006 John Murray.
11. *...had a home and editing studio at a house on the Black lake where she' moved to escape the bombing in Germany.* Riefenstahl's home and editing studio is now a rentable holiday home. www.hotel-seebichl.at
12. *He was spotted by a Major in the United States army who remembered his bald egg shaped head.* Photograph of Oberg just after capture on May 26th, 1945, The United States Holocaust memorial Museum. https://collections.ushmm.org. Oberg was finally released from prison in 1962 and died three years later.
13. *...some the men were involved in salvaging the remains of a B25 bomber that had crashed.* No Task Too Great In France. Chapter IV of the History of the 97th Engineer Battalion (Construction) 2014. 220th Aviation Company https://catkillers.org